Arthur Schnitzler

FOUR MAJOR PLAYS

A Smith and Kraus Book
Published by Smith and Kraus, Inc.
PO Box 127, Lyme, NH 03768

Copyright ©1999 Carl R. Mueller
All rights reserved
Manufactured in the United States of America

Cover and Text Design by Julia Hill Gignoux, Freedom Hill Design
Cover Illustration: *The Kiss,* Gustav Klimt

First Edition: January 1999
10 9 8 7 6 5 4 3 2 1

The Library of Congress Cataloging-In-Publication Data
Schnitzler, Arthur, 1862–1931.
[Plays. English. Selections]
Arthur Schnitzler: four plays / translated by Carl R. Mueller — 1st ed.
p. cm. — (Great translations series)
Contents: La ronde — Anatol — The green cockatoo — Flirtation.
ISBN 1-57525-180-9
1. Schnitzler, Arthur, 1862–1931 — Translations into English. I. Mueller, Carl Richard. II. Title.
III. Title: Four Plays. IV. Series: Great translations for actors series.
PT2637.N5 (A2–29 M+)
832' .8—dc21 98-52961
CIP

Arthur Schnitzler

>–‹›–◦–‹›–‹

FOUR MAJOR PLAYS

Translated by Carl R. Mueller

Great Translations Series

SK
A Smith and Kraus Book

FOR
MARTIN MAGNER

Contents

I have been aware for several years of the extensive concurrence which exists between your views and mine regarding some psychological and erotic problems.... I have often asked myself in wonder where you could have found this or that secret knowledge which I was able to discover only after arduous examination of the object, and ended up feeling envious of the poet for whom I had always had the deepest admiration. You cannot imagine the pleasure and delight I obtained from your lines in which you tell me that you, on your part, have received inspiration from my writings. I feel quite resentful that I had to wait for my fiftieth birthday before discovering such a unique honor.

Sigmund Freud in a letter to Schnitzler
dated May 8, 1906, thanking him for a fiftieth birthday greeting.
It represents their first contact with one another.

Introduction

The Austrian playwright Arthur Schnitzler (1862–1931) is one of the seminal forces both in German-speaking and world drama. He was in every sense a total man of letters: playwright, novelist and short-story writer. But he was also a physician, and perhaps this is the real basis for his acute perception into the mind and soul of *fin-de-siècle* Vienna.

THE HISTORICAL CONTEXT

His father, a well-known Jewish throat specialist who founded a leading medical journal of the day, deeply influenced his son in regard to his initial profession, causing him to study medicine at the world-renowned University of Vienna, from which he was graduated in 1885, his dissertation having been written on the hypnotic treatment of neurosis. Once he became actively engaged in his literary career, Schnitzler continued to review medical publications on such diverse topics as hysteria, hypnosis, sexual pathology, and psychotherapy, and it is these interests that allowed the literary man to dissect his characters as incisively as if he were conducting a delicate surgical operation.

All this occurred in a Vienna also inhabited by Sigmund Freud, whose clinical interests were virtually parallel to those of Schnitzler. Ironically, their first contact was a fiftieth birthday greeting sent to Freud by Schnitzler in 1906. Even so, they met only a few times, though they lived within walking distance of each other. It has been suggested rather aptly that Schnitzler the doctor and Freud with his artist's imagination were entirely too similar for comfort ever to be close. In reply to the birthday greeting, Freud admits that he has frequently been struck by the insights both psychological and erotic that Schnitzler displays in his work, insights that he, Freud, "was able to discover only after arduous examination of the object," and admitting "feeling envious of the poet for whom I had always had the deepest admiration." Precisely as is Freud's work, Schnitzler's literary output is inextricable from the social and intellectual milieu of his time, the end of the Austro-Hungarian Empire, the *fin-de-siècle* decadence and pleasure-seeking atmosphere that frequently crosses the border into disease. It is the age of the Viennese Secessionists, the development of modern music through such composers as Berg, Webern, and Schoenberg, the seductive and decadent graphic images of Gustav Klimt and Oskar Kokoschka. The foundations of modern architecture were being developed, modern statecraft was being established, and Theodor Herzl founded Zionism. As a centerpiece to all this ferment, the theories of sexuality as promulgated by Freud were introduced into a welcoming as well as an unwilling world. It was a dizzying time. It was out of this maelstrom that Schnitzler wrote. Nonetheless, he wrote with charm and grace and, what is more important, with great compassion, when faced with the tender, though often brutal frailty of humankind.

His characters are determined by the pleasure principle; their aim is to squeeze from life its ultimate drop of sensual gratification. Yet at their back hovers always the Angel of Death, that baroque morality figure, poised to descend and annihilate at any moment. It is a precarious view that life can be snuffed out in a single breath. This pervasive presence of the Angel of Death manifests itself in a multitude of forms. In *Flirtation* he is the husband of Fritz's mistress; he is austere, foreboding, judgmental. In *La Ronde* it is the omnipresent fear that tomorrow's sun may never rise. In the series of one-act plays titled *Anatol* it is time that is relentless and waits for no man; the moment is all. Sex in Schnitzler's plays is frenetic, it represents a desperate attempt to escape from the knowledge that life lived solely out of the pleasure principle is an empty shell that allows no cushioning to fall back on. On a more external plane, the constant indulgence in the sexual aspect of life is an attempt to escape from the innate knowledge that their way of life is crumbling at their feet and that there is nothing they can do about it. The characters in Schnitzler's plays represent an aristocratic ostrich with its head in the sand. In every way it is a picture of the Vienna in which Schnitzler wrote. Vienna was one of the few remaining baroque cities of the world, a city that still lived the baroque tradition, that set itself apart from modernization, that resisted not only the railroad but the telephone, a city that suffered repression, and compensation for repression, like no place else: Vienna, City of Dreams. Is it any wonder that Vienna is the city in which, at the same time as Schnitzler wrote the plays in this volume, Sigmund Freud was formulating his understanding of hysteria? In studying hysteria in his patients Freud was in reality delineating the psychosis of the society in which he lived and worked. And where else but in the City of Dreams could that epochal work *The Interpretation of Dreams* have been gestated? Had psychoanalysis developed anywhere but Vienna, it might well have taken another turn. And so, if much in these plays and the narrative fiction by Schnitzler appears sentimental, even precious, it is so not by default but by careful design: Schnitzler, like Freud, is holding the mirror up to his age and his society. Beneath that fun-loving exterior of whirling waltzes lurk cruelty, duplicity, bitterness, ruthlessness, skepticism, and, ultimately, despair. Freud's final, transcendent, civilization-condemning works *The Future of an Illusion* and *Civilization and Its Discontents* hold the mirror up to meet the eyes of us all, but especially to the eyes of his Vienna in the last years of the nineteenth and the early years of the twentieth centuries.

One of Schnitzler's principal themes is the Pirandellian confusion between reality and illusion. As in the Italian playwright's work, and in the life of his society, illusion in Schnitzler is the one sure means of escaping personal and corporate incapacity to deal with reality; it is at best a veil, and at worst a shutting of the eyes entirely. Inevitably illusion reverses itself into hard, cruel reality. In *The Green Cockatoo* what starts as playacting ends as reality of the most terrible and bloody sort, the French Revolution, on one warm summer night.

Schnitzler, then, is the biographer of an age that has passed; but it is an age that has fired the imagination and interest of the present as no other. We are in the process of re-evaluating Vienna at the turn of the century as the crucible of all that is modern. In this repressive, and repressed, dream-oriented and reality-hating city the Age of Modernism hit with a vengeance, indeed like a revolt of the Freudian Id against the sickness of the demand for the retention of tradition by its authoritarian Superego, the Austrian monarchy and its social system. Schnitzler's contribution to our understanding of that fascinating and troublesome period cannot be overestimated.

THE PLAYS

La Ronde, published in 1903 and first produced in 1912, met with considerable benighted censorship problems from the time it was first written, between 1897–98. Possibly because Schnitzler felt the play was highly susceptible to misinterpretation, he had it privately printed in 1900, in an edition of 200 copies, for distribution to his friends. As copies were transferred from one individual to another, it soon became a literary sensation. In 1903 Schnitzler permitted a trade edition to be printed, but it was summarily attacked as subversive and obscene. The press refused to review it; a public reading in Vienna was curtailed by the police; Germany confiscated and banned the publication. When an unauthorized production was mounted in Budapest in 1912, it was offensively and tastelessly performed and consequently banned by the police. The play caused subsequent riots in Munich and Berlin, occasioned a trial, and was even discussed in the Austrian Parliament. Finally, in 1921, it received its Viennese première, causing further demonstrations, including proto-Nazi protests that it was "Jewish filth."

The play is a series of ten "dialogues," each between a man and a woman, and each leading to sexual intercourse. The ten participants bridge the entire range of society, from the Prostitute, to the Soldier, the Parlor Maid, the Young Gentleman, the Young Wife, the Husband, the Sweet Young Thing, the Poet, the Actress, and the Count. Beginning with the Prostitute and the Soldier, each successive scene utilizes the person representative of the next highest class from the scene before. Thus the second scene engages the Soldier and the Parlor Maid. In the final scene the Count and the Prostitute of scene one are brought together: The highest and lowest are effectively reduced to a common denominator.

Schnitzler's most famous play, *La Ronde* (in German *Reigen*) is more than a series of sexual encounters; it is a keen and incisive picture of its time fully and succinctly realized as drama of psychological-sociological criticism. The uniting thread of the "dialogues" is the deception involved in the supposed act of love. The guiding motive behind each couple's physical union is the ideal of love, but in the end only animal passion has been expended. The final coup is insensitivity and egocentric unconcern for the other. Systematically, perhaps even to the point of cruelty, Schnitzler lays bare the inadequacy of mere sexual encounter and demonstrates with extreme dramatic economy the emptiness of the life of his time. It is a play of profound disillusionment.

Anatol constitutes Schnitzler's first attempts at dramatic writing, and it might well be considered his most charming. Neither planned nor composed as a whole, *Anatol* was turned out scene by scene between the years 1888 and 1892. And, yes, Schnitzler was aware that his work was a mirror of his time. Of *La Ronde,* his masterpiece, he wrote that "if disinterred after a couple of hundred years, [it] may illuminate in a unique way aspects of our culture."

If *La Ronde* is clinical and perhaps even cold in its freedom from sentimentality, *Anatol* is gentler in tone and mode, but not one whit less ironic in its depiction of the futile search for sexual gratification that, in Schnitzler's world, is uniformly destined to failure and disillusionment. Sweetness promises always to be around the next dark corner, chiefly in Schnitzler's nostalgic depiction of the Viennese Sweet Young Thing, whose charms are as abundant as lilacs in spring, but whose expectations are seldom met if only because of the ego-centeredness of the male's need for a little diversion from his conventional state of ennui. The disappointment on both sides is both comic and tragic, and thus ineffably sad, but, implies Schnitzler, that's life. Anatol, however, is only one half of the paradigm of the central hero, and the other half is not the female eternally sought, but his sidekick Max who looms large in five of the play's seven scenes. It is he who plays Mephisto to Anatol's Faust; the realist to his friend's fashionable romantic dissatisfaction. Max is the sounding board for Anatol's delusions of grandeur. "I thought," boasts Anatol, "of myself as one of the great men of history. Those girls and women — I ground them underfoot as I strode across the earth. I thought of it as a law of nature. My way lies over these bodies." To which Max replies with no small sense of irony though no less a sense of humor: "The storm wind that scatters the blossoms." At which corrective Anatol collapses into being just another *mensch*.

The Green Cockatoo, a one-act play written in 1898, takes place in a sordid Paris cabaret-theater in 1789, on the night of the storming of the Bastille. Various actors from local theaters are performing impromptu scenes of crime for the debased delectation of the slumming Parisian aristocracy. One actor, whom they believe to be pursued, tells of pickpockets at work outside; another relates how he set fire to a house; a third, how he came upon a murder. The host of the establishment derides his noble guests as rogues and pigs and says he hopes they are next in line for extinction by the citizens. No one knows whether he is acting for the gentry's delight or if he is serious. Henri, a good-natured actor, reveals to the shuddering guests how he has just murdered a nobleman who was his wife's lover. The host knows this affair to be a fact; what he does not know is whether Henri is acting or telling the truth. As it happens, Henri is only acting, but not for long, for he soon learns the truth, and when that same nobleman enters the tavern, Henri stabs him to death. Havoc breaks loose and is further amplified by the stormers of the Bastille rushing in, causing the frightened gentry to flee for their lives.

The Green Cockatoo is one of Schnitzler's most skillful pieces, particularly because of the tension generated through the fluctuating uncertainty between reality and illusion and the fact that in the end illusion, true or otherwise, bursts out into bloody reality. Carl Schorske describes brilliantly the basic premise upon which the play is based: "Too much dedication to the life of the senses has destroyed in the upper class the power to distinguish politics from play, sexual aggression from social revolution, art from reality. Irrationality reigns supreme over the whole." In writing this piece, Schnitzler looked squarely at the problem of Austria's psyche and society, but he did so "abstractly, lightly, ironically."

Flirtation, written in 1895 under the untranslatable title *Liebelei,* takes place, like most of Schnitzler's plays, in the Vienna of his time. It centers around Christine, a young, gentle, and sensitive girl of the lower middle class who makes the mistake of taking her lover and their affair seriously. She is the Sweet Young Thing revisited. This time, however, she fails to play the game of love according to the well-established rules of the time. She falls in love with a dashing Viennese gentleman, Fritz, who is already engaged in an amorous affair with a married woman. The woman's husband challenges him to a duel. Fritz is killed, and Christine, believing in his love for her, yet realizing too late that it was mere illusion on her part and that she was merely a pastime, commits suicide.

Flirtation, though sentimental on its surface, is at its base a solid and bitter indictment of society, of its superficial and delusory orientation. A play about morals, there is no moralizing. Schnitzler's dissection of social and sexual mores of imperial Vienna at the turn of the century is graceful yet always directed at his desired end. He shows in Christine's violent, passionate, but always human revolt against convention (the acceptance of the rules of the game) the end of an age. Her act tears a rent so wide in the curtain of bourgeois respectability that it can never again be mended. Perhaps this has made this work one of Schnitzler's most popular and resilient plays.

CARL R. MUELLER
Summer 1998
Department of Theater
School of Theater, Film and Television
University of California, Los Angeles

La Ronde

A Play in Ten Dialogues

CAST OF CHARACTERS

The Prostitute
The Soldier
The Parlor Maid
The Young Gentleman
The Young Wife
The Husband
The Sweet Young Thing
The Poet
The Actress
The Count

TIME AND PLACE

Vienna in the 1890s

La Ronde

I. THE PROSTITUTE AND THE SOLDIER

Late evening. On the Augarten Bridge. The SOLDIER comes along whistling, on his way back to the barracks.

PROSTITUTE: (*Seductively, interested.*) Hey! (*The SOLDIER turns to look, then continues on.*) How about it?

SOLDIER: Who? Me?

PROSTITUTE: See anyone else? Come on.

SOLDIER: Can't. Got to get back to the barracks.

PROSTITUTE: Barracks can wait. I'm better than an empty bunk.

SOLDIER: (*Close to her.*) Could be.

PROSTITUTE: Psst! Police snoop around here.

SOLDIER: So? I got my bayonet.

PROSTITUTE: Let's go.

SOLDIER: Cut it out! I'm broke.

PROSTITUTE: Who needs money?

SOLDIER: (*Stops; they are near a street lamp.*) Who are you?

PROSTITUTE: Civilians I charge. Guys like you get it free.

SOLDIER: Huber told me about you.

PROSTITUTE: Who's Huber?

SOLDIER: You took him home one night? From the cafe in Schiffgasse?

PROSTITUTE: Oh, *him!*

SOLDIER: Let's go.

PROSTITUTE: You in a rush? Now you can't wait?

SOLDIER: Gotta be back by ten.

PROSTITUTE: Been in long?

SOLDIER: Knock it off. You live far?

PROSTITUTE: Mmm, ten minutes.

SOLDIER: Forget it. Kiss me.

PROSTITUTE: (*Kisses him.*) That's always the best when you like a guy.

SOLDIER: You're weird. Sorry, too far.

PROSTITUTE: Tomorrow afternoon?

SOLDIER: Great. What's the address?

PROSTITUTE: You won't come.

SOLDIER: Promise.

PROSTITUTE: In that case — how about — over there. By the Danube. (*Points toward the river.*)

SOLDIER: What's over there?

PROSTITUTE: It's quiet. And deserted.

SOLDIER: Forget it.

PROSTITUTE: Come on. Don't go. We could be dead tomorrow.

SOLDIER: Okay. But make it quick.

PROSTITUTE: Careful. It's dark. Slip and you end up in the river.

SOLDIER: Sounds great.

PROSTITUTE: Psst! Not so fast. There's a bench somewhere.

SOLDIER: Right at home, uh?

PROSTITUTE: You'd be a good lover.

SOLDIER: I'd make you jealous.

PROSTITUTE: I can handle that.

SOLDIER: You think so.

PROSTITUTE: Shh! Police. Imagine. The middle of Vienna.

SOLDIER: Over here. Come on.

PROSTITUTE: Watch it. You want to fall in the water?

SOLDIER: (*Takes hold of her.*) You little —

PROSTITUTE: Hold tight.

SOLDIER: Don't worry.

• • •

PROSTITUTE: We should've used the bench.

SOLDIER: Who cares. Get up.

PROSTITUTE: What's the rush?

SOLDIER: The barracks. I'm late.

PROSTITUTE: What's your name?

SOLDIER: Shit!

PROSTITUTE: Mine's Leocadia.

SOLDIER: Jesus Christ!

PROSTITUTE: Watch it!

SOLDIER: What?

PROSTITUTE: How about a tip for the parlor maid?

SOLDIER: I'm a banker now?!

PROSTITUTE: Bastard! Son of a bitch!

II. THE PARLOR MAID AND THE SOLDIER

The Prater. Sunday evening. A path leading from the amusement park out into a dark avenue of trees. The confused sounds of the park are still audible, along with the music of "The Five Crosses Dance," a banal polka played by a brass band.

PARLOR MAID: Why'd we have to leave so early? (*The SOLDIER laughs stupidly, embarrassed.*) I liked it in there. I love dancing. (*The SOLDIER puts his arm around her waist. She doesn't resist.*) But we're not dancing now. Why are you holding me so tight?

SOLDIER: What's your name? Kathy?

PARLOR MAID: No!

SOLDIER: Oh, yeah. Marie?

PARLOR MAID: It's dark. I'm afraid.

SOLDIER: I'm here. Come on. Leave it to me.

PARLOR MAID: Where're we going? There's nobody — come on. Let's go back. It's dark.

SOLDIER: (*Draws on his Virginia cigar, making the tip glow red.*) How's that for light? (*Laughs.*) You're really something.

PARLOR MAID: What are you — ? No! I didn't —

SOLDIER: You're so soft, Marie!

PARLOR MAID: You should know.

SOLDIER: You notice little things like that, dancing. And more.

PARLOR MAID: All evening you danced with that stupid blonde!

SOLDIER: A friend of a friend.

PARLOR MAID: The one with the mustache?

SOLDIER: The guy with the big mouth. At the table earlier. Civilian.

PARLOR MAID: The fresh one.

SOLDIER: Did he — ? What'd he do?

PARLOR MAID: I saw him with the others.

SOLDIER: Miss Marie?

PARLOR MAID: You'll burn me.

SOLDIER: Sorry. Miss Marie? Why are we so stuffy?

PARLOR MAID: We just met.

SOLDIER: People who can't stand each other aren't as stuffy as us.

PARLOR MAID: Maybe next time, when — oh, Mr. Franz!

SOLDIER: Aha. So you *do* know my name.

PARLOR MAID: But, Mr. Franz!

SOLDIER: *Franz*, Miss Marie! *Franz!*

PARLOR MAID: Then don't be so — stop it! What if someone comes.

SOLDIER: It's pitch black out here.

PARLOR MAID: Where are you — taking me?

SOLDIER: Look. Two others. Just like us.

PARLOR MAID: Where? I can't see.

SOLDIER: There. Right ahead.

PARLOR MAID: You said "two just like us."

SOLDIER: They like each other.

PARLOR MAID: Careful. What — ? I almost fell.

SOLDIER: Just the railing.

PARLOR MAID: Stop pulling. I'll fall.

SOLDIER: Shh! Not so loud.

PARLOR MAID: Stop it! I'll scream! What are you — doing? What — !

SOLDIER: We're all alone.

PARLOR MAID: Then let's find some —

SOLDIER: Who needs them? Marie! We need — come on. Come on. (*He laughs.*)

PARLOR MAID: No — no. Mr. Franz, no. Please. Listen! If I'd — if I'd —. Oh! Oh! Yes!

• • •

SOLDIER: (*Blissfully.*) Oh! Don't stop. Don't — ah — ah —

PARLOR MAID: I can't see you.

SOLDIER: Who cares.

. . .

SOLDIER: You going to lay there all night, Miss Marie?

PARLOR MAID: Help me.

SOLDIER: Come on. Get up.

PARLOR MAID: God, Franz!

SOLDIER: Aha! So now it's "Franz!"

PARLOR MAID: You're terrible, Franz!

SOLDIER: Yeah, sure. Hey, wait for me!

PARLOR MAID: Why'd you let go of me?

SOLDIER: Can I light my cigar?!

PARLOR MAID: It's dark.

SOLDIER: It'll be light tomorrow.

PARLOR MAID: You could at least say you like me.

SOLDIER: You sayin' you didn't feel nothin'? Miss Marie? (*He laughs.*)

PARLOR MAID: Where're we going?

SOLDIER: Back.

PARLOR MAID: Please, not so fast!

SOLDIER: What now? I don't like the dark.

PARLOR MAID: Franz? Do you — care for me?

SOLDIER: What'd I just say?

PARLOR MAID: Kiss me?

SOLDIER: (*Condescendingly.*) There. Listen. You can hear the music.

PARLOR MAID: You're going back? Dancing?

SOLDIER: Why not?

PARLOR MAID: But — I have to get home. They'll be mad as it is. My mistress is such a — she never wants us to go out.

SOLDIER: Hm.

PARLOR MAID: It's — well — lonely walking home alone.

SOLDIER: Where do you live?

PARLOR MAID: Not far. Porzellangasse.

SOLDIER: Yeah, well. We're going in the same direction, all right. But it's still early. They're dancing. I want to have some fun. I got a late pass. Till midnight. I'm going back.

PARLOR MAID: Back after that stupid blonde.

SOLDIER: She ain't so stupid.

PARLOR MAID: Men! I hate you! You treat us like scum!

SOLDIER: Such hard words from such a pretty little mouth.

PARLOR MAID: Franz, please, not tonight. Stay with me?

SOLDIER: Okay. Okay. But first — I dance.

PARLOR MAID: I couldn't dance with any other man.

SOLDIER: Almost there.

PARLOR MAID: Where?

SOLDIER: The Svoboda. We must've run. (*He laughs.*) Listen! They're still playing it! Tatata*tum*! Tatata*tum*! (*He sings along.*) If you want to wait, okay. If not. See you!

(*They enter the dance hall.*)

SOLDIER: Miss Marie, treat yourself to a glass of beer, uh? (*He turns to a blonde as she dances past in the arms of a young man.*) How about a dance?

III. THE PARLOR MAID
AND THE YOUNG GENTLEMAN

A hot summer afternoon. His parents are already off to the country for the season. The cook is having her day off. The PARLOR MAID is in the kitchen writing a letter to the soldier who is her lover. A bell rings from the Young Gentleman's room. She rises and goes to answer. The YOUNG GENTLEMAN is reclining on the divan, smoking and reading a French novel.

PARLOR MAID: You rang, sir?

YOUNG GENTLEMAN: Oh. Yes, Marie, yes. Of course. Now what was I — ? Ah. The blinds. Would you lower them, please? Marie? It's cooler with the blinds down. (*The PARLOR MAID goes to the windows and lowers the blinds. The YOUNG GENTLEMAN continues reading.*) What are you doing, Marie? Yes, well. Now it's too dark to read.

PARLOR MAID: You're always so studious, sir.

YOUNG GENTLEMAN: (*Listens with an air of superiority.*) That will be all. (*The PARLOR MAID goes out. The YOUNG GENTLEMAN tries to continue reading; soon, however, he drops his book and rings again. The PARLOR MAID appears.*) Oh! Marie. Now what was I going to — ? Ah, yes! Would there be any cognac in the house?

PARLOR MAID: Yes, but it would be locked away.

YOUNG GENTLEMAN: Then who has the key?

PARLOR MAID: Lini has the key.

YOUNG GENTLEMAN: Who would Lini be?

PARLOR MAID: Lini would be the cook, Mr. Alfred.

YOUNG GENTLEMAN: Well, then, ask Lini to open it.

PARLOR MAID: It's Lini's day off, sir.

YOUNG GENTLEMAN: Aha.

PARLOR MAID: Shall I fetch some from the café?

YOUNG GENTLEMAN: No, no. It's hot enough. Who needs cognac. Ah, but, Marie, you might bring me a glass of water. Psst, Marie! Let it run till it's nice and cold.

(*The PARLOR MAID goes off. The YOUNG GENTLEMAN watches her leave. At the door she turns to him; the YOUNG GENTLEMAN looks into space. The PARLOR MAID turns on the water and lets it run. Meanwhile she goes into her small room, washes her hands, and arranges her curls in front of the mirror. She then brings the YOUNG GENTLEMAN his glass of water. She goes to the divan. The YOUNG GENTLEMAN rises up halfway; the PARLOR MAID hands him the glass of water. Their fingers touch.*)

YOUNG GENTLEMAN: Thank you. Well? What is it? Be careful. Put the glass back on the saucer. (*He lies back and stretches out.*) What time is it?

PARLOR MAID: Five o'clock, sir.

YOUNG GENTLEMAN: Ah, five o'clock. Good.

(*The PARLOR MAID goes out, but turns in the doorway. The YOUNG GENTLEMAN has followed her with his eyes; she notices this, and smiles. The YOUNG GENTLEMAN remains on the divan for a while, then suddenly rises. He walks as far as the door, then returns, lies down again on the divan. He tries to continue reading. After a moment he rings again. The PARLOR MAID appears with a smile that she does not attempt to hide.*)

YOUNG GENTLEMAN: Ah, Marie. I forgot to ask you. Did Dr. Schüller
come by this morning?

PARLOR MAID: No one came by this morning.

YOUNG GENTLEMAN: Hm. Strange. You're certain he didn't come by?
Would you know him if you saw him?

PARLOR MAID: The tall man with the black beard.

YOUNG GENTLEMAN: Yes. Was he by?

PARLOR MAID: No, sir.

YOUNG GENTLEMAN: (*Decisively.*) Come here, Marie.

PARLOR MAID: (*Steps a bit closer.*) Sir?

YOUNG GENTLEMAN: I thought — well, I thought — your blouse.
What's it made of? Come closer, I don't bite.

PARLOR MAID: (*Goes to him.*) Is something wrong with my blouse? Don't
you like it, sir?

YOUNG GENTLEMAN: (*Takes hold of her blouse and pulls her down to
him.*) Blue? What a lovely blue. (*Simply.*) You're nicely dressed, Marie.

PARLOR MAID: Oh, but, sir —

YOUNG GENTLEMAN: What? (*He has opened her blouse; directly.*) You
have lovely white skin, Marie.

PARLOR MAID: You flatter me, sir.

YOUNG GENTLEMAN: (*Kisses her breasts.*) No harm — in this.

PARLOR MAID: No.

YOUNG GENTLEMAN: You're sighing. Why are you sighing, Marie?

PARLOR MAID: Oh, sir.

YOUNG GENTLEMAN: And what nice slippers.

PARLOR MAID: But — but, sir. What if — what if — what if someone rings?

YOUNG GENTLEMAN: You needn't be embarrassed with me. You needn't
be embarrassed with anyone. You're too lovely. My God, Marie, you're so —
even your hair smells lovely.

PARLOR MAID: Mr. Alfred —

YOUNG GENTLEMAN: Don't be silly, Marie. I've seen you. (*He gestures.*)
One night. Just after I'd come home. I went to the kitchen for a glass of
water. The door to your room was — open — and —

PARLOR MAID: (*Hides her face.*) Oh, God, Mr. Alfred.

YOUNG GENTLEMAN: I saw everything, Marie. Here. And here. And
here. And —

PARLOR MAID: Oh — ?

YOUNG GENTLEMAN: Come, come here. Come. There. That's better.

PARLOR MAID: But someone might ring.

YOUNG GENTLEMAN: Stop that! We simply won't answer.

. . .

(*The bell rings.*)

YOUNG GENTLEMAN: Good lord! Couldn't he make a little *more* noise! He probably rang earlier and we didn't hear.

PARLOR MAID: I was listening the whole time, sir.

YOUNG GENTLEMAN: Well, go and see who it is. Through the peep-hole.

PARLOR MAID: Mr. Alfred, you're — you're a terrible man!

YOUNG GENTLEMAN: Will you go and see.

(*The PARLOR MAID goes out. The YOUNG GENTLEMAN opens the blinds.*)

PARLOR MAID: (*Enters.*) He must have left. There's no one there. Maybe it was Dr. Schüller.

YOUNG GENTLEMAN: (*Disagreeable.*) That will be all. (*The PARLOR MAID approaches him. He avoids her.*) By the way, Marie. I'm going off to the café now.

PARLOR MAID: (*Tenderly.*) So soon — Mr. Alfred?

YOUNG GENTLEMAN: (*Sternly.*) I'm off to the café. If Dr. Schüller should call, I'll — I'll be at the café. (*He goes into the neighboring room.*) (*The PARLOR MAID takes a cigar from the smoking-table, puts it in her pocket, and goes out.*)

IV. THE YOUNG GENTLEMAN
AND THE YOUNG WIFE

Evening. A salon in a house in Schwindgasse, furnished with cheap elegance. The YOUNG GENTLEMAN has just entered, and, while still wearing his topcoat and with hat still in hand, lights the candles. He then opens the door to the adjoining room and looks in. The light from the candles in the salon falls across the inlaid floor to the four-poster against the back wall. The reddish glow from a fireplace in the corner of the room diffuses itself on the curtains of the bed. The YOUNG GENTLEMAN also inspects the bedroom. He removes an atomizer from the dressing table and sprays the pillows on the bed with a fine mist of violet perfume. Then he goes through both rooms with the atomizer, pressing continuously on the little bulb, until both rooms smell of violet. He removes his topcoat and hat, sits in a blue velvet armchair, and smokes. After a short while, he rises again, and assures himself that the green shutters are lowered. Suddenly he returns to the bedroom and opens the drawer of the night table. He feels around in it for a tortoise-shell hairpin. He looks for a place to hide it, then puts it in the pocket of his topcoat. He then opens a cabinet in the salon, removes a tray with a bottle of cognac on it and two small liqueur glasses that he places on the table. He goes to his topcoat and removes a small white package from the pocket. Opening it, he places it beside the cognac. He returns to the cabinet, and removes two small plates and eating utensils. From the package he takes a marron glacé and eats it. He then pours himself a glass of cognac and drinks it. He looks at his watch. He paces the room several times. He stops in front of the large mirror and combs his hair and small mustache with a pocket comb. Now he goes to the door leading to the hallway and listens. Not a sound. The bell rings. The YOUNG GENTLEMAN starts suddenly. He then sits in the armchair and rises only when the door is opened and the YOUNG WIFE enters. She is heavily veiled. Closing the door behind her, she remains standing there for a moment while she brings her left hand to her heart as though to master an overwhelming emotion. The YOUNG GENTLEMAN goes to her, takes her left hand in his and imprints a kiss on her white black-trimmed glove.

YOUNG GENTLEMAN: (*Softly.*) Thank you.

YOUNG WIFE: Alfred! Alfred!

YOUNG GENTLEMAN: Come in, dear lady. Come in, my dear, dear Emma!

YOUNG WIFE: Please leave me here a while! Please, Alfred! (*She remains standing at the door. The YOUNG GENTLEMAN stands in front of her holding her hand.*) Where am I?

YOUNG GENTLEMAN: With me.

YOUNG WIFE: This is a frightful house, Alfred!

YOUNG GENTLEMAN: Why? It's a distinguished house.

YOUNG WIFE: I passed two gentlemen on the stairs!

YOUNG GENTLEMAN: Did you recognize them?

YOUNG WIFE: I don't know. It's possible.

YOUNG GENTLEMAN: Wouldn't you recognize your own friends?

YOUNG WIFE: I couldn't see!

YOUNG GENTLEMAN: Your best friends wouldn't have recognized you in that veil. Not even me.

YOUNG WIFE: Two veils!

YOUNG GENTLEMAN: Do come in. And at least take off your hat.

YOUNG WIFE: Oh, I couldn't possibly! When I agreed to come, I said five minutes. Not a moment longer.

YOUNG GENTLEMAN: Then your veil.

YOUNG WIFE: Two veils.

YOUNG GENTLEMAN: Both veils, then. But at least let me see you.

YOUNG WIFE: Do you love me, Alfred?

YOUNG GENTLEMAN: (*Deeply hurt.*) Emma, how *can* you.

YOUNG WIFE: It's terribly warm in here.

YOUNG GENTLEMAN: It's your fur cape. You'll catch cold if you —

YOUNG WIFE: (*Finally enters the room and throws herself into the armchair.*) I'm exhausted.

YOUNG GENTLEMAN: May I?

(*He removes her veils, takes the pin out of her hat, and places the hat, the pin, and the veils to one side. The YOUNG WIFE does not hinder him. The YOUNG GENTLEMAN stands in front of her and shakes his head.*)

YOUNG WIFE: What — ?

YOUNG GENTLEMAN: You're lovely.

YOUNG WIFE: I don't —

YOUNG GENTLEMAN: Just being alone with you, Emma. (*He kneels beside the armchair, takes her hands in his and covers them with kisses.*)

YOUNG WIFE: No. I have to go. You've had your wish. (*The YOUNG GENTLEMAN lets his head sink into her lap.*) You promised you'd behave.

YOUNG GENTLEMAN: Yes.

YOUNG WIFE: I'm about to suffocate.

YOUNG GENTLEMAN: (*Rises.*) It's your fur cape.

YOUNG WIFE: Put it next to my hat.

YOUNG GENTLEMAN: (*Takes off her fur cape and places it beside the other things on the divan.*) There.

YOUNG WIFE: And now — good-bye.

YOUNG GENTLEMAN: Emma! Emma!

YOUNG WIFE: You've had your five minutes.

YOUNG GENTLEMAN: But I haven't!

YOUNG WIFE: I want to know the time, Alfred.

YOUNG GENTLEMAN: A quarter to seven exactly.

YOUNG WIFE: I should be at my sister's!

YOUNG GENTLEMAN: Your sister sees you all the time.

YOUNG WIFE: Why did you bring me here!

YOUNG GENTLEMAN: Because I worship you, Emma.

YOUNG WIFE: And I'm the first, I suppose?

YOUNG GENTLEMAN: You are now.

YOUNG WIFE: I can't believe what I've become. A week ago — even yesterday. I wouldn't have thought it possible.

YOUNG GENTLEMAN: The day before yesterday you agreed.

YOUNG WIFE: You tormented me into it. I didn't want to. God knows I didn't. I swore yesterday that — yesterday evening I wrote you a long letter.

YOUNG GENTLEMAN: It never arrived!

YOUNG WIFE: I destroyed it. Oh, I should have sent it!

YOUNG GENTLEMAN: It's better this way.

YOUNG WIFE: No, it's disgraceful of me. I just don't understand myself. Alfred, let me go now. Good-bye. (*The YOUNG GENTLEMAN embraces her and covers her face with passionate kisses.*) Is this how you — keep your promise?

YOUNG GENTLEMAN: Just one more kiss. Just one.

YOUNG WIFE: And the last. (*He kisses her; she returns the kiss; their lips remain locked together for a long while.*)

YOUNG GENTLEMAN: Emma! This is the first time I've ever known happiness! (*The YOUNG WIFE sinks back into the armchair. The YOUNG GENTLEMAN sits on the arm of the chair, placing his arm lightly around her neck.*) Or rather, I — know what happiness *could* be.

YOUNG WIFE: (*Sighs deeply; the YOUNG GENTLEMAN kisses her again.*) Oh, Alfred, I don't like what you've made of me.

YOUNG GENTLEMAN: Are you uncomfortable? We're safe. Better than meeting outside.

YOUNG WIFE: Don't remind me of it.

YOUNG GENTLEMAN: Those were wonderful times. I'll remember them. Every moment with you is precious.

YOUNG WIFE: Do you remember the Industrial Ball?

YOUNG GENTLEMAN: Remember?! I sat beside you during supper. Close beside. Your husband ordered champagne. (*The YOUNG WIFE looks at him in protest.*) I was only going to mention the champagne. A glass of cognac?

YOUNG WIFE: A drop. With a glass of water first.

YOUNG GENTLEMAN: Hm! Now, where is the — ah! (*He pushes aside the curtains and enters the bedroom. He then returns with a decanter of water and two drinking glasses.*)

YOUNG WIFE: Where did you go?

YOUNG GENTLEMAN: The — the next room. (*Pours a glass of water.*)

YOUNG WIFE: Now, Alfred, I — I want you to tell me the truth.

YOUNG GENTLEMAN: Promise.

YOUNG WIFE: Have there been other women here?

YOUNG GENTLEMAN: But this house is twenty years old.

YOUNG WIFE: You know what I mean. With you. Here. With you.

YOUNG GENTLEMAN: With me?! Here?! Emma! How can you — !

YOUNG WIFE: Then you — no, I'd rather not ask. I'm to blame. Nothing goes unavenged.

YOUNG GENTLEMAN: What? I don't understand. What doesn't go unavenged?

YOUNG WIFE: No, no, no, I must come to my senses! Or I'll die of shame!

YOUNG GENTLEMAN: (*Holding a water decanter, shakes his head slowly.*)

Emma, how can you hurt me like this! (*The YOUNG WIFE pours herself a glass of cognac.*) I have something to say, Emma. If you're ashamed to be here, if I mean nothing to you, if you don't know that you're everything in the world to me — then — you should leave.

YOUNG WIFE: Thank you, I will.

YOUNG GENTLEMAN: (*Taking her by the hand.*) But if you know that I can't live without you, that to kiss your hand means more than all the women in the world! Emma, I'm not like those other young men who know how to court women. Maybe I'm too naive. I —

YOUNG WIFE: Suppose you *were* like all those other young men?

YOUNG GENTLEMAN: Then you wouldn't be here. Because you're not like other women.

YOUNG WIFE: Are you so sure?

YOUNG GENTLEMAN: (*Has pulled her to the divan and sat down beside her.*) I've thought about you a lot. I know you're unhappy. (*The YOUNG WIFE is pleased.*) Life is so empty, so futile! And then — so short! So terribly short. There's only one happiness. Finding someone who loves you. (*The YOUNG WIFE has taken a candied pear from the table and puts it in her mouth.*) Give me half.

YOUNG WIFE: (*Offers it to him with her lips, then takes hold of his hands threatening to go astray.*) What are you doing, Alfred? Is this keeping your promise?

YOUNG GENTLEMAN: (*Swallowing the pear; then more boldly.*) Life is so short —

YOUNG WIFE: (*Weakly.*) But there's no reason to —

YOUNG GENTLEMAN: (*Mechanically.*) Oh, but there is —

YOUNG WIFE: (*More weakly.*) Alfred, you promised to behave. And it's so light.

YOUNG GENTLEMAN: Come, my dear, my only. (*He lifts her from the divan.*)

YOUNG WIFE: What are you — ?

YOUNG GENTLEMAN: It's dark in there.

YOUNG WIFE: Another room? Alfred?

YOUNG GENTLEMAN: (*Takes her with him.*) A beautiful room — and very dark —

YOUNG WIFE: I want to stay here. (*The YOUNG GENTLEMAN is already through the curtains with her, into the bedroom, and begins to unbutton her blouse.*) You're so — oh, God, what are you — ! Alfred!

YOUNG GENTLEMAN: I worship you, Emma!

YOUNG WIFE: Please wait! Wait! (*Weakly.*) Go on. I'll call you.

YOUNG GENTLEMAN: Please. Let me — let me — let me help you —

YOUNG WIFE: You're tearing my clothes.

YOUNG GENTLEMAN: You're not wearing a corset!

YOUNG WIFE: *No!* And neither does Duse! You can unbutton my shoes. (*The YOUNG GENTLEMAN unbuttons her shoes and kisses her feet. The YOUNG WIFE has slipped into bed.*) Oh, it's cold!

YOUNG GENTLEMAN: Not for long!

YOUNG WIFE: (*Laughing softly.*) Oh?

YOUNG GENTLEMAN: (*Suddenly in a bad mood; to himself.*) Why did she say that! (*He undresses in the dark.*)

YOUNG WIFE: (*Tenderly.*) Come — come — come —

YOUNG GENTLEMAN: (*Suddenly in a better mood.*) In a second.

YOUNG WIFE: I smell violets.

YOUNG GENTLEMAN: No. *You* smell like violets. Yes. (*To her.*) You!

YOUNG WIFE: Alfred! Alfred!

• • •

YOUNG GENTLEMAN: I just love you too much, that's all! I feel like I'm going insane!

YOUNG WIFE: —

YOUNG GENTLEMAN: I've felt that way recently. I knew it would happen!

YOUNG WIFE: Don't be upset.

YOUNG GENTLEMAN: No. It's only natural for a man to —

YOUNG WIFE: There now. There. You're all excited. Calm down.

YOUNG GENTLEMAN: Do you know Stendhal?

YOUNG WIFE: Stendhal?

YOUNG GENTLEMAN: His *Psychology of Love.*

YOUNG WIFE: Why?

YOUNG GENTLEMAN: There's a story in it. Very significant.

YOUNG WIFE: Tell me about it.

YOUNG GENTLEMAN: Well, there's a large group of cavalry officers that's gotten together.

YOUNG WIFE: And?

YOUNG GENTLEMAN: And they tell about their love affairs. And each reports that with the woman he loves most — most passionately — Well. The same thing happened to them that just happened to us.

YOUNG WIFE: Yes —

YOUNG GENTLEMAN: There's more. One of them claims that it *never* happened to him. But Stendhal adds that he was a notorious braggart.

YOUNG WIFE: Aha.

YOUNG GENTLEMAN: But it's still a shock. Even if it doesn't mean anything. Stupid.

YOUNG WIFE: Yes, and you did promise you'd behave.

YOUNG GENTLEMAN: You're laughing! You don't know — !

YOUNG WIFE: I'm not. That bit about Stendhal was very interesting. I only thought it happened to older men. Who — who've lived a good deal.

YOUNG GENTLEMAN: That's got nothing to do with it. Besides, I didn't tell you the best story. One of the cavalry officers tells how he spent three nights — or was it six? — with a woman he'd wanted for weeks. And all they did was cry with happiness. Both of them.

YOUNG WIFE: Both of them?

YOUNG GENTLEMAN: Yes! Amazing! It makes so much sense. When you're in love.

YOUNG WIFE: But there must be many who don't cry.

YOUNG GENTLEMAN: (*Nervous.*) Well, of course. That was an exception.

YOUNG WIFE: Ah! I thought Stendhal said that *all* cavalry officers cry. Under the circumstances.

YOUNG GENTLEMAN: You're making fun of me!

YOUNG WIFE: Alfred! Don't be childish!

YOUNG GENTLEMAN: I'm nervous! And — and — it's all you're thinking about! I'm ashamed!

YOUNG WIFE: It never occurred to me.

YOUNG GENTLEMAN: You're lying! I'm not even sure you love me!

YOUNG WIFE: What else can I do?

YOUNG GENTLEMAN: You always make fun of me!

YOUNG WIFE: How silly. Come. Let me kiss that sweet face.

YOUNG GENTLEMAN: I like that.

YOUNG WIFE: Do you love me?

YOUNG GENTLEMAN: I'm *so* happy!

YOUNG WIFE: But you don't have to cry, too.

YOUNG GENTLEMAN: (*Pulling away from her; agitated.*) There. You see? And I even begged you.

YOUNG WIFE: All I said was you shouldn't cry.

YOUNG GENTLEMAN: You said: "You don't have to cry, *too!*"

YOUNG WIFE: Sweetheart, you're nervous.

YOUNG GENTLEMAN: I know!

YOUNG WIFE: But why? I love the idea that — well, that we're friends.

YOUNG GENTLEMAN: There you go again!

YOUNG WIFE: That was one of our first talks. We wanted to be good friends. Just friends. What a lovely time. It was at my sister's. The big ball in January. During the quadrille. Oh, God, I should be at my sister's now! What will she say? Good-bye, Alfred!

YOUNG GENTLEMAN: Emma! You can't leave me! Like *this!*

YOUNG WIFE: But I can.

YOUNG GENTLEMAN: Just five more minutes.

YOUNG WIFE: All right. Just five more minutes. But promise me not to move. Agreed? I'll give you a kiss when I leave. Shh! Quiet. Don't move. Or I'll leave at once, my sweet — sweet —

YOUNG GENTLEMAN: Emma! My dear, dear —

• • •

YOUNG WIFE: Dear Alfred.

YOUNG GENTLEMAN: You're heavenly! Heavenly!

YOUNG WIFE: I have to go now.

YOUNG GENTLEMAN: Your sister can wait.

YOUNG WIFE: No! Home! It's too late for my sister's. What time is it?

YOUNG GENTLEMAN: (*Dumbfounded.*) Well, I don't know!

YOUNG WIFE: Try your watch.

YOUNG GENTLEMAN: It's in my waistcoat.

YOUNG WIFE: Then get it.

YOUNG GENTLEMAN: (*Gets out of bed with a mighty push.*) Eight.

YOUNG WIFE: (*Rises quickly.*) Oh, God! Hurry, Alfred! My stockings! What will I tell him? They're waiting for me at home! Eight o'clock!

YOUNG GENTLEMAN: When will I see you again?

YOUNG WIFE: Never.

YOUNG GENTLEMAN: Emma! You don't love me!

YOUNG WIFE: Of course I love you. Hand me my shoes.

YOUNG GENTLEMAN: But *never?* (*Hands her the shoes.*) Here.

YOUNG WIFE: There's a buttonhook in my bag. Hurry! Please!

YOUNG GENTLEMAN: (*Hands her the buttonhook.*) Here.

YOUNG WIFE: Alfred, this situation could become serious.

YOUNG GENTLEMAN: (*Disagreeable.*) Why?

YOUNG WIFE: What will I tell my husband? And he'll ask!

YOUNG GENTLEMAN: You've been at your sister's.

YOUNG WIFE: I can't lie. I never could.

YOUNG GENTLEMAN: There's no other way.

YOUNG WIFE: If only you were worth it. Oh, come here. I want to kiss you again. (*She embraces him.*) And now — leave me alone. Go in the other room. I can't dress with you here. (*The YOUNG GENTLEMAN goes into the salon and dresses. He eats some of the pastry and drinks a glass of cognac. The YOUNG WIFE calls after a while.*) Alfred?

YOUNG GENTLEMAN: My dear?

YOUNG WIFE: I'm glad we didn't cry.

YOUNG GENTLEMAN: (*Smiling not without pride.*) Oh! Women!

YOUNG WIFE: What will happen — if by chance we meet one day at a party?

YOUNG GENTLEMAN: By chance? One day? But you'll be at Lobheimer's tomorrow.

YOUNG WIFE: Yes. You?

YOUNG GENTLEMAN: Yes. May I have the cotillion?

YOUNG WIFE: Oh, I *can't* go! You're mad! I'd — (*She enters the salon, fully dressed, and takes a chocolate pastry.*) — I'd die of embarrassment!

YOUNG GENTLEMAN: Tomorrow at Lobheimer's. It will be lovely.

YOUNG WIFE: No! I'll excuse myself! I'll —

YOUNG GENTLEMAN: Then the day after tomorrow. Here.

YOUNG WIFE: You're joking.

YOUNG GENTLEMAN: At six.

YOUNG WIFE: Are there any cabs at the corner?

YOUNG GENTLEMAN: As many as you like. The day after tomorrow. At six. Here. Say yes, my dear, my sweet.

YOUNG WIFE: We'll discuss it tomorrow. During the cotillion.

YOUNG GENTLEMAN: (*Embraces her.*) Angel!

YOUNG WIFE: Don't muss my hair.

YOUNG GENTLEMAN: Tomorrow at Lobheimer's. And the day after tomorrow here. In my arms.

YOUNG WIFE: Good-bye.

YOUNG GENTLEMAN: (*Suddenly troubled again.*) What will you tell your husband?

YOUNG WIFE: Don't ask! Don't ask! I can't bear to think! Why do I love you so? Good-bye! If I meet anyone on the stairs, I'll have a stroke! Ah! (*The YOUNG GENTLEMAN kisses her hand once again. The YOUNG WIFE goes off. The YOUNG GENTLEMAN stays behind, alone. Then he sits on the divan.*)

YOUNG GENTLEMAN: (*Smiles and says to himself.*) Finally! An affair with a respectable woman!

V. THE YOUNG WIFE AND THE HUSBAND

A comfortable bedroom. It is 10:30 P.M. The YOUNG WIFE is in bed reading. The HUSBAND enters in his bathrobe.

YOUNG WIFE: (*Without looking up.*) Finished?

HUSBAND: Yes. I'm exhausted. Besides —

YOUNG WIFE: What besides?

HUSBAND: Suddenly I felt lonely. Like — I need you.

YOUNG WIFE: (*Looks up.*) Oh?

HUSBAND: (*Sits beside her on the bed.*) Don't read any more. You'll ruin your eyes.

YOUNG WIFE: (*Closes the book.*) Do you have a problem?

HUSBAND: No. Just that I love you. But you know that.

YOUNG WIFE: There are times I could forget.

HUSBAND: There are times you *have* to forget.

YOUNG WIFE: Why?

HUSBAND: Otherwise marriage would be imperfect. It would — it would — lose its sanctity.

YOUNG WIFE: Oh.

HUSBAND: It's true. If during our five years of marriage we hadn't occasionally forgotten that we were in love — maybe we wouldn't be.

YOUNG WIFE: I don't quite —

HUSBAND: It's like this. We've had — oh — ten or twelve love affairs together. Wouldn't you say?

YOUNG WIFE: I haven't been counting.

HUSBAND: If we'd carried our first affair to its conclusion, if I'd surrendered to my passion for you, we'd have ended like every other pair of lovers. We'd have been finished.

YOUNG WIFE: Ah. Yes. I see.

HUSBAND: Early in our marriage I was afraid it would turn out just that way.

YOUNG WIFE: Me, too.

HUSBAND: You see. I was right. That's why it's good to live together. As friends. Occasionally.

YOUNG WIFE: I see.

HUSBAND: That way we always have *new* honeymoons. Because I never let our honeymoons —

YOUNG WIFE: Grow stale.

HUSBAND: Yes.

YOUNG WIFE: Is another of those "friendship" phases coming to a close?

HUSBAND: (*Tenderly pressing her to him.*) Could be.

YOUNG WIFE: But what if I didn't — agree?

HUSBAND: But you *do* agree! You're the cleverest, enchantingest creature there is! I'm lucky to have found you!

YOUNG WIFE: I rather like the way you — court me — occasionally.

HUSBAND: (*Has climbed into bed.*) I've been around a bit in the world. Come, lay your head on my shoulder. And, well, marriage is something much more mysterious for me than for a young girl from a good family.

You come to us pure and — to a certain degree — ignorant. And so you have a clearer idea of love than we men.

YOUNG WIFE: (*Laughing.*) Oh!

HUSBAND: It's true. Men are forced into all sorts of experiences before marriage. And it confuses us. Makes us insecure. You women hear a lot and know much too much. You *read* too much. But you don't understand what men are forced into. Love becomes disgusting. Because of the creatures we become dependent upon.

YOUNG WIFE: Who are — ?

HUSBAND: (*Kisses her on the forehead.*) You're lucky you're ignorant of such relationships. They're most pitiable creatures. We shouldn't cast stones.

YOUNG WIFE: Why pitiable? It hardly seems appropriate.

HUSBAND: (*Gently.*) They deserve it. You protected young girls from good families know nothing of the misery that drives these poor creatures into sin.

YOUNG WIFE: They all sell themselves?

HUSBAND: Not exactly. But I don't mean merely material misery. There's such a thing as moral misery. The failure to know what's proper. And especially what's noble.

YOUNG WIFE: But why are they pitiable? They seem to be doing rather well.

HUSBAND: Where do you get your ideas! It's because they're destined by nature to sink deeper and deeper. There's no end to it.

YOUNG WIFE: (*Snuggles close to him.*) Sounds like fun.

HUSBAND: (*A bit pained.*) Emma! For a respectable woman there should be nothing more repulsive than a woman who is not — respectable.

YOUNG WIFE: I was only joking, Carl! But I do enjoy hearing you talk. Talk to me.

HUSBAND: About what?

YOUNG WIFE: About these — creatures.

HUSBAND: You can't be serious.

YOUNG WIFE: When we were first married I begged you to tell me about your youth.

HUSBAND: But why?

YOUNG WIFE: Because you're my husband. And because it's only fair for me to know.

HUSBAND: You can't really expect me to — ! Emma, that's enough! I could never —

YOUNG WIFE: I wonder how many women you've held like you're holding me?

HUSBAND: Women, yes. But not like you.

YOUNG WIFE: Answer me one question — or — or — no honeymoon.

HUSBAND: You have a way with words, Emma! And remember that you're a mother. And that our little girl is asleep in the next room.

YOUNG WIFE: (*Snuggling close to him.*) I think I'd like to have a boy, too.

HUSBAND: Emma!

YOUNG WIFE: Old grouch! So I'm your wife. Why can't I be your mistress, too.

HUSBAND: Would you?

YOUNG WIFE: First my question.

HUSBAND: (*Accommodating.*) Yes?

YOUNG WIFE: Was there ever a — married woman among your — ?

HUSBAND: I — I don't understand.

YOUNG WIFE: I think you do.

HUSBAND: (*Mildly disturbed.*) Why?

YOUNG WIFE: I know that there *are* such women. But did *you* ever — ?

HUSBAND: (*Seriously.*) Do you know any?

YOUNG WIFE: I'm not sure.

HUSBAND: One of your friends?

YOUNG WIFE: How can I know?

HUSBAND: Well, when women get together they — did one of them confess?

YOUNG WIFE: (*Uncertainly.*) No.

HUSBAND: Have you ever suspected that — ?

YOUNG WIFE: Ah! Suspected! Hm.

HUSBAND: You have!

YOUNG WIFE: No! I don't think them capable of it!

HUSBAND: Not a one?

YOUNG WIFE: Not *my* friends!

HUSBAND: Promise me, Emma.

YOUNG WIFE: What?

HUSBAND: That you'll have nothing to do with a woman you even slightly suspect of —

YOUNG WIFE: You're mad!

HUSBAND: I know you'd never seek out such — but it could happen that — well, women like that seek out women who are respectable. As a relief. And as a sign of their longing for virtue.

YOUNG WIFE: Virtue —

HUSBAND: But you can be sure of one thing. These women are terribly unhappy.

YOUNG WIFE: Why?

HUSBAND: How can you ask! How *can* you! The existence they lead! Lies! Viciousness! Vulgarity! Danger!

YOUNG WIFE: Yes, I suppose you're right.

HUSBAND: They *pay* for their happiness — their —

YOUNG WIFE: Pleasure —

HUSBAND: Pleasure? Pleasure?

YOUNG WIFE: There must be *something* to recommend it. Or why would they do it?

HUSBAND: *Nothing — nothing* recommends it! Intoxication!

YOUNG WIFE: (*Reflectively.*) Intoxication —

HUSBAND: No! *Not* intoxication! But the price is high.

YOUNG WIFE: Is this from personal experience?

HUSBAND: Yes. I'm sorry to say.

YOUNG WIFE: Who? Tell me. Do I know her?

HUSBAND: How can you?

YOUNG WIFE: How long — before you married me?

HUSBAND: Don't ask. Please.

YOUNG WIFE: But, Carl!

HUSBAND: She's dead.

YOUNG WIFE: Dead?

HUSBAND: It's ridiculous, I know. But I have the feeling that *all* of these women die young.

YOUNG WIFE: Did you love her very much?

HUSBAND: You don't love a liar.

YOUNG WIFE: Then why — do you — ?

HUSBAND: Intoxication.

YOUNG WIFE: Then it *does* have something to —

HUSBAND: Don't, please. It's past. I've only loved one woman. You can only love purity and truth.

YOUNG WIFE: Carl!

HUSBAND: Beautiful! You're beautiful! Come here! (*He puts out the light.*)

YOUNG WIFE: Do you know what I keep thinking about tonight?

HUSBAND: What, my sweet?

YOUNG WIFE: About — about — about — Venice.

HUSBAND: The first night —

YOUNG WIFE: Yes! It was so —

HUSBAND: What? Tell me.

YOUNG WIFE: Do you love me the same way now?

HUSBAND: The same.

YOUNG WIFE: Oh! If you'd always —

HUSBAND: What?

YOUNG WIFE: Dear Carl!

HUSBAND: What? If I'd always — ?

YOUNG WIFE: — always —

HUSBAND: What would happen if I would always — ?

YOUNG WIFE: Then I'd always know that you love me.

HUSBAND: But you know that already. I can't always be the loving husband. At times I have to brave the hostile world, struggle for an existence. In marriage everything has its place. That's the beauty of it. There aren't many couples who after five years can still remember their — their Venice.

YOUNG WIFE: Of course.

HUSBAND: And now — good night, my sweet.

YOUNG WIFE: Good night!

VI. THE HUSBAND
AND THE SWEET YOUNG THING

A private room in the Riedhof Restaurant. Comfortable, modest elegance. The gas stove is burning. On the table are the remains of a meal, meringues with whipped cream, fruit, cheese. The HUSBAND smokes a Havana cigar as he leans into a corner of the divan. The SWEET YOUNG THING sits beside him on a chair and spoons whipped cream out of a bowl, sucking it up with great delight.

HUSBAND: Taste good?

SWEET YOUNG THING (*Not allowing herself to be disturbed.*) Ohhh!

HUSBAND: How about another?

SWEET YOUNG THING: Too much is too much!

HUSBAND: You're out of wine. There. (*He pours wine.*)

SWEET YOUNG THING: No. I just couldn't take another drink, sir.

HUSBAND: You said "sir" again.

SWEET YOUNG THING: Oh? I guess I just always forget. Don't I, sir?

HUSBAND: Carl!

SWEET YOUNG THING: What?

HUSBAND: "Don't I, *Carl,*" not "Don't I, *sir!*" Sit over here by me.

SWEET YOUNG THING: In a minute. I'm not through yet. (*The HUS-BAND rises, stands behind the chair and embraces her, while she turns her head toward him.*) Something wrong?

HUSBAND: A kiss?

SWEET YOUNG THING: (*Gives him a kiss.*) You're very daring, sir. I mean, Carl.

HUSBAND: You're just finding that out?

SWEET YOUNG THING: No. I knew on the street. What you must think of me, sir!

HUSBAND: *Carl!*

SWEET YOUNG THING: Carl.

HUSBAND: Why?

SWEET YOUNG THING: For being so easy. Coming here with you. A private room and all.

HUSBAND: It wasn't all *that* easy.

SWEET YOUNG THING: But you have a nice way of —

HUSBAND: Do you think so?

SWEET YOUNG THING: And who cares.

HUSBAND: Right.

SWEET YOUNG THING: What's the difference if we go for a walk or —

HUSBAND: Oh, it's too cold for a walk.

SWEET YOUNG THING: Yes, too cold.

HUSBAND: And it's cozy here. (*He has sat down again, puts his arms around the SWEET YOUNG THING and pulls her to his side.*)

SWEET YOUNG THING: (*Weakly.*) Oh —

HUSBAND: Have you noticed me before?

SWEET YOUNG THING: Sure. In Singerstrasse.

HUSBAND: Not just today. Yesterday. The day before. When I followed you.

SWEET YOUNG THING: Lots of men follow me.

HUSBAND: I imagine. *Did* you notice me?

SWEET YOUNG THING: The other day my cousin's husband followed me. In the dark. And didn't recognize me.

HUSBAND: Did he talk to you?

SWEET YOUNG THING: Silly. All men aren't as fresh as you.

HUSBAND: Hm. But you answered *me*.

SWEET YOUNG THING: Are you sorry?

HUSBAND: (*Kisses her violently.*) Your lips taste like whipped cream.

SWEET YOUNG THING: They're always sweet.

HUSBAND: How many other men have told you that?

SWEET YOUNG THING: How many?

HUSBAND: How many men have kissed you?

SWEET YOUNG THING: You'd never believe me.

HUSBAND: Why?

SWEET YOUNG THING: Guess.

HUSBAND: Well, let's say — you won't be angry?

SWEET YOUNG THING: Angry?

HUSBAND: Mmm. Twenty?

SWEET YOUNG THING: (*Pulling away from him.*) Oh, sure! Why not a hundred!

HUSBAND: I was guessing.

SWEET YOUNG THING: You're a bad guesser!

HUSBAND: Ten.

SWEET YOUNG THING: (*Insulted.*) A girl who lets herself be picked up! And goes to a place like this right off!

HUSBAND: Don't be childish. What's the difference? The streets or here? We're in a private room. In a restaurant. The waiter could come in any time. So what?

SWEET YOUNG THING: That's what I said. So what.

HUSBAND: Have you been in places like this before? A *chambre séparée*?

SWEET YOUNG THING: Well — yes.

HUSBAND: Good. At least you're honest about it.

SWEET YOUNG THING: It's not what you think. It was with my girl-friend and her husband. During Carnival. Last year.

HUSBAND: Would the world have collapsed if it had been with a lover?

SWEET YOUNG THING: No. The world wouldn't collapse. But I haven't got a lover.

HUSBAND: Do hens lay eggs?

SWEET YOUNG THING: I *don't!*

HUSBAND: Do you expect me to — ?

SWEET YOUNG THING: What? I *don't* have one. At least not for the last six months.

HUSBAND: Before that? Who?

SWEET YOUNG THING: Nosy!

HUSBAND: It's because I love you.

SWEET YOUNG THING: You mean that?

HUSBAND: Of course. You must have noticed. Tell me about it? (*He presses her close to him.*)

SWEET YOUNG THING: Why should I?

HUSBAND: Do I always have to beg? I just want to know.

SWEET YOUNG THING: (*Laughing.*) Oh — a man.

HUSBAND: Who!

SWEET YOUNG THING: He looked like you. A little.

HUSBAND: I see.

SWEET YOUNG THING: If you hadn't —

HUSBAND: What then?

SWEET YOUNG THING: Why ask, if you know?

HUSBAND: (*Understands.*) That's why you let me talk to you?

SWEET YOUNG THING: I guess.

HUSBAND: I don't know whether to be pleased or angry.

SWEET YOUNG THING: I'd be pleased.

HUSBAND: Yes.

SWEET YOUNG THING: Even the way you talk reminds me of him. The way you look.

HUSBAND: Who was he?

SWEET YOUNG THING: And your eyes.

HUSBAND: What was his name?

SWEET YOUNG THING: Don't look at me like that.

HUSBAND: (*Embraces her; a long passionate kiss.*) Where are you going?

SWEET YOUNG THING: Home. Time.

HUSBAND: Later.

SWEET YOUNG THING: I really have to. What will my mother say?

HUSBAND: Your mother? You live with her?

SWEET YOUNG THING: Of course. Where else?

HUSBAND: I see. Well. Just the two of you?

SWEET YOUNG THING: Just the five of us, you mean. Two brothers and two sisters.

HUSBAND: Why are you sitting way over there? Are you the eldest?

SWEET YOUNG THING: Second oldest. Kathy's first. She works in a flower shop. And then me.

HUSBAND: Where do you work?

SWEET YOUNG THING: I stay at home.

HUSBAND: All the time?

SWEET YOUNG THING: *Somebody* has to.

HUSBAND: Of course. What do you tell your mother? When you're late.

SWEET YOUNG THING: It doesn't happen often.

HUSBAND: Tonight, then. Won't she ask?

SWEET YOUNG THING: You bet! I can be quiet as a mouse, but she hears me every time.

HUSBAND: What'll you tell her?

SWEET YOUNG THING: Say I went to the theater.

HUSBAND: She'll believe that?

SWEET YOUNG THING: Why not? I go to the theater a lot. Like last Sunday. With my girlfriend and her husband and my oldest brother.

HUSBAND: Where'd you get the tickets?

SWEET YOUNG THING: My brother's a hairdresser.

HUSBAND: At the theater?

SWEET YOUNG THING: Questions, questions!

HUSBAND: I'm interested. What does your other brother do?

SWEET YOUNG THING: School. Wants to be a teacher. Imagine! A teacher!

HUSBAND: And then you have a younger sister.

SWEET YOUNG THING: Oh, what a brat! You can't take your eyes off her. The things they learn in school these days! The other day I found her out. With a boy!

HUSBAND: What?

SWEET YOUNG THING: From the school across the street from us. Out walking with him one evening. The little brat!

HUSBAND: What did you do?

SWEET YOUNG THING: She got a spanking, she did.

HUSBAND: You're that strict?

SWEET YOUNG THING: I *have* to be. My older sister works and my mother nags. I have to do *everything!*

HUSBAND: God, you're sweet! (*He grows tender and kisses her.*) You remind me of someone, too.

SWEET YOUNG THING: Oh! Who?

HUSBAND: It doesn't matter. Maybe my youth. Here. Have some wine.

SWEET YOUNG THING: How old are you? And I don't even know your name.

HUSBAND: Carl.

SWEET YOUNG THING: Carl?!

HUSBAND: Was *his* name Carl?

SWEET YOUNG THING: I don't believe it! It's a miracle! It's — it's your eyes. You look — (*Shakes her head.*)

HUSBAND: Tell me who he was.

SWEET YOUNG THING: He was a terrible man or he wouldn't have left me.

HUSBAND: Did you love him a lot?

SWEET YOUNG THING: Of course I loved him a lot.

HUSBAND: He was a lieutenant, I suppose?

SWEET YOUNG THING: No, they wouldn't take him. His father had a house in — Why are you asking?

HUSBAND: (*Kisses her.*) Your eyes are gray. At first I thought they were black.

SWEET YOUNG THING: Don't you like them? (*The HUSBAND kisses her eyes.*) No! No! I can't stand that! Oh, please! No! Let me up! Just for a minute. Please.

HUSBAND: (*More and more tenderly.*) No — no — no —

SWEET YOUNG THING: Please, Carl. Please —

HUSBAND: How old are you? Eighteen? Hm?

SWEET YOUNG THING: Nineteen.

HUSBAND: Nineteen. And how old am I?

SWEET YOUNG THING: You're — thirty.

HUSBAND: More or less. But let's not talk about that.

SWEET YOUNG THING: He was thirty-two when I met him.

HUSBAND: How long ago?

SWEET YOUNG THING: I don't remember. But I think there was something in that wine.

HUSBAND: Oh?

SWEET YOUNG THING: I'm all — well, you know. My head's spinning.

HUSBAND: Hold tight to me. There. (*He presses her to him and grows more tender.*) How about leaving. Hm?

SWEET YOUNG THING: Yes. For home.

HUSBAND: That wasn't what I had in mind.

SWEET YOUNG THING: I don't know what you mean. Oh, no! No no no! Not me! You terrible men!

HUSBAND: Listen. Next time we'll arrange it so that — (*He has sunk to the floor, his head in her lap.*) I like that. I like that.

SWEET YOUNG THING: What are you doing? (*She kisses his hair.*) I knew there was something in the wine. I'm so — so sleepy. What if I can't get up? Oh, but — oh, no! Carl! What if someone comes in! Oh, please! The waiter —

HUSBAND: No waiter — 'll come in here — if he knows what's —

$$\bullet \quad \bullet \quad \bullet$$

(*The SWEET YOUNG THING leans with closed eyes into the corner of the divan. The HUSBAND walks back and forth in the small room after lighting a cigarette. Long silence.*)

HUSBAND: (*Looks at the SWEET YOUNG THING for a long while; to himself.*) I wonder what she's really like. Damn! It happened so fast. I wasn't very careful either. Hm.

SWEET YOUNG THING: (*Her eyes shut.*) I knew there was something. In the wine.

HUSBAND: Why?

SWEET YOUNG THING: Otherwise —

HUSBAND: Why blame it on the wine?

SWEET YOUNG THING: Where are you? You're so far away. Come here. (*The HUSBAND sits next to her.*) Do you like me?

HUSBAND: Do you have to ask? (*Quickly interrupting himself.*) Of course.

SWEET YOUNG THING: You know — I still — what was in the wine?

HUSBAND: I don't go around poisoning people.

SWEET YOUNG THING: Then why — ? I'm just not like that. I swear. And if you think I —

HUSBAND: There, there. It's all right. I don't think badly of you. It's because you like me.

SWEET YOUNG THING: Yes.

HUSBAND: When two young people are together. Like this. Alone. There's no need for anything in the wine.

SWEET YOUNG THING: I was just talking.

HUSBAND: Why?

SWEET YOUNG THING: (*Rather obstinately.*) I was ashamed of myself.

HUSBAND: Oh, God! But I remind you of your first lover.

SWEET YOUNG THING: Yes.

HUSBAND: Your first.

SWEET YOUNG THING: Yes.

HUSBAND: Who were the others?

SWEET YOUNG THING: There weren't any.

HUSBAND: You're joking.

SWEET YOUNG THING: Don't pester me.

HUSBAND: Cigarette?

SWEET YOUNG THING: No, thanks.

HUSBAND: Do you know the time?

SWEET YOUNG THING: What?

HUSBAND: Eleven thirty.

SWEET YOUNG THING: Oh?

HUSBAND: I was thinking of your mother. But she must be used to it.

SWEET YOUNG THING: You're sending me home? Already?

HUSBAND: But you —

SWEET YOUNG THING: You sure change fast. What'd I do?

HUSBAND: What? What is it?

SWEET YOUNG THING: It was your eyes. Your look. A lot of men beg me to go to places like this with them.

HUSBAND: Would you like to come here again? Soon? Or somewhere else?

SWEET YOUNG THING: I don't know.

HUSBAND: What do you mean "I don't know"?

SWEET YOUNG THING: Why'd you ask?

HUSBAND: Good. When? Unfortunately I don't live in Vienna. I come here now and then. For a few days.

SWEET YOUNG THING: Go on! You're not Viennese?

HUSBAND: Well, yes, I'm *from* Vienna. I just don't live in town.

SWEET YOUNG THING: Then where?

HUSBAND: Why are you interested?

SWEET YOUNG THING: You think I'll come spying on you?

HUSBAND: Come any time.

SWEET YOUNG THING: Really?

HUSBAND: Does that surprise you?

SWEET YOUNG THING: Married?

HUSBAND: (*Taken aback.*) Why?

SWEET YOUNG THING: Just thought you might be.

HUSBAND: Wouldn't that bother you?

SWEET YOUNG THING: Well, sure, I'd rather have you single. You're married.

HUSBAND: Why?

SWEET YOUNG THING: Oh — you don't live in Vienna — you don't have time —

HUSBAND: So?

SWEET YOUNG THING: I never believe them when they say that.

HUSBAND: Would it bother you to make a man unfaithful to his — ?

SWEET YOUNG THING: Oh, God! She does the same thing!

HUSBAND: How dare you!

SWEET YOUNG THING: Thought you weren't married!

HUSBAND: You don't say things like — (*Rises.*)

SWEET YOUNG THING: Oh, now, what's the matter? Don't be mad. I didn't really know you were married. I just said it. Be nice.

HUSBAND: (*Goes to her after a few seconds.*) Women! What strange creatures. (*He becomes tender again at her side.*)

SWEET YOUNG THING: No. Please. It's late.

HUSBAND: Listen. Talk seriously now. I want to see you again. Often.

SWEET YOUNG THING: Oh?

HUSBAND: But I have to depend on you. I can't be careful *all* the time.

SWEET YOUNG THING: I can take care of myself.

HUSBAND: You're not exactly inexperienced. You're young and — men are an unscrupulous lot.

SWEET YOUNG THING: Oh, Lord!

HUSBAND: Not in a moral sense, of course. But you know what I'm —

SWEET YOUNG THING: What do you really think of me?

HUSBAND: Well. If you *do* want to love me — just me — we might arrange something. Even if I do live in Graz. A place like this isn't right. (*The SWEET YOUNG THING snuggles close to him.*) Next time it'll be somewhere else.

SWEET YOUNG THING: Sure.

HUSBAND: Where we can't be disturbed.

SWEET YOUNG THING: All right.

HUSBAND: (*Embraces her passionately.*) We'll talk it over walking home. (*Rises and opens the door.*) Waiter! The check!

VII. THE SWEET YOUNG THING AND THE POET

A small room furnished in comfortable good taste. The drapes maintain a level of semidarkness. Red curtains. A large writing-table scattered with papers and books. An upright piano against the wall. The SWEET YOUNG THING and the POET enter together. The POET locks the door.

POET: So here we are. (*Kisses her.*)

SWEET YOUNG THING: (*In hat and cape.*) Oh, I like it! But I can't see anything.

POET: You get used to it. Your sweet little eyes. (*Kisses her eyes.*)

SWEET YOUNG THING: My sweet little eyes won't have time for that.

POET: What?

SWEET YOUNG THING: I can stay only a minute.

POET: At least take off your hat.

SWEET YOUNG THING: It's a waste of time.

POET: (*Removes the pin from her hat and places the hat at a distance.*) And your cape.

SWEET YOUNG THING: Don't. I told you. I can't stay.

POET: Rest a while. We walked for three hours.

SWEET YOUNG THING: Drove. Not walked. So there.

POET: On the way back, maybe. But earlier we walked for three full hours. Sit down. Anywhere. How about the writing-table? No, no. That's not — here. The divan. There. (*He urges her onto the divan.*) Your sweet little head on the pillow.

SWEET YOUNG THING: (*Laughing.*) I'm not tired.

POET: How would you know? And if you're sleepy, you can take a nap. I'll be quiet as a mouse. I know. I'll play a lullaby. One I wrote. (*He goes to the piano.*)

SWEET YOUNG THING: One you wrote?

POET: Yes.

SWEET YOUNG THING: But, Robert, I thought you were a doctor.

POET: I said I was a writer.

SWEET YOUNG THING: But doctors are *always* writers.

POET: Not me. What made you think of that?

SWEET YOUNG THING: You said you wrote the lullaby.

POET: Well, not *wrote* exactly. But who cares? As long as it's beautiful.

SWEET YOUNG THING: Yes. As long as it's beautiful.

POET: Do you know what I meant by that?

SWEET YOUNG THING: What?

POET: What I just said.

SWEET YOUNG THING: (*Sleepily.*) Oh. Sure.

POET: (*Rises, goes to her and strokes her hair.*) You didn't understand a word.

SWEET YOUNG THING: I'm not stupid.

POET: Of course you're stupid. It's why I love you. A woman needs to be stupid. I mean *beautifully*. In *your* way.

SWEET YOUNG THING: Why are you making fun of me?

POET: Angel! You sweet, sweet angel! Do you like lying on soft Persian rugs?

SWEET YOUNG THING: Yes. Are you going to play? The piano?

POET: It's nicer here. (*Strokes her hair.*)

SWEET YOUNG THING: Shouldn't you light a lamp?

POET: No. The twilight's comforting. We spent the day bathed in sunlight.

And now we've climbed from the bath and wrap the — the twilight about us like a robe. (*Laughs.*) No, that's bad. Ah, well. Do you agree?

SWEET YOUNG THING: Don't ask *me*.

POET: (*Gently moving from her.*) What divine stupidity! (*He takes out a pocket notebook and jots down a few words.*)

SWEET YOUNG THING: What're you doing? (*Turning toward him.*) What're you writing?

POET: (*Softly.*) Sun. Bath. Twilight. Robe. There. (*Pockets the notebook; aloud.*) Nothing. Tell me, sweet angel. What would you like to eat? Or drink?

SWEET YOUNG THING: I'm not thirsty. But I could eat.

POET: Hm. Too bad. There's cognac in the house. I have to go out for the food.

SWEET YOUNG THING: Send for it.

POET: The maid's left. Oh, I'll go myself. What's your wish, fair damsel?

SWEET YOUNG THING: No, don't bother. I have to get home anyway.

POET: No, please. Listen. We'll have supper on the way back. After we leave.

SWEET YOUNG THING: It's late. And where would we go? We might run into friends.

POET: You have that many friends?

SWEET YOUNG THING: If even *one* of them saw us!

POET: What if they did?

SWEET YOUNG THING: Well, my mother!

POET: Oh, there are places. Restaurants. With private rooms.

SWEET YOUNG THING: (*Singing.*) "Dining in a *chambre séparée!*"

POET: Ever been to one? A *chambre séparée?*

SWEET YOUNG THING: Well — to be honest. Yes.

POET: And who was the lucky man?

SWEET YOUNG THING: No man. Well. My girlfriend and her husband. They took me along once.

POET: You must think I'm a fool.

SWEET YOUNG THING: Believe it or not.

POET: You're blushing. Do you like the dark? I can't even see your face now. (*Touches her cheek.*) But this is better.

SWEET YOUNG THING: Just don't mix me up with someone else.

POET: Strange. I don't remember what you look like.

SWEET YOUNG THING: Thanks a lot.

POET: (*Seriously.*) Isn't that remarkable. I don't even have an image of you. In a sense, I've forgotten you. And then, if I didn't recognize the tone of your voice — what would you be? Near and far. At the same time. Remarkable.

SWEET YOUNG THING: What are you talking about.

POET: Nothing, sweet angel. Nothing. Where are your lips? (*He kisses her.*)

SWEET YOUNG THING: Would you — light a lamp?

POET: No. (*He grows very tender.*) Do you love me?

SWEET YOUNG THING: Oh — so — so much.

POET: More than anyone else? Ever?

SWEET YOUNG THING: I told you. No.

POET: (*Sighs.*) But — (*He sighs.*)

SWEET YOUNG THING: Well. He was my fiancé.

POET: Don't — don't think about him.

SWEET YOUNG THING: What — what are you doing? Look, I —

POET: Let's pretend we're in a — a castle in India.

SWEET YOUNG THING: They can't be any worse than you.

POET: Silly. You're divine! I wish you knew what you meant to me.

SWEET YOUNG THING: Well?

POET: You push me away and I haven't touched you. Yet.

SWEET YOUNG THING: Mm. My corset hurts.

POET: (*Simply.*) Take it off.

SWEET YOUNG THING: Promise you'll behave?

POET: Yes. (*The SWEET YOUNG THING has risen and removes her corset in the dark. The POET meanwhile sits down on the divan.*) Don't you care to know my last name?

SWEET YOUNG THING: Sure. What?

POET: No. Not my name. What I call myself.

SWEET YOUNG THING: What's the difference?

POET: The name I write under.

SWEET YOUNG THING: You need another name for that? (*The POET is close to her.*) Now — stop that — no — !

POET: You smell like heaven. Sweet as honey. (*He kisses her breasts.*)

SWEET YOUNG THING: You're tearing my — blouse!

POET: Here. Let me. We don't need this.

SWEET YOUNG THING: But — Robert —

POET: And now — into our Indian castle!

SWEET YOUNG THING: First tell me you love me.

POET: I worship you! (*Kisses her passionately.*) I worship you! My sweet! My springtime! My —

SWEET YOUNG THING: Robert — Robert —

• • •

POET: Oh, God, there are no words. Ah —

SWEET YOUNG THING: Robert! My Robert!

POET: I write under the name Biebitz.

SWEET YOUNG THING: Why Biebitz?

POET: My *name* isn't Biebitz. It's only my *nom de plume*. Don't you recognize it?

SWEET YOUNG THING: No.

POET: The name Biebitz means nothing to you?! Oh, how delicious! Really? You're joking!

SWEET YOUNG THING: I swear, I never heard the name.

POET: Don't you go to the theater?

SWEET YOUNG THING: Yes. A while back I went with — with the uncle of a girlfriend. To the Opera. *Cavalleria Rusticana.*

POET: Not to the Burgtheater?

SWEET YOUNG THING: Nobody gives me tickets.

POET: I'll send you one.

SWEET YOUNG THING: Oh, do! But don't forget. And make it a comedy.

POET: A comedy. I see. You wouldn't consider anything else? Sad?

SWEET YOUNG THING: Not really.

POET: Not even if I wrote it?

SWEET YOUNG THING: Oh! You? You're a playwright?

POET: Excuse me. I'll light a candle. I haven't seen you since we became lovers. Angel! (*He lights a candle.*)

SWEET YOUNG THING: No, don't! I'm ashamed! At least give me a cover!

POET: Later. (*He approaches her with a candle and looks at her for a long while.*)

SWEET YOUNG THING: (*Hides her face with her hands.*) Robert! Don't!

POET: You're beautiful! You're beauty! Nature herself! Sacred simplicity!

SWEET YOUNG THING: Ouch! You're dripping on me! Look at that! Be careful!

POET: (*Puts the candle aside.*) I've wanted what you are for so long! You love *me*, and only *me!* If I worked in a dry-goods shop you'd love *me!* Thank God! I never knew till now! Didn't you even suspect that I was Biebitz?

SWEET YOUNG THING: Look. I don't know what you're after. But Biebitz I never heard of.

POET: So much for fame! But forget everything, even the name. I'm Robert. That's all. I was joking. (*Lightly.*) I'm not even a writer. I'm a shop assistant. In a dry-goods store. And in the evening I play piano. For folk singers.

SWEET YOUNG THING: Now you're *really* mixing me up. Why do you look at people that way? What? What's the matter?

POET: Strange. It's almost never happened. I feel like crying. You move me very deeply. We'll stay together for now. We'll love each other.

SWEET YOUNG THING: Do you really play the piano for folk singers?

POET: Yes. But no more questions. If you love me, you won't ask questions. Could you be free for a couple of weeks?

SWEET YOUNG THING: "Free?"

POET: Could you get away? From home?

SWEET YOUNG THING: Oh! Impossible! What would mother say! Without *me* around the house, everything would fall to pieces.

POET: I'd like to be alone with you. Somewhere quiet. In the woods. With nature. For a few weeks. Live there with you. Nature! Hm. And then one day just say good-bye. Part. Without knowing where.

SWEET YOUNG THING: We just met and you're already talking about — I thought you loved me?

POET: That's *why!* (*He bends down and kisses her on the forehead.*) Precious creature.

SWEET YOUNG THING: Yes! Hold me tight! I'm so cold!

POET: Time to get dressed. Wait. I'll light more candles.

SWEET YOUNG THING (*Rises.*) Don't look!

POET: No. (*At the window.*) Are you happy?

SWEET YOUNG THING: I don't —

POET: In general, I mean. Are you happy?

SWEET YOUNG THING: It could be better.

POET: You don't understand. I know about the conditions at home. And I know you're no princess. But apart from that. Do you feel alive? Do you really feel like you're living?

SWEET YOUNG THING: Got a comb?

POET: (*Goes to the dressing table, hands her a comb, then looks at her.*) God, you're charming!

SWEET YOUNG THING: Now! Don't!

POET: Don't go yet. Stay a while. I'll get something for supper and —

SWEET YOUNG THING: It's late.

POET: Not even nine.

SWEET YOUNG THING: Oh! I *have* to go!

POET: Will we see each other again?

SWEET YOUNG THING: When do you *want* to see me?

POET: Tomorrow.

SWEET YOUNG THING: What's tomorrow?

POET: Saturday.

SWEET YOUNG THING: Oh, I can't. Have to take my little sister out to see her guardian.

POET: Sunday, then? Hm? But I must explain something. I'm not really Biebitz. Biebitz is a friend of mine. I'll introduce you sometime. But there's a play of his. Next Sunday. I'll send you some tickets and pick you up afterward. At the theater. And you can tell me what you thought of the play. All right?

SWEET YOUNG THING: Biebitz, Biebitz! I must be stupid!

POET: I'll only really know you when I hear what you thought of the play.

SWEET YOUNG THING: There. I'm ready.

POET: Come, my sweet.

(*They go out.*)

VIII. THE POET AND THE ACTRESS

A room in a country inn. It is an evening in springtime; the moon shines across the hills and meadows. The windows are open. Total silence. The POET and the ACTRESS enter, and as they do, the candle in the POET's hand goes out.

POET: Oh!

ACTRESS: What?

POET: The candle. But we won't need it. The moon's so bright. Beautiful. (*The ACTRESS suddenly sinks to her knees beside the window, her hands folded.*) What are you doing? (*The ACTRESS is silent. The POET goes to her.*) What?

ACTRESS: (*Indignant.*) I'm praying!

POET: Do you believe in God?

ACTRESS: Do I look like an atheist?

POET: Hm.

ACTRESS: Here. Kneel beside me. It won't hurt you. You won't drop dead. I promise. (*The POET kneels beside her and puts his arms around her.*) Libertine! (*The POET rises.*) Any idea what I was praying to?

POET: God, I suppose.

ACTRESS: (*With great scorn.*) Oh! I was praying to you!

POET: You were looking out of the window.

ACTRESS: Where have you hauled me off to? Seducer!

POET: It was your idea. You wanted to go to the country. You insisted on coming here.

ACTRESS: And?

POET: It's charming. And only two hours from Vienna. The quiet is — wonderful! The country!

ACTRESS: Yes. If you had any talent, you could write poetry out here.

POET: You've been here before?

ACTRESS: Been here before? I lived here! For years!

POET: Who with?

ACTRESS: Fritz. Of course.

POET: Fritz. I see.

ACTRESS: Oh, I worshipped that man!

POET: So you've said.

ACTRESS: Well, I can leave if I bore you.

POET: Don't you know what you mean to me? You're my world! You're divinity! You're spirit! You're — you're sacred simplicity! *You!* Just don't mention Fritz!

ACTRESS: That *was* a mistake. Well!

POET: I'm glad you —

ACTRESS: Give me a kiss. (*The* POET *kisses her.*) It's time to say good night. Good-bye, sweet!

POET: I don't — ?

ACTRESS: I'm going to bed.

POET: Fine. But good night? Where will *I* sleep?

ACTRESS: There must be other rooms.

POET: The hell with "other rooms"! I won't stay in "other rooms"! And I think I'll light a lamp.

ACTRESS: Fine.

POET: (*Lights the lamp on the night table.*) Lovely room! What pious people! All these holy pictures. Living around here could be interesting. It's another world. We know so little about our fellow creatures.

ACTRESS: You're talking silly. Hand me my bag from the table.

POET: Here, my precious love. (*The ACTRESS takes a small framed picture from her bag and places it on the night table.*) What's that?

ACTRESS: A picture of the Madonna.

POET: Do you carry it with you always?

ACTRESS: It's my talisman. Off with you now, Robert!

POET: You must be joking. I want to help you.

ACTRESS: But I want you to go.

POET: And when should I — ?

ACTRESS: Ten minutes.

POET: (*Kisses her.*) Good-bye.

ACTRESS: Where will you be?

POET: Wearing out the grass beneath your window. I love walking at night. My best ideas come to me then. And especially when I'm near you. Your arms around me! Your longing! Your art!

ACTRESS: Out, out! And don't get involved with the waitress. (*The POET goes out. The ACTRESS undresses. She hears the POET as he descends the wooden stairs and walks back and forth beneath her window. As soon as she is undressed, she goes to the window, looks down and sees him standing there. The ACTRESS calls down to him in a whisper.*) Ready! (*The POET hurries upstairs and rushes to her. She has in the meanwhile climbed into bed and put out the lamp. He locks the door.*) Now. I want you to sit next to me. Here. And talk to me.

POET: (*Sits beside her on the bed.*) Should I close the window? Are you cold?

ACTRESS: No.

POET: What should I talk about?

ACTRESS: Oh — who you're being unfaithful to tonight.

POET: To no one. Unfortunately.

ACTRESS: Well, I am.

POET: I'm sure.

ACTRESS: Who do you think?

POET: I have no idea.

ACTRESS: Guess?

POET: Let me see. Mmm. Your director.

ACTRESS: I'm not a chorus girl!

POET: Just a guess.

ACTRESS: Guess again.

POET: You're being unfaithful to — one of your colleagues. To — Benno!

ACTRESS: Benno?! But, my dear, he doesn't care for women! Didn't you know? He's having an affair with his postman!

POET: Seriously?

ACTRESS: Well, I suppose so. Give us a kiss. (*The POET embraces her.*) What — what are you doing?

POET: Then stop tormenting me!

ACTRESS: Robert? Come to bed with me? (*The POET groans in relief.*) Hurry-hurry-hurry!

POET: I thought you'd never ask! Do you hear that?

ACTRESS: What?

POET: The crickets.

ACTRESS: But there are no crickets here.

POET: Listen!

ACTRESS: You're wasting time.

POET: Here I am! (*Goes to her.*)

ACTRESS: Now lie there quietly. No. I said quietly.

POET: You're insane!

ACTRESS: Are you suggesting — ?

POET: How did you ever guess!

ACTRESS: Many men have wanted —

POET: At the moment the odds are entirely in my favor.

ACTRESS: Come, little cricket! I'll call you little cricket from now on.

POET: Fine with me.

ACTRESS: So! Who am I being unfaithful to?

POET: Who? Me, maybe?

ACTRESS: Be serious!

POET: Someone — you've never seen. Someone — you don't know. Someone — destined for you, whom you'll never find.

ACTRESS: You needn't make a fairy tale out of it.

POET: Amazing! Even you! And I'd have thought — but changing you would mean taking away all that's best about you. Come. Come. Come.

• • •

ACTRESS: This is much nicer than acting in those idiotic plays.

POET: Oh, there are intelligent plays. Occasionally.

ACTRESS: *Your* play? Arrogant puppy!

POET: Why not?

ACTRESS: (*Seriously.*) It's a magnificent play!

POET: Aha!

ACTRESS: Yes, Robert, you're a genius!

POET: While we're on the subject. Why did you cancel your performance two evenings ago? And don't tell me you were ill.

ACTRESS: I wanted to antagonize you.

POET: Why? What did I do?

ACTRESS: You were arrogant.

POET: I what?!

ACTRESS: Everyone at the theater thinks so.

POET: I see.

ACTRESS: "But," I said to them, "that man has every right to be arrogant!"

POET: And what did they say?

ACTRESS: How should I know. I never speak to them.

POET: Really?

ACTRESS: They all want to poison me. But they won't succeed.

POET: Forget other people for now. Be happy we're here. And tell me that you love me.

ACTRESS: What more proof do you need?

POET: You don't prove such things.

ACTRESS: Marvelous! What more do you want?

POET: How often have you tried to prove it? Like this. Did you love them all?

ACTRESS: No. I've never loved more than one man!

POET: (*Embracing her.*) My —

ACTRESS: Fritz.

POET: My name is Robert! How can you think of Fritz! At a time like this?! At least I know what I mean to you!

ACTRESS: You're a whim!

POET: That's nice to know.

ACTRESS: Aren't you proud? Hm?

POET: Proud? Of what?

ACTRESS: You should be! My!

POET: *This?*

ACTRESS: I should think so! And the chirping? Are they still chirping outside?

POET: Nonstop! Don't you hear them?

ACTRESS: Of course. But those are frogs, my darling.

POET: Wrong. Frogs croak.

ACTRESS: Yes. They're croaking.

POET: But not here, my love. They're chirping.

ACTRESS: You are the *stubbornest* man I've ever known! Kiss me! Little frog!

POET: Don't call me that. It makes me nervous.

ACTRESS: What shall I call you?

POET: By my name! Robert!

ACTRESS: Then kiss me! Robert! Oh! (*She kisses him.*) Are you happy now, my little frog? (*She laughs lightly.*)

POET: May I have a cigarette?

ACTRESS: Me, too. (*He removes the cigarette case from the drawer of the night table, takes out two cigarettes, lights both, and hands one to her.*) By the way. You haven't mentioned my performance last night.

POET: Performance?

ACTRESS: Really!

POET: Oh, *that* one! I wasn't *at* the theater last night.

ACTRESS: You and your little jokes.

POET: Not at all. After you canceled the day before yesterday, I assumed you wouldn't be in top form. So I didn't go.

ACTRESS: You really missed something.

POET: Did I?

ACTRESS: I was sensational! The audience turned pale!

POET: How could you tell?

ACTRESS: Benno said: "My dear, you were an absolute goddess!"

POET: Hm. And so ill the day before.

ACTRESS: Yes, I was! And do you know why? Because I wanted you!

POET: You said you canceled to antagonize me.

ACTRESS: You have no idea how I love you! And you don't care! I had a hundred and four temperature! All night!

POET: Some temperature for a whim.

ACTRESS: Whim?! I'm dying of love for you, and you call it a whim!

POET: What about Fritz?

ACTRESS: Fritz?! Don't mention that cretin to me!

IX. THE ACTRESS AND THE COUNT

The Actress's bedroom. Very sumptuously decorated. It is noon. The blinds are still drawn and a candle still burns on the small night table. The ACTRESS lies in her canopied bed. Numerous newspapers are strewn across the bed. The COUNT enters in the uniform of a Captain of the Dragoons. He remains standing at the door.

ACTRESS: Ah! My dear Count!

COUNT: Your kind mother gave me permission. Or I would never have —

ACTRESS: Please. Come closer.

COUNT: I kiss your hand. I beg your pardon. Coming from the street, I can't see a thing. Ah, here we are. (*At the bed.*) I kiss your hand.

ACTRESS: Do sit down, my dear Count.

COUNT: Your mother tells me you aren't well. I trust it's nothing serious.

ACTRESS: Nothing serious? I was at death's door!

COUNT: Oh, surely not.

ACTRESS: But how nice that you came.

COUNT: At death's door! And last night you acted like a goddess!

ACTRESS: Yes, it was a triumph, wasn't it!

COUNT: Stupendous! The audience was ecstatic. I can't tell you what I feel.

ACTRESS: Thank you for the flowers.

COUNT: My pleasure.

ACTRESS: (*Glancing at a basket of flowers on a small table near the window.*) There they are.

COUNT: Yesterday you were overwhelmed with flowers and bouquets.

ACTRESS: They're still in my dressing room. Yours are the only ones I've brought home.

COUNT: (*Kisses her hand.*) How sweet of you.

ACTRESS: (*Suddenly takes his hand and kisses it.*) Don't be frightened, Count. You're under no obligation.

COUNT: You extraordinary creature! You're an enigma! Really!
(*Pause.*)

ACTRESS: I suppose Miss Birken is rather less complicated.

COUNT: Our little Birken offers no problem at all. Of course, I — scarcely know her.

ACTRESS: Ha!

COUNT: Believe me. But you — are a conundrum. And I love conundrums. I didn't realize the pleasure I'd missed by not seeing you act before this.

ACTRESS: Is that possible?

COUNT: Yes. I find it difficult to get to the theater. I dine late. And when I do arrive the best of the play is over.

ACTRESS: From now on you must dine earlier.

COUNT: I've considered that. Or perhaps not dine at all. Actually, dining bores me these days.

ACTRESS: What does a young dotard like you do for pleasure?

COUNT: I ask myself the same question. Though I'm not an old man. There must be another reason than age for loss of pleasure.

ACTRESS: Really?

COUNT: For example. Lulu says I'm a philosopher. What he means is I think too much.

ACTRESS: Think. Yes, well. That *is* a misfortune.

COUNT: I have too much time on my hands. And so I think. But I assumed if they transferred me to Vienna things would be different. The amusements here, the stimulation. But it's no different.

ACTRESS: From where?

COUNT: Hungary. The small towns I was generally stationed in.

ACTRESS: What were you doing in Hungary.

COUNT: The Army, of course.

ACTRESS: But why did you stay so long?

COUNT: Did I have a choice?

ACTRESS: That could drive one insane.

COUNT: No, no. There's more to do there than here. Training recruits, breaking in horses. And the region's not as bad as they say. It's quite lovely. The plains. And those sunsets! Pity I'm not a painter. If I were, I'd have painted them. There was a young man in the regiment. Splany! He could have done it. But why bore you with these dull stories.

ACTRESS: Oh, but it amuses me.

COUNT: May I say, dear lady, that it's not at all difficult talking to you. Lulu assured me it wouldn't be. And that's rare.

ACTRESS: In Hungary, I suppose it might be.

COUNT: It's the same in Vienna. People are the same no matter where. Only in Vienna the crowds are larger. Are you fond of people?

ACTRESS: Fond? I loathe people! I can't look at a human being! I never see anyone! I'm always alone! No one ever enters this house!

COUNT: Then I was right. You're a misanthrope. It must be common among artists. When one exists in those higher regions. Well. It's all right for you. At least you have a reason for living.

ACTRESS: Where did you hear that! I have no idea why I'm living!

COUNT: But that can't be. You're famous. Celebrated.

ACTRESS: You call that happiness?

COUNT: But there's no such thing as happiness. The things people talk about most don't really exist. Love, for example. It's the same with happiness.

ACTRESS: You're right.

COUNT: Pleasure. Intoxication. Fine. No complaints. You can depend on them. If I take pleasure in something, fine, at least I *know* I take pleasure in it. Or if I feel intoxicated. Wonderful. That's something you can depend on, too. And when it's over — well, then, it's over.

ACTRESS: (*Grandly.*) Over!

COUNT: But as soon as you fail to live for the moment, and begin thinking about the future or the past — well then, pleasure's as good as dead. The future is — sad — the past uncertain. In short — it only confuses one.

ACTRESS: (*Nods, her eyes large with wonder.*) I think you may have hit on something there.

COUNT: So you see, dear lady, once you've perceived the truth of all this, it makes little difference whether you live in Vienna or Pussta. Or even Steinamanger. For example. Excuse me. Where can I put my cap? Ah. Thank you. Now. What were we saying?

ACTRESS: Steinamanger.

COUNT: Ah! Steinamanger! As I said. The difference is slight. I don't care whether I spend my evenings in the casino or the club.

ACTRESS: Where does love come into this?

COUNT: If you believe in love, you can always find someone to love you.

ACTRESS: Miss Birken, for example?

COUNT: Why do you always drag poor Miss Birken into the picture?

ACTRESS: But she's your mistress.

COUNT: Who says so?

ACTRESS: Everyone!

COUNT: Except me! Isn't that amazing!

ACTRESS: You even fought a duel for her once.

COUNT: And was I also killed and failed to notice?

ACTRESS: Count, you're a man of honor. Won't you sit closer?

COUNT: May I?

ACTRESS: Here. (*She draws him to her and runs her fingers through his hair.*) I knew you'd come today.

COUNT: Really?

ACTRESS: I knew last night. At the theater.

COUNT: Did you see me in the audience?

ACTRESS: My dear man. I was playing straight toward you.

COUNT: How can that be?

ACTRESS: I felt I was floating when I saw you in the front row.

COUNT: Floating? Because of me? I didn't know you even saw me.

ACTRESS: You and your dignity could drive a woman to desperation.

COUNT: But, my dear.

ACTRESS: "But, my dear." At least take off your saber.

COUNT: If I may. (*He unbuckles the belt and leans the saber against the bed.*)

ACTRESS: Oh! I wish I'd never seen you!

COUNT: This is much better.

ACTRESS: Count, you are a *poseur*.

COUNT: I? How so?

ACTRESS: Think how happy most men would be to find themselves where you are now.

COUNT: And I'm very happy.

ACTRESS: I thought there was no happiness? Don't look at me like that. I do believe you're afraid of me, Count.

COUNT: As I said, madam. You're an enigma.

ACTRESS: Spare me your philosophizing. Come here. And now, ask me for something. Anything you like. You're far too handsome for me to —

COUNT: Your permission to — (*Kisses her hand.*) — return tonight.

ACTRESS: Tonight? I'm acting tonight.

COUNT: *After* the theater.

ACTRESS: Is that all you want?

COUNT: After the theater I'll want all you have.

ACTRESS: (*Offended.*) And you'll want for a long time, you *poseur*.

COUNT: We've been so open with each other that I thought, well, it would be so much more pleasant after the theater. More comfortable. I feel like the door could open at any moment.

ACTRESS: It doesn't open from the outside.

COUNT: It seems careless to spoil from the start what might be quite beautiful.

ACTRESS: "Might be"!

COUNT: The fact is, I find love in the morning rather ghastly.

ACTRESS: You're the most insane man I've ever met.

COUNT: I don't mean just *any* woman. In general it hardly matters. But women like you? No. Call me a fool if you like. Women like you aren't to be had before breakfast. And so —

ACTRESS: God, you're sweet.

COUNT: I think you know what I mean. As I see it —

ACTRESS: *Tell* me how you see it.

COUNT: I thought after the theater I'd pick you up in a carriage — and we could drive somewhere for supper.

ACTRESS: I'm not your Miss Birken.

COUNT: I didn't say you were. But the mood is so important. And I'm always in the mood after supper. It's always nicer that way. After supper you drive home together — and then —

ACTRESS: And then — ?

COUNT: Well. Then it depends on how things develop.

ACTRESS: Sit closer. Closer.

COUNT: (*Sitting on the bed.*) The perfume from your pillow is very — mignonette, isn't it?

ACTRESS: Is it too warm in here for you? (*The COUNT bends down and kisses her throat.*) But, my dear Count. That's not on your program. (*She draws him to her.*)

COUNT: Yes. It's quite warm.

ACTRESS: Yes. And so dark. Almost — like evening. It's night. Close your eyes if it's too light. Come. Come.

• • •

ACTRESS: How's your mood now, you *poseur*.

COUNT: Little devil!

ACTRESS: What a thing to say!

COUNT: Then an angel!

ACTRESS: You should have been an actor. Really. You understand women. Do you know what I'm going to do now?

COUNT: What?

ACTRESS: Tell you that I'll never see you again.

COUNT: But why?

ACTRESS: No, no. You're too dangerous. You'd drive a woman insane. Look at you! Standing in front of me now! As if nothing had happened!

COUNT: But —

ACTRESS: And I've just become your mistress.

COUNT: I'll never forget it.

ACTRESS: And what about tonight?

COUNT: Tonight?

ACTRESS: You said you'd wait for me after the theater.

COUNT: Yes. Well. What about tomorrow?

ACTRESS: Tomorrow? We were talking about tonight.

COUNT: But there's no sense in it.

ACTRESS: Dotard!

COUNT: Don't misunderstand. I mean — well — from the spiritual stand-
point.

ACTRESS: What has your soul got to do with it?

COUNT: But the soul's a part of it. It's a dreadful mistake to think that the
physical and the spiritual should be kept apart.

ACTRESS: Spare me your philosophizing. If I'm interested, I'll read books.

COUNT: Books teach you nothing.

ACTRESS: That's true. And that's why we should meet this evening. We just
might get your soul into some kind of working order.

COUNT: In that case, I'll have my carriage waiting.

ACTRESS: After the theater.

COUNT: Of course. (*He buckles on his saber.*)

ACTRESS: What are you doing?

COUNT: It's time I were going. For a formal call, I seem to have overstayed
my visit.

ACTRESS: Tonight — will *not* be a formal call.

COUNT: Really?

ACTRESS: I'll see to that. Now give me another kiss, my little philosopher.
Here, you seducer. You sweet, sweet little — you slave driver. Little pole-
cat. You — (*After having kissed him vigorously several times, she pushes him
vigorously from her.*) Count, it was a great honor.

COUNT: I kiss your hand, madam! (*At the door.*) *Au revoir!*

ACTRESS: *Adieu*, Steinamanger!

X. THE COUNT AND THE PROSTITUTE

Morning, around 6:00 A.M. A miserable little room with one window. The dirty yellow blinds are down; worn green curtains on the window. A chest of drawers with a few photographs on it and a particularly tasteless, cheap woman's hat. A number of tawdry Japanese fans behind the mirror. On the table covered with a reddish cloth sits a kerosene lamp, still feebly alight and omitting odor; it is crowned with a yellow paper lamp shade. Beside it is a jug with leftover beer and a half-empty glass. On the floor beside the bed is a disarray of female clothing, as if hastily tossed there. The PROSTITUTE is asleep in the bed; she breathes quietly. Fully dressed on the divan lies the COUNT in his overcoat, his hat on the floor at the head of the divan.

COUNT: (*Stirs, rubs his eyes, sits up quickly, looks around.*) How did I get — Oh! Yes. Then I did go home with that girl. (*He rises quickly and sees her bed.*) And there she is. Imagine! A thing like that happening to a man my age! I can't remember. Did they carry me up here? No. I saw — I came into the room. Yes. I was still awake. Or — or does this room remind me of somewhere else? My God! Yes! Yes! I saw it last night. (*Looks at his watch.*) Hm. Last night. A couple of hours ago. But I knew something had to happen. I felt it. Last night when I began drinking, I felt that something — and what *did* happen? Nothing. Or did I — ? My God! I haven't — I haven't forgotten anything that's happened to me in ten years! Well. In any case, I was drunk. If only I could remember when it began. At least I remember when I went into that whores' café with Lulu and — No. No. It was after we left the Sacher. And then on the way — yes, that's right. I was riding along with Lulu. But why am I racking my brains! It doesn't matter! Just get yourself out of here! (*He rises; the lamp shakes.*) Oh! (*He looks at the sleeping girl.*) At least *she's* sleeping soundly — I can't remember a thing. But I'll put the money on the night table just in case. And so good-bye. (*He stands looking at her face for a long while.*) I've known a lot of her kind that didn't look half as virtuous in their sleep. Lulu would say I'm philosophizing again! But it's true! — seems to me Sleep washes away all differences. Like his brother Death. Hm. I wish I knew whether — No, I'd remember that. Amazing how sometimes all women look alike! — Well, time to go. (*He is about to leave.*) Ah! I forgot. (*Takes out his wallet and is about to remove a bill.*)

PROSTITUTE: (*Wakes up.*) What! Who's — ! What are you doing here so early? (*Recognizing him.*) Oh! Hello!

COUNT: Good morning. Sleep well?

PROSTITUTE: (*Stretching.*) Oh, come here. Give us a kiss.

COUNT: (*Bends down to her, considers, pulls back.*) I was just going.

PROSTITUTE: Going?

COUNT: It's time.

PROSTITUTE: You want to go? Just like that?

COUNT: (*Embarrassed.*) Well —

PROSTITUTE: Okay. Bye. Come back some other time.

COUNT: Yes. Good-bye. Won't you give me your hand? (*The PROSTITUTE extends her hand from under the covers. The COUNT takes her hand and kisses it mechanically; becomes aware of himself, and laughs.*) Like a princess, if all you saw was —

PROSTITUTE: Why are you looking at me like that?

COUNT: If all you saw was that dear little head. Just as it is now. When they wake, one woman looks as innocent as another. My God! One could imagine all sorts of things if only there weren't this — kerosene smell.

PROSTITUTE: That lamp's always a nuisance.

COUNT: How old are you?

PROSTITUTE: Guess.

COUNT: Twenty-four.

PROSTITUTE: You bet.

COUNT: Older?

PROSTITUTE: I'm almost twenty.

COUNT: And how long have you — ?

PROSTITUTE: About a year.

COUNT: You started young.

PROSTITUTE: Better too young than too old.

COUNT: (*Sits on her bed.*) Tell me. Are you happy?

PROSTITUTE: What?

COUNT: I mean — how are you getting on?

PROSTITUTE: Right now, fine.

COUNT: I see. Did you ever think of doing something else?

PROSTITUTE: Like what?

COUNT: Well — you're a very lovely girl. You could have a lover.

PROSTITUTE: You think I don't have?

COUNT: Yes. Well. One who — who'd support you. So you wouldn't have to — go with just anyone.

PROSTITUTE: I *don't* go with just anyone. I'm not *that* hard up. I pick and choose. (*The COUNT looks around the room, which she notices.*) Next month we're moving into town. Spiegelgasse.

COUNT: Who's we?

PROSTITUTE: The madam and the girls who still live here.

COUNT: Other girls?

PROSTITUTE: Next door. Listen. That's Milli. She was at the café last night.

COUNT: Someone's snoring.

PROSTITUTE: That's Milli. She snores up a storm till ten at night. Then goes off to the café.

COUNT: What a terrible life.

PROSTITUTE: Sure is. The madam gets pissed at her, too. I'm on the street by noon every day.

COUNT: What do you do on the street at noon?

PROSTITUTE: What else. Walk my beat.

COUNT: I see. Of course. (*He rises, takes out his wallet, and places a bill on the night table.*) Good-bye.

PROSTITUTE: Going already? So long! Come back again soon. (*Turns on her side.*)

COUNT: (*Stops again.*) Tell me. Does it mean anything to you anymore?

PROSTITUTE: What?

COUNT: I mean, there's no more enjoyment in it for you.

PROSTITUTE: I'm sleepy.

COUNT: It makes no difference whether a man is young or old.

PROSTITUTE: Questions, questions!

COUNT: Well. (*Suddenly struck by a thought.*) My God! I remember who you remind me of!

PROSTITUTE: I remind you of someone?

COUNT: It's uncanny! Uncanny! Please. Don't talk. For a moment. (*Looks at her.*) The same face exactly. Hm. (*He suddenly kisses her on the eyes.*)

PROSTITUTE: Hey!

COUNT: What a pity you're not something else. You could make a fortune.

PROSTITUTE: You're just like Franz.

COUNT: Franz?

PROSTITUTE: The waiter at the café.

COUNT: How am I like Franz?

PROSTITUTE: He's always saying I could make a fortune. Says I should get married.

COUNT: Why don't you?

PROSTITUTE: Married? No thanks. Not me. Not for all the money in the world. Later, maybe.

COUNT: Your eyes. It's your eyes that — Lulu would say I'm a fool. But I want to kiss your eyes. Just once more. There. And now, good-bye. I really have to go.

PROSTITUTE: Bye.

COUNT: (*At the door.*) Mm. Tell me. Does it surprise you that —

PROSTITUTE: That what?

COUNT: That I don't want anything from you?

PROSTITUTE: A lot of men aren't in the mood in the morning.

COUNT: I suppose. (*To himself.*) Silly I should have wanted to surprise her. Well. Good-bye. (*He is at the door.*) Still, it does annoy me. I know girls like her do it only for the money. But why did I say "girls like her"? I'm glad at least that she — that she doesn't pretend. That she should please me. (*To her.*) Look. I'll — I'll come back again soon.

PROSTITUTE: (*Eyes closed.*) Good.

COUNT: When are you at home?

PROSTITUTE: Most of the time. Just ask for Leocadia.

COUNT: Leocadia. Fine. Well, then. Good-bye. (*At the door.*) I can still feel that wine. Amazing. Here I am with one of her kind — and all I did was kiss her eyes. Just because she reminded me of someone. (*Turns to her again.*) Leocadia. Do men often leave you — like this?

PROSTITUTE: Like what?

COUNT: Like me.

PROSTITUTE: In the morning?

COUNT: No. I wondered whether men often come to you — and — don't ask for anything?

PROSTITUTE: Never.

COUNT: What do you think? Do you think I don't like you?

PROSTITUTE: Why shouldn't you like me? You liked me all right last night.

COUNT: I don't understand.

PROSTITUTE: Why the silly questions?

COUNT: Last night. Well. Didn't I collapse onto the divan the moment I arrived?

PROSTITUTE: You sure did. With me.

COUNT: You?

PROSTITUTE: Don't remember, uh?

COUNT: You mean I — that we — Yes.

PROSTITUTE: But you went right off to sleep.

COUNT: Right off to sleep. I see. So that's the way it was.

PROSTITUTE: Sure, lovey. You must've had a real load on, not to remember.

COUNT: I see. Still, there *is* a faint resemblance. (*He listens.*) What's that noise?

PROSTITUTE: The parlor maid's up already. Give her a little something on the way out. The door's open, so you'll save on the doorkeeper.

COUNT: Yes. (*In the entrance hall.*) Well. It would have been beautiful even if I'd only kissed her eyes. It was almost an adventure. But maybe not meant for me. (*The PARLOR MAID stands at the main door, holding it open for him.*) Oh! (*Hands her some change.*) Here you are. Good night.

PARLOR MAID: Good morning!

COUNT: Yes, of course. Good morning! Good morning!

END OF PLAY

ANATOL

A Play in Seven Scenes

CAST OF CHARACTERS

Anatol
Max
Cora
Gabrielle
Bianca
Emilie
Annie
Elsa
Franz
Ilona

TIME AND PLACE

Vienna in the 1890s

Anatol

I. QUESTIONING FATE

Anatol's Room.

MAX: Anatol, I envy you. (*ANATOL smiles.*) I'm — I'm flabbergasted. I used to think it was nonsense. But you actually put her to sleep. She danced when you said she was a ballerina. Cried when you told her her lover was dead. And pardoned a criminal when you crowned her queen.

ANATOL: That's the way it goes.

MAX: You're a magician.

ANATOL: As are we all.

MAX: Unbelievable.

ANATOL: No more than life itself. No more than centuries of other discoveries. Think of our ancestors. When they discovered the earth turned.

MAX: But that was *everyone's* concern.

ANATOL: Suppose we'd just discovered spring. Who'd believe it? Green trees and flowers not withstanding. Not to mention love.

MAX: You're being evasive. Be reasonable. But magnetism —

ANATOL: Hypnotism.

MAX: — is quite another matter. You'll never find *me* being hypnotized.

ANATOL: Don't be childish. I tell you to go to sleep. You lie down. You relax.

MAX: And suddenly I'm a chimney sweep. Climbing up. Getting all sooty.

ANATOL: Practical jokes. What's important is its scientific application. Unfortunately we're not that far along yet.

MAX: Explain.

ANATOL: Me, for example. I put that girl into a dozen different worlds today. But can I do the same for myself?

MAX: Why not?

ANATOL: Not for lack of trying. I've stared at this diamond in my ring for minutes on end, mumbling: "Anatol, go to sleep. And when you wake, every thought of that distressing female will have vanished from your mind."

MAX: And?

ANATOL: Never got to sleep.

MAX: You're still involved with her?

ANATOL: Involved! I'm desperate! I'm insane!

MAX: Then you still have doubts?

ANATOL: Doubts? No. She deceives me right and left. When we're kissing. When she caresses my hair. When we're — deception, deception!

MAX: You're mad.

ANATOL: Don't be a fool.

MAX: Then prove it.

ANATOL: I *sense* it! I *feel* it! *That's* how I know!

MAX: Very logical, I must say.

ANATOL: Women are unfaithful. It's their nature. And they don't even realize it. *I* read two or three books at once. *They* have two or three love affairs at once.

MAX: Does she love you?

ANATOL: Passionately! But the point is, she's unfaithful.

MAX: With whom?

ANATOL: How should I know? With a prince she met on the street. With a poet from the suburbs.

MAX: You're a fool.

ANATOL: And why not? She's like all the others. Loves life. But not a thought in her head. I ask if she loves me. She says yes. And she means it. Are you faithful? I ask. Of course, she says. And she means it. Because she's forgotten the others. At least for the moment. And what girl has ever admitted to being unfaithful? They're unfathomable! And if one *were* to admit being faithful —

MAX: Hmm?

ANATOL: — it would be pure coincidence.

MAX: But if she loves you?

ANATOL: Dear, naive Max! As if that were a reason.

MAX: Well?

ANATOL: Rather ask why am *I* unfaithful to *her*. I'm certainly in love with her.

MAX: But you're a man.

ANATOL: That old cliché. We insist on women being different from us. Well, maybe those whose mothers locked them up. Or ones with no spirit. But we're alike. If I say to a woman that I love her and only her, well, it's not really lying. Even if I did spend last night curled around someone else.

MAX: Well, of course, *you!*

ANATOL: *Me, yes!* But not *you*, I suppose. Nor my dear Cora, I suppose. It's driving me mad! What if I got down on my knees and told her that I forgive her in advance, if only she'll tell me the truth. Nonsense. She'd lie just the same. Do you suppose no girl has ever asked me if I'm being true to her? I answer, of course. But I lie. Quietly. With a sweet smile on my face. And the clearest of consciences. Why upset them? And they believe me and are happy.

MAX: So there you are.

ANATOL: But *I* don't believe it. And *I'm* not happy. Oh, I might be. If there were some way of bringing these stupid, lovable, despicable creatures to confess. Or some other way of discovering the truth. But there *is* none. None but chance.

MAX: What about hypnosis?

ANATOL: What?

MAX: Hypnosis. Put her to sleep and demand the truth.

ANATOL: Good God!

MAX: You ask her if she loves you? Is there anyone else? Where does she come from? Where is she going? What's the other fellow's name? Etcetera, etcetera, and so forth.

ANATOL: Max! Max!

MAX: Well?

ANATOL: I'd be a magician. I'd actually worm an honest word from a woman's mouth!

MAX: There you are. Salvation is in sight. Cora will make an excellent medium. By this evening you'll know whether she's faithful, or —

ANATOL: Or I'm the luckiest man alive. Max, I could kiss you. I'm free. I'm a new man. Power over a woman at last.

MAX: I'm really quite curious.

ANATOL: Oh? Do you suspect anything?

MAX: Ah, so only *you* are allowed to have doubts?

ANATOL: Of course. If a husband walks out of his house having discovered his wife in bed with her lover, and a friend comes by and says, "I suspect your wife's having an affair," the husband's not going to say, "I know; I've just seen them," but, "You, sir, are a bastard!"

MAX: Yes. I forgot. The first duty of a friend is to preserve illusion.

ANATOL: Shh!

MAX: What?

ANATOL: Footsteps in the hall. I recognized them the moment they entered downstairs.

MAX: I don't hear anything.

ANATOL: They're coming closer. They're on the stairs now. (*He opens the door.*) Cora!

CORA: (*From outside the door.*) Good evening. Oh! You have company.

ANATOL: My friend Max.

CORA: (*Entering.*) Good evening. Sitting in the dark?

ANATOL: It's dusk. You know how fond I am of this light.

CORA: (*Caressing his hair.*) My little poet.

ANATOL: Dear Cora.

CORA: Still, I think I'll light the candles. Do you mind? (*She lights the candles in the candelabra.*)

ANATOL: (*To MAX.*) Isn't she ravishing?

MAX: Ah!

CORA: What have you two been up to? Been talking long?

ANATOL: Half an hour.

CORA: Good. (*She removes her hat and coat.*) What about? Or shouldn't I ask?

ANATOL: This and that.

MAX: Hypnosis, as a matter of fact.

CORA: Oh! Not again! I'll go insane!

ANATOL: Well!

CORA: Anatol, dear. Would you hypnotize me? Sometime?

ANATOL: *I?* Hypnotize *you?*

CORA: I'd love it. As long as it was you.

ANATOL: Thanks.

CORA: I'd never let a stranger. Well. You know.

ANATOL: Yes, well. I'll — I'll hypnotize you.

CORA: When?

ANATOL: Now.

CORA: Wonderful. What do I do?

ANATOL: Sit quietly. Here. In this armchair. And be willing to fall asleep.

CORA: I'm willing.

ANATOL: I'll stand here in front of you. And you'll look at me. Well? Look at me. And I'll lightly stroke your forehead. And your eyes. There.

CORA: And then?

ANATOL: That's all. You must be willing to fall asleep.

CORA: It feels so strange. You stroking my eyes like that.

ANATOL: Be still. Don't talk. Sleep. You're very tired.

CORA: No —

ANATOL: You are. Just a bit.

CORA: Yes. Just a bit.

ANATOL: Your eyelids are growing heavy. Very heavy. You can scarcely lift your hands.

CORA: (*Softly.*) Yes —

ANATOL: (*Continues to stroke her forehead and eyes; in a monotone.*) Tired. You're very tired. Go to sleep now. Sleep. (*He turns towards MAX, looking on in amazement, with a triumphant expression.*) Sleep. Your eyes are tightly closed. You can't even open them. (*CORA tries to open her eyes.*) Don't even try. You are asleep. Just sleep quietly. There.

MAX: (*Wanting to ask something.*) Anatol —

ANATOL: Shh! (*To CORA.*) Sleep. Deep, deep sleep. (*He stands for a while in front of CORA who breathes softly while she sleeps.*) There. Now you can ask your question.

MAX: Is she really asleep?

ANATOL: See for yourself. We'll wait a few moments, though. (*He stands in front of CORA and looks at her quietly. Long pause.*) Cora! You will answer me now. Answer me. What is your name?

CORA: Cora.

ANATOL: Cora, we are in the forest.

CORA: Oh, the forest! How beautiful! Green trees and — and nightingales!

ANATOL: Cora, you will tell me the truth. No matter what I ask. What will you do, Cora?

CORA: I will tell you the truth.

ANATOL: You will answer every question. Truthfully. And when you wake up you will have forgotten everything. Do you understand?

CORA: Yes.

ANATOL: Just sleep. Sleep. (*To MAX.*) I'll ask her now.

MAX: How old is she?

ANATOL: Nineteen. Cora, how old are you?

CORA: Twenty-one.

MAX: Haha!

ANATOL: Shh! Extraordinary. Well! That only goes to show you.

MAX: Little did she know what a good subject she'd make.

ANATOL: The suggestion worked. I'll ask her another question. Cora? Do you love me? Cora? Do you love me?

CORA: Yes.

ANATOL: (*Triumphantly.*) Did you hear?

MAX: And the big question? Is she faithful?

ANATOL: Cora! (*Turning around.*) The question is stupid.

MAX: Why?

ANATOL: I can't just ask it like that.

MAX: Aha.

ANATOL: I need to phrase it differently.

MAX: Sounds fine to me.

ANATOL: No. It's not fine at all.

MAX: Why?

ANATOL: If I asked if she were faithful to me, she might take it much too generally.

MAX: And so?

ANATOL: She could take it to refer to her entire past. A time when she was in love with someone else. And answer no.

MAX: That could be interesting.

ANATOL: Thanks a lot. I know that Cora knew others before me. She said once that, had she known that one day she would meet me, she would have —

MAX: But she *didn't* know.

ANATOL: No.

MAX: And your question?

ANATOL: Yes, the question. It's a bit clumsy. In it's present form.

MAX: In that case, ask her: "Cora, have you been true to me since we met?"

ANATOL: Hmm. Not bad. (*In front of CORA.*) Cora, have you been — Oh, that's silly.

MAX: Silly?

ANATOL: Really now. You need to visualize the circumstances that brought us together. We had no idea we'd fall so desperately in love. During those first days we thought of it as a passing fancy. Who knows —

MAX: Who knows what?

ANATOL: Who knows whether she didn't start loving me just as she stopped loving someone else? And who knows what happened to her on the day we met. Before we'd even exchanged a word. Was she able to break loose from the old affair without further involvement? Or did she have to drag around those old chains for days. Even weeks.

MAX: Hmm.

ANATOL: And I'll go even further. At first it was only a whim on her part. And on mine. Neither of us saw it as anything else. All we asked of each other was a moment of sweet, fleeting happiness. If at the time she committed an indiscretion, am I to blame for it? Well. Hardly.

MAX: You're very lenient, I must say.

ANATOL: Not at all. It's just inappropriate to take advantage of the situation.

MAX: How noble. May I help extricate you from this — dilemma?

ANATOL: What?

MAX: All you need to say is: "Cora, since you've been in love with me, have you been true?"

ANATOL: That seems clear enough.

MAX: Well, then.

ANATOL: But it's not.

MAX: I see.

ANATOL: Well. Just suppose that yesterday she was riding in a train compartment. And a man sitting opposite her touched the tip of her shoe with his. Now. With the characteristic heightening of perception brought on by sleep, and with the greatly sensitized condition of the medium's mind during hypnosis, it is not at all impossible for her to consider even *this* a breach of fidelity.

MAX: Great heavens!

ANATOL: All the more so since she's come to know my *own* perhaps exaggerated views on the matter. I've as much as told her: "Cora, if you even *look* at another man, you're being unfaithful to me."

MAX: And her reply?

ANATOL: She laughed. Asked how I could possibly *think* she'd even look at another man.

MAX: Yet you still think — ?

ANATOL: Accidents happen. Just suppose some arrogant man should come along some night and kiss her on the neck.

MAX: Well. Yes. Of course.

ANATOL: It's not all *that* impossible.

MAX: What you're saying is that you don't want to ask her.

ANATOL: I *do*, but —

MAX: Your objections are nonsense. When you ask a woman if she's been faithful, she knows what you're saying. Whisper tenderly in her ear: "Are you true to me?" and the man's foot or the importunate kiss would instantly flee her mind. Her understanding of infidelity is no different from yours. Which gives you the advantage of asking additional questions that will make her answers perfectly clear.

ANATOL: Then I should question her?

MAX: It's you who want to know.

ANATOL: Something else just occurred to me.

MAX: Yes?

ANATOL: The unconscious.

MAX: The unconscious?

ANATOL: I believe that there are unconscious states of mind.

MAX: And so?

ANATOL: Such states of mind arise naturally. But they may also be induced by artificial means. Means that dull or exhilarate the senses.

MAX: I'm afraid I don't —

ANATOL: Imagine a mysterious, twilit room.

MAX: Twilit. Mysterious. Yes. I'm imagining.

ANATOL: And in that room — there is she — and another —

MAX: How did she get there?

ANATOL: We'll come back to that. There are ways. In any case, it *could* happen. And then — a couple of glasses of Rhine wine. A certain heaviness in the air that seems to weigh on everything. The fragrance of cigarettes. Perfumed wallpaper. The dim light of frosted chandeliers reflecting red silk curtains. Solitude. Silence. The whisper of tender words —

MAX: Aha —

ANATOL: Others have been had in such circumstances. Better ones than she. More placid than she —

MAX: How do I reconcile fidelity and her being in that scene with another man?

ANATOL: Life has its enigmas.

MAX: Anatol! You have the opportunity to resolve the enigma that the world's wisest men have beaten their heads over! If only you'd ask the question. *One question* will tell you whether you are among the few who are loved exclusively by one woman, the identity of your rival in love, and by what means he succeeded. And yet you refuse! You have the power to question fate! But you *won't!* The truth is at your fingertips! And you do nothing! Do you know why? Because the woman you love is the same as you suppose all women to be. And because illusion is a thousand times more dear to you than the truth. Let's stop this. Wake her up, and be satisfied that — that you might have accomplished a miracle.

ANATOL: Max!

MAX: Am I wrong? Your words are empty phrases, Anatol, that deceived neither of us. That's what all this has been about.

ANATOL: (*Quickly.*) But, Max. I *do* want to ask her. I *will* ask her.

MAX: Aha.

ANATOL: Don't be angry with me, Max. Just not with you in the room.

MAX: What?

ANATOL: When she tells me she's been unfaithful, I want to be the only one to hear it. Unhappiness is only half of the misfortune. Being pitied for it is *total* misery. I couldn't bear that. You're my best friend. I don't want your pity telling me how miserable I am. Maybe I'm just ashamed in front of you. You'll know the truth in any case. If it's true, you'll never see her again. I just want to hear it by myself.

MAX: Of course. (*He shakes ANATOL's hand.*) I'll go.

ANATOL: Dear Max. (*He accompanies MAX to the door.*) I won't be more than a minute. (*MAX goes out. ANATOL stands in front of CORA, looking at her for a long while.*) Cora! (*Shakes his head and walks about.*) Cora! (*Kneels in front of her.*) Cora! My sweet Cora! — Cora! (*He rises; with resolution.*) Wake up! Kiss me!

CORA: (*Rises, rubs her eyes and throws her arms around ANATOL's neck.*) Anatol! Was I asleep long? Where's Max?

ANATOL: Max!

MAX: (*Entering from the adjoining room.*) Here I am.

ANATOL: Yes, quite a while. And you talked in your sleep.

CORA: Oh, I didn't! Anything interesting?

MAX: You answered the questions he put to you.

CORA: What did he ask?

ANATOL: All sorts of things.

CORA: And I answered them?

ANATOL: Every one.

CORA: Well, what did you ask?

ANATOL: None of your business. Tomorrow I'll hypnotize you again.

CORA: Oh, no. Not me. It's witchcraft. You wake up and don't know what you've said. All I know is I talked a lot of nonsense.

ANATOL: For example. That you love me.

CORA: Oh?

MAX: Doesn't believe it herself. Too much!

CORA: I didn't need to be asleep to tell you that.

ANATOL: My angel!

(*They embrace.*)

MAX: Dear friends, I bid you good night.

ANATOL: Going? So soon?

MAX: I must.

ANATOL: Forgive me if I don't show you out.

CORA: See you.

MAX: My pleasure. (*At the door.*) I've learned one thing for certain. That women are capable of lying even under hypnosis. But they're happy. And that's all that matters. Good-bye, my dears.

(*They fail to hear MAX because they are entwined in a passionate embrace.*)

II. CHRISTMAS SHOPPING

It is six o'clock on a Christmas Eve in the streets of Vienna. Light snowfall.

ANATOL: Madam? Madam?

GABRIELLE: I beg your — ? Oh! It's you!

ANATOL: Yes. I'm following you. I can't bear to have you carry all those things. Here. Give me those packages.

GABRIELLE: No, no. Thank you. I can manage.

ANATOL: Why are you making it so difficult? All I want is to be gallant for a change.

GABRIELLE: Well. Perhaps this one.

ANATOL: This? Oh, come now. Give them to me. There. And that one. And that one there.

GABRIELLE: That's quite enough. Really. You're much too kind.

ANATOL: And you're kind for letting me help. It happens far too seldom.

GABRIELLE: In your case only in the street. And when it's snowing.

ANATOL: And night coming on. And just by chance Christmas Eve.

GABRIELLE: I can't believe it's you.

ANATOL: What you mean is, I haven't called on you all season.

GABRIELLE: Yes. Something like that.

ANATOL: My dear lady. I'm not making calls this season. None. And how is your husband? And the children?

GABRIELLE: Why not spare yourself all this? You're not the least bit interested.

ANATOL: How perceptive. Uncanny.

GABRIELLE: I know you.

ANATOL: Not as well as I could wish.

GABRIELLE: I could do without your observations.

ANATOL: But I can't help myself.

GABRIELLE: Please. My packages.

ANATOL: No, don't be angry. Please. I'll behave. (*They walk along in silence.*)

GABRIELLE: You can *talk*, you know. I didn't mean *that*.

ANATOL: Yes. Well. When madam commands —

GABRIELLE: Entertain me. It's been so long. What have you been up to?

ANATOL: Nothing. As usual.

GABRIELLE: Nothing?

ANATOL: Not a thing.

GABRIELLE: Pity!

ANATOL: And you couldn't care less.

GABRIELLE: You know that, do you?

ANATOL: Loafing my life away. And whose fault is that? Whose?

GABRIELLE: The packages. Please.

ANATOL: It was only a question.

GABRIELLE: Do you walk often?

ANATOL: "Walk?" You ask that with such contempt. It's a marvelous pastime. Such an aimless word. Unfortunately today I'm not aimless. Today I'm busy. As you are, dear lady.

GABRIELLE: Oh?

ANATOL: Buying Christmas presents. Like you.

GABRIELLE: You?

ANATOL: But nothing suits me. Evening after evening I've poured over Vienna's shop windows. Up one street. Down another. There's not a tasteful or imaginative item to be had.

GABRIELLE: That's for the buyer to supply. You should invent for yourself. You certainly have the time. And order your presents during the autumn.

ANATOL: Not my style, I'm afraid. How am I to know in autumn who I'll give presents to at Christmas? No thanks. So here I am again. Two hours before candle lighting. And still no idea. Not a one.

GABRIELLE: May I help?

ANATOL: You're an angel. Just leave me with the packages. All right?

GABRIELLE: No.

ANATOL: Ah! Then I *can* call you angel. Nice. Angel!

GABRIELLE: Just be quiet.

ANATOL: I'll sit on my tongue.

GABRIELLE: Give me some hints. Who's the gift for?

ANATOL: That's a difficult one.

GABRIELLE: A lady? Of course.

ANATOL: Yes. As a matter of fact. You're very perceptive. Once again.

GABRIELLE: Exactly what *sort* of lady? A *real* one?

ANATOL: Depends on how you define your terms. If by *lady* you mean a woman of the great world, then the definition falls short.

GABRIELLE: The small world then?

ANATOL: You might say that.

GABRIELLE: What else?

ANATOL: You're being catty.

GABRIELLE: I know your taste. Thin and blonde. The other side of the tracks.

ANATOL: Blonde? Yes. I must admit.

GABRIELLE: Blonde it is. You're very consistent. All those girls from the suburbs.

ANATOL: Is that my fault? My dear?

GABRIELLE: Shall we drop the subject? I like people who stick with their kind. Imagine forsaking the scene of your triumphs.

ANATOL: I have no choice. I'm loved only in the suburbs.

GABRIELLE: And do they *understand* you? In the suburbs?

ANATOL: Not at all. I'm loved in the suburbs. In the great world I'm only understood. You know how it is.

GABRIELLE: I'm afraid I don't. Nor do I care to. Ah! Here we are! Just the shop we're looking for. Your little miss shall have a lovely present.

ANATOL: You're too kind.

GABRIELLE: Why, look here. A fancy little box with three different perfumes. Or this! With six cakes of soap. Patchouli. Chypre. Jockey Club. That should be just the thing.

ANATOL: You're very cruel, my dear.

GABRIELLE: No, no. Look here. A small brooch with six paste diamonds. Just imagine! Six! And how it glitters! Or this bracelet. With the divine trinkets dangling from it. One the head of a moor. That should go down well. In the suburbs.

ANATOL: You're quite wrong, I'm afraid — dear lady. You don't understand this sort of girl. They're quite different from what you imagine.

GABRIELLE: And there! Oh, how charming! Come closer. Well? What do you think of the hat? Three years ago the style was an absolute rage. The sweeping feathers! What do you think? This will be a sensation in the provinces!

ANATOL: I don't believe we were discussing the provinces, madam. And besides, you underestimate the taste even of the provinces.

GABRIELLE: Yes. Well. You're not being very helpful. Any suggestions?

ANATOL: How can I? Your answer would be a condescending smile.

GABRIELLE: Listen to you! I want to learn about her. Is she vain? Is she modest? Is she large? Is she small? Does she like bright colors — ?

ANATOL: I should never have accepted your kind offer. You're mocking me.

GABRIELLE: But I'm all ears. Tell me about her.

ANATOL: I don't dare.

GABRIELLE: Don't dare? Since when?

ANATOL: Shall we change the subject?

GABRIELLE: No. But I insist. How long have you known her?

ANATOL: For some time.

GABRIELLE: Must I drag it out by the tail? Tell me.

ANATOL: There's nothing to tell.

GABRIELLE: Where, how, when you met her. What sort of person she is. Well?

ANATOL: Fine. But you may find it boring. I've warned you.

GABRIELLE: I won't be bored. I want to learn about that world. What's it like? I'm really quite ignorant.

ANATOL: You wouldn't understand.

GABRIELLE: You're off again.

ANATOL: You have contempt for everything outside your little circle. And you're very wrong.

GABRIELLE: I can be taught. No one ever tells me anything. How can I be expected to —

ANATOL: And yet you're always afraid of losing something if you go too far. A kind of silent enmity.

GABRIELLE: No one takes from me what I don't want to lose.

ANATOL: You may not want it. Yet you don't want anyone else having it.

GABRIELLE: Oh!

ANATOL: That, my dear, is being feminine. And being feminine, it's very noble and beautiful and profound.

GABRIELLE: Where do you come by your irony?

ANATOL: I'll tell you. I, too, was innocent once. Full of trust. Without scorn. And I suffered my wounds silently.

GABRIELLE: Don't romanticize.

ANATOL: Honest wounds, that is. I could endure a "No" spoken at the right time. Even from lips I loved dearly. But a "No" when the eyes have said "Perhaps" a hundred times over — when the lips have smiled "Maybe" a hundred times over — when the tone of voice sounded "Yes" a hundred times over — such a "No" is enough to —

GABRIELLE: We were buying a present.

ANATOL: Such a "No" makes a man either a fool or a cynic.

GABRIELLE: You were going to — tell me —

ANATOL: Very well. If you insist.

GABRIELLE: Of course I insist. How did you meet her?

ANATOL: Good God! The same way one meets anyone. In the street. At a dance. On a bus. Under an umbrella —

GABRIELLE: Yes. Of course. But — it's this particular case I'm interested in. We were to buy a present for this particular case. Remember?

ANATOL: Over there — in that "small world" — there *are* no particular cases. No more than in the "great world." You're all so true to type.

GABRIELLE: Sir, you're beginning to —

ANATOL: That's no insult. Not at all. I'm true to type myself.

GABRIELLE: What type?

ANATOL: Frivolous melancholic.

GABRIELLE: And? And I?

ANATOL: You? Easy. Lady of fashion.

GABRIELLE: I see. And she?

ANATOL: She? She is — the sweet young thing.

GABRIELLE: Sweet. Did you say sweet? Then that leaves me simply a — a lady of fashion.

ANATOL: A wicked lady of fashion, if you insist.

GABRIELLE: Well. Do tell me about this — sweet young thing.

ANATOL: She's not fascinatingly beautiful. She's not particularly elegant. And she's certainly not bright.

GABRIELLE: I'm not interested in what she's *not*.

ANATOL: But she has the gentle charm of a spring evening. The grace of an enchanted princess. The spirit of a girl who knows how to love.

GABRIELLE: The kind of spirit that is rather commonplace in your "small world."

ANATOL: There's no way you could understand. As a young girl you were told too little. And as a young woman too much. Consequently you're rather naive.

GABRIELLE: But I've already told you. I want to learn. I'm willing to believe in your "enchanted princess." But do tell me about the magic garden she reclines in.

ANATOL: Well. You mustn't imagine a glittering drawing room with heavy curtains and pale velvets. Nor the affected twilight of a dying afternoon.

GABRIELLE: Please don't tell me what I *mustn't* imagine.

ANATOL: Fine! Then imagine a small — a very small, dim room with painted walls. Somewhat too light in tone. A few dreadful engravings with faded lettering hanging here and there. And a lamp with a shade. From the window at evening you have a view of roofs and chimneys receding into the dusk. And — when spring comes, the garden opposite will burst into blossom and send out its fragrance.

GABRIELLE: How happy to think of May on Christmas Eve.

ANATOL: Yes. I'm happy there occasionally.

GABRIELLE: But enough of this. It's getting late. And we were buying her something. Something for the room with the painted walls?

ANATOL: It has all it needs.

GABRIELLE: For *her* taste, yes. But I'd like to decorate the room to — to suit *your* taste.

ANATOL: *My* taste!

GABRIELLE: With Persian carpets —

ANATOL: In the suburbs! Really!

GABRIELLE: — and a red and green cut-glass lamp.

ANATOL: Hm.

GABRIELLE: And vases of fresh flowers.

ANATOL: But I wanted something for *her*.

GABRIELLE: Yes. Of course. How silly of me. Decisions, decisions! I suppose she's waiting for you? This very moment?

ANATOL: I'm sure.

GABRIELLE: Is she really?! But tell me. How does she welcome you?

ANATOL: Oh — the usual way, I suppose.

GABRIELLE: Listens for your footsteps on the stairs? Hm?

ANATOL: Sometimes. Yes.

GABRIELLE: And waits by the door?

ANATOL: Yes!

GABRIELLE: And then falls into your arms. Kisses you. And says — tell me what she says.

ANATOL: What one usually says.

GABRIELLE: For example.

ANATOL: I can't think of one.

GABRIELLE: Well. Yesterday.

ANATOL: Oh — nothing in particular. It sounds stupid without the sound of her voice.

GABRIELLE: In that case I'll imagine it. I'm waiting. What did she say?

ANATOL: "I'm so happy to have you again."

GABRIELLE: "I'm so happy" — what was it?

ANATOL: — "to have you again."

GABRIELLE: That's quite sweet. Really. Quite sweet.

ANATOL: Yes. It's sincere.

GABRIELLE: And she's — alone, is she? You can see each other without being — disturbed?

ANATOL: Yes. She's independent. No father. No mother. Not even an aunt.

GABRIELLE: And you — are her everything?

ANATOL: I suppose. Today.

GABRIELLE: It's getting late. The streets are empty.

ANATOL: I'm sorry. I've kept you. You should be home by now.

GABRIELLE: Yes. I should. They're waiting for me. But what shall we do about the present?

ANATOL: Oh — I'll pick up something or other.

GABRIELLE: You never know. Still, I did say I'd choose something for your — for the — girl.

ANATOL: Don't bother. Please.

GABRIELLE: I wish so much I could be there when you give her her Christmas present. To see her tiny room and — and the sweet young thing. She has no idea how lucky she is.

ANATOL: — ?

GABRIELLE: I can take my parcels now. It's quite late —

ANATOL: Certainly. Here you are. But —

GABRIELLE: Could you hail that cab?

ANATOL: Why the rush all of a sudden?

GABRIELLE: Please. Please. (*He motions for the cab.*) Thank you very much. Oh, but the present. (*The cab has stopped beside them.* ANATOL *starts to open the door.*) Wait. I'd like to send her something myself.

ANATOL: You?! But, my dear lady!

GABRIELLE: Why shouldn't I? Take these. These flowers. Just these flowers. It's only a greeting. Nothing more. But you must promise to give her a message with them.

ANATOL: You're very kind.

GABRIELLE: Promise you'll tell her — in these exact words —

ANATOL: Of course.

GABRIELLE: Promise?

ANATOL: My pleasure. Why not?

GABRIELLE: (*Has opened the cab door.*) Tell her —

ANATOL: Yes — ?

GABRIELLE: Tell her: "These flowers, my — sweet young thing, are a gift from a woman who might have loved as much as you — but who hadn't the courage."

ANATOL: Dear — lady!

(*She has climbed into the cab and it moves off. The streets are nearly deserted. He looks in the direction of the cab until it turns a far corner — stands there for a while, looks at his watch and hurries away.*)

III. EPISODE

Max's room decorated in generally dark tones. Dark red wallpaper, dark red curtains hanging over doorways. Upstage center, a door. Another door stage left. In the center of the room there is a large writing-table with a shaded lamp, books, and papers. Downstage right, a tall window. In a niche, stage right, a fireplace in which a fire burns. In front of it, two low armchairs and a casually arranged dark red fire screen.

MAX: (*Sitting at the writing-table reading a letter and smoking a cigar.*) "My dear Max! I'm back again. Our company will be in town for three months. As you have probably read in the papers. My first evening here belongs to you and to our friendship. See you tonight. Bibi — Bibi — that's — ah, Bianca! Well, then, I'll expect her. (*A knock at the door.*) Good God! Already? Come in.

ANATOL: (*Enters somberly, a large package under his arm.*) Evening.

MAX: Ah. What's that?

ANATOL: I'm seeking a refuge for my past.

MAX: I'm afraid I don't — ? (*ANATOL holds out the package to him.*) Well?

ANATOL: I'm bringing you my past. My entire youth. Guard it for me.

MAX: Delighted. But would you mind explaining?

ANATOL: May I sit down?

MAX: Of course. But why the formality?

ANATOL: (*Having sat down.*) Do you mind if I smoke a cigar?

MAX: Here. Have one of mine. This year's harvest.

ANATOL: (*Lights one of the cigars.*) Ah! Excellent!

MAX: (*Pointing at the package that ANATOL has placed on the writing-table.*) And that?

ANATOL: My house is too small for these memories of my youth. I'm leaving town.

MAX: I see.

ANATOL: I'm beginning a new life for an indefinite period. To do so I must be free and alone. And that's why I'm cutting all ties with the past.

MAX: I presume you have a new mistress?

ANATOL: No. The old one just isn't around any longer. (*Indicating the package.*) And therefore I'm leaving all of this nonsense with you, my dear friend Max.

MAX: Why nonsense? Why not burn it?

ANATOL: I can't.

MAX: How childish.

ANATOL: No, no. It's my way of being faithful. I want to remember every single woman I've loved. When I rummage in these letters and flowers and locks of hair — you will allow me to come and rummage from time to time, won't you, Max? — suddenly I'm with them all again. They come alive. And I worship them as in the past.

MAX: In other words you're asking to use my apartment as a trysting place to meet your ex-mistresses.

ANATOL: (*Scarcely hearing him.*) What if there were a magic phrase to make them all reappear. Conjure them up out of nowhere.

MAX: That would be a lot of nowheres.

ANATOL: I would say the magic phrase —

MAX: Such as: "My only love!"

ANATOL: "My only love!" And they'd come. One from a small house in the suburbs. Another from her husband's splendid drawing room. And one from her dressing room at the theater.

MAX: Several, in other words —

ANATOL: Of course. Several. One from a milliner's shop —

MAX: One from the arms of a new lover —

ANATOL: One from the grave. One from here, one from there, until they've all come.

MAX: Just don't say the word! It could be awkward. Because they've stopped loving you, doesn't mean they've stopped being jealous of each other.

ANATOL: True. Well then — rest in peace.

MAX: But where will I find a place for this stately package?

ANATOL: You'll have to divide it up. (*He tears open the package and several small packets tied with ribbons tumble out.*)

MAX: Ah.

ANATOL: Everything's neatly arranged.

MAX: In alphabetical order?

ANATOL: No, no. Each packet has its own inscription. A rhyme. A single word. An observation that calls back the whole affair. No names. Any one of them could be Marie or Anna —

MAX: Let me see.

ANATOL: Will I recognize you all again? I haven't seen some of these for years.

MAX: (*Picks up one of the packets and reads.*)
"Wonder of the world, my dear,
Passionate, wild, untamed,
I enfold and hold you near,
Who are Matilda named!"
What a name! Matilda?

ANATOL: Matilda, yes. Oh, she was called something else. But I did manage to kiss her neck.

MAX: Who was she?

ANATOL: Don't ask. I held her in my arms. That's all that matters.

MAX: Away with Matilda, then! A very slender packet at that.

ANATOL: It's only a lock of hair.

MAX: No letters?

ANATOL: From Matilda?! I doubt she could write her name. Besides, what if all women took it in their heads to write us letters. Away with Matilda!

MAX: (*Reading.*) "In one sense women are all alike: They grow impertinent when you catch them in a lie."

ANATOL: True enough.

MAX: Who was she? It's a heavy packet.

ANATOL: Lies eight pages long. Away with them!

MAX: Was she impertinent, too?

ANATOL: Yes, when I found her out. Away with her!

MAX: Away with the impertinent liar!

ANATOL: No insults. She lay in my arms. She's sacred!

MAX: Not a bad reason, I suppose. But let's continue. (*Reading.*)

> "To take my mind from all that's sad,
> To make the day go lighter,
> I call to mind that silly lad,
> Your fiancé the fighter."

ANATOL: (*Smiling.*) Ah, yes, that was the one.

MAX: What's in it?

ANATOL: A photograph. Of her and the fiancé.

MAX: Did you know him?

ANATOL: Of course. How else could I have laughed? He was a knucklehead.

MAX: (*Seriously.*) He lay in her arms — he's sacred.

ANATOL: That's enough of that.

MAX: Away with the sweet young thing and her knucklehead fiancé! (*Picks up another packet.*) What's this? Two little words?

ANATOL: Let's see —

MAX: "Boxed ears."

ANATOL: Oh, how I remember that!

MAX: That, I presume, was the end of it?

ANATOL: No. The beginning.

MAX: I see. And this one? "It's easier to change the direction of a flame than to light it." Care to explain?

ANATOL: Well. I changed the direction of the flame. Someone else lit it.

MAX: Away with the flame! "She always brought her curling iron." (*Looks questioningly at ANATOL.*)

ANATOL: Why, yes. She always brought along her curling iron. Just in case. All I have to remember her by is a piece of veil.

MAX: (*Feeling the package.*) That's what it feels like, all right. (*Continues reading.*) "How did I lose you?" Well? How *did* you lose her?

ANATOL: Damned if I know. Suddenly she was gone. Vanished from my life. It happens like that sometimes. Like forgetting your umbrella somewhere and only remembering it a few days later. Though by that time you've forgotten where.

MAX: Farewell, vanished girl! (*Reading.*)
"You were a sweet and lovely creature —"

ANATOL: (*Continuing dramatically.*)
"Maiden with the needle-pricked fingers."

MAX: That was Cora. Right?

ANATOL: Yes. You knew her.

MAX: Do you know what happened to her?

ANATOL: I ran into her sometime later. The wife of a cabinetmaker.

MAX: Is that right.

ANATOL: That's how it is with these girls with needle-pricked fingers. Loved in the city, wed in the suburbs. She was a darling.

MAX: Farewell! And what's this? "Episode." Nothing in it? Dust!

ANATOL: (*Taking the envelope in his hand.*) Oh, nothing. A random thought. It was just an episode. A romance of two hours' duration. Nothing! Dust! It's sad to think that this is all that's left of so much sweetness. — Hm?

MAX: Yes. Sad. But why episode? You could have written that on any of these.

ANATOL: True. But I was never so conscious of it as with her. Often when I was with one or another of them — especially when I was young and still thought a lot of myself — I would think, "You poor child — you poor child — !"

MAX: Why?

ANATOL: I thought of myself as one of the great men of history. Those girls and women — I ground them underfoot as I strode across the earth. I thought of it as a law of nature. My way lies over these bodies.

MAX: The storm wind that scatters the blossoms.

ANATOL: I raged. I fumed. That's why I always thought: "You poor, poor child!" I had deceived myself. I know now that I'm not one of the great characters of history. And what's so sad is — I've become reconciled to the thought. Ah! But in those days!

MAX: And the episode?

ANATOL: That was one of them. A creature I found on my path.

MAX: And destroyed?

ANATOL: You know, the more I think about it, the more I realize that I really *did* destroy her.

MAX: Aha.

ANATOL: Just listen. It's got to be the most beautiful thing I've ever experienced. I can't even talk about it.

MAX: Why not?

ANATOL: Because it's so commonplace. Because it's — nothing. You could never see the beauty in it. The secret of it is that it happened to *me*.

MAX: Well?

ANATOL: I was sitting at the piano. In the little room I lived in in those days. It was evening. I'd known her for only two hours. My green and red lamp was burning. I mention the green and red lamp because it's part of the story.

MAX: Well?

ANATOL: Well. There I was at the piano. She — was at my feet. So that I couldn't use the pedal. Her head was in my lap. Her tousled hair reflected the green and red from the lamp. I was improvising at the piano. But only with my left hand. She was pressing my right hand to her lips.

MAX: Well?

ANATOL: That infernal "well" of yours is going to drive me insane! And — that's all there is. I'd known her for only two hours. But I also knew that after that evening I'd probably never see her again. She told me so herself. And yet, I felt that at that moment I was passionately loved. I felt surrounded by it. The air was drunk and heavy with love. Do you understand?

(*MAX nods.*) And again I had that stupidly divine thought: "You poor
— poor child!" The episodic nature of the experience came very clear to
me. While I felt her warm breath on my hand, I had the sensation that
I was remembering it all from a distance. As though it were already past.
She was another one of those that I crushed underfoot. That's when the
word episode occurred to me. But at the same time I was eternal. And I
knew that that "poor child" would never forget that hour. I was never
more sure of that than with her. One often feels that tomorrow he'll be
forgotten. But this was something else. For this — this girl at my feet I
was all the world. I felt surrounded by the sacred, enduring love that
came from her at that moment. One feels such things. I'm certain of it.
And I'm also certain that at that moment all her thought was for me.
Only me. But for me she was already a thing of the past. Fleeting. An
episode.

MAX: Who was she?

ANATOL: Who was she? You knew her. We got to know her one night at a
party. And you said at the time you'd known her before.

MAX: But who? I've known several women "before." The way you describe
her in the lamplight, she must be a fairy princess.

ANATOL: No. Not really. Do you know what she did? Now, of course, I'm
about to destroy the whole illusion.

MAX: What did she do?

ANATOL: (*Smiling.*) She worked in — ?

MAX: The theater?

ANATOL: No. The circus.

MAX: I don't believe it.

ANATOL: Yes. Bianca. I never told you that I saw her again. After that
evening when I practically ignored her.

MAX: You seriously believed that Bibi loved you?

ANATOL: No question about it. A week or so after the party we met on the
street. The next morning she was scheduled to leave for Russia with the
company.

MAX: Obviously there was no time to lose.

ANATOL: You see? I knew it would spoil the illusion. You haven't yet discovered the true mystery of love.

MAX: And where does one find the secret to this mystery known as woman?

ANATOL: In the proper "atmosphere."

MAX: Ah. Dim lights. Your green and red lamp. A piano —

ANATOL: That's it! That's why I find life so exciting, so varied. Where a single color can transform the world. What would this girl with the sparkling hair have meant to you? Or to the thousands like you? Or the lamp you scoff at? No more than a circus rider and a green and red glass shade with a light behind it! What magic is there in that? Oh, you can live that way. But you'll never *really* live. You blunder into an adventure brutally. With your eyes open. But your senses are shut. And it's all so colorless. But my soul sheds a thousand lights and colors across the scene. And I *feel*. Where you only — taste.

MAX: This atmosphere, as you call it, is like a magic spring. Those who've dipped into it have the power to bring strange and wonderful adventures back to intoxicate them.

ANATOL: Take it however you like.

MAX: And as for your circus rider. You'll have to prove to me that your green and red lamp had the same effect on her as it did on you.

ANATOL: I know what she felt in my arms.

MAX: Yes. Well. I knew this Bianca of yours, too. And better than you.

ANATOL: Better?

MAX: Better. Because we weren't in love. To me she's no fairy tale princess. She's another of those fallen women that your dreamer's imagination endows with a new virginity. To me she's no better than a hundred other women, who jump through hoops or dance in a tutu for the final circus number.

ANATOL: I see.

MAX: And she *was* nothing more. It wasn't *I* who overlooked some remarkable quality in her. It was *you* who saw in her what didn't exist. You projected the richness and variety of your youthful imagination onto her pallid soul. And the light you basked in was nothing but the glow of your own reflection.

ANATOL: No. I've had that experience. But not this time. I didn't want to make her out any better than she was. But I was neither the first nor the last. I was —

MAX: Well? What were you? One of many. She was the same in your arms as in the arms of others. A woman at the moment of her highest ful-fillment.

ANATOL: Why did I tell you this? You don't understand.

MAX: Oh, no. It's *you* who don't understand *me*. All I said was, *you* may have felt all the exquisite things you claim. But for *her* it was no different from all the other times. Did *she* see the world as a kaleidoscope of colors?

ANATOL: You knew her well?

MAX: Yes. We met frequently. At parties. You came with me once.

ANATOL: That was all?

MAX: That was all. But we were good friends. She was fun. We enjoyed talking together.

ANATOL: And that was all?

MAX: That was all.

ANATOL: And yet — she *loved* me —

MAX: Shall we get on with these? (*Picks up a packet.*) "Could I but know the meaning of your smile, you green-eyed —"

ANATOL: Did you know that the circus was back in town?

MAX: Of course. And she's with them.

ANATOL: I suppose so.

MAX: No question about it. I'm seeing her this evening.

ANATOL: What? You? You know where she lives?

MAX: No. She wrote me. She's coming here.

ANATOL: (*Leaping to his feet.*) What? And you're only telling me now?

MAX: What's it got to do with you? You want to be "free and alone," I think you said?

ANATOL: Oh, good God!

MAX: And there's nothing sadder than a warmed-over love.

ANATOL: You mean — ?

MAX: I mean you should take every precaution not to see her.

ANATOL: Because I might be attracted to her again.

MAX: No. Because that one time was so — beautiful. Go home with your memories, Anatol. Never try to revive the past.

ANATOL: You can't seriously believe that I'd give up seeing her. When it's so easy.

MAX: She's wiser than you. She didn't write to you. Maybe because — she's forgotten about you.

ANATOL: Nonsense.

MAX: You think it's impossible?

ANATOL: It's laughable.

MAX: Not everyone lives in the rarefied atmosphere of your existence.

ANATOL: Oh! That glorious hour!

MAX: What?

ANATOL: It was a moment out of time.

MAX: Do you hear steps in the hall?

ANATOL: Is it — ?

MAX: You can leave through my bedroom.

ANATOL: I'd be a fool —

MAX: Go. Why destroy the magic?

ANATOL: I'm staying.

> (*A knock at the door.*)

MAX: Go on. Quick. (*ANATOL shakes his head.*) Then at least stand over there. Where she won't see you right away. Over there. (*MAX pushes ANATOL to the fireplace where he is partially hidden by the screen.*)

ANATOL: (*Leaning against the mantel.*) Oh, all right.

> (*A knock.*)

MAX: Come in.

BIANCA: (*Enters vivaciously.*) Max! My dear friend! Good evening!

MAX: (*Hands extended to her.*) Good evening, my dear Bianca! How nice of you. How really nice.

BIANCA: I trust you got my letter? You're the very first. The only one, in fact.

MAX: And you can imagine how proud I am.

BIANCA: And the others? The Sacher Gang, as we called them. Still around? Will we get together again every evening after the performance?

MAX: (*Helping her off with her hat and coat.*) Ah, but there were evenings when you couldn't be found.

BIANCA: After the performance?

MAX: Yes, when you disappeared immediately after.

BIANCA: (*Smiling.*) Yes. I remember. How nice to be reminded of such things. And without the least bit of jealousy. Everyone should have a friend like you.

MAX: Yes, I think so, too.

BIANCA: Friends who like you but don't torment you.

MAX: That didn't happen to you often.

BIANCA: (*Becoming aware of ANATOL's shadow.*) I see you're not alone.
(*ANATOL comes forward and bows.*)

MAX: An old acquaintance.

BIANCA: (*Lorgnette at her eye.*) Ah!

ANATOL: (*Approaching.*) Miss —

MAX: What do you think of the surprise, Bibi?

BIANCA: (*A bit embarrassed, searching her memory.*) Yes, of course — we
know each other —

ANATOL: Naturally — Bianca.

BIANCA: Certainly — we know each other quite well —

ANATOL: (*Excitedly takes her right hand in both of his.*) Bianca —

BIANCA: Now where was it we met — where — oh, of course —

MAX: Do you remember?

BIANCA: Yes, it was — it was in St. Petersburg, wasn't it — ?

ANATOL: (*Quickly dropping her hand.*) It was — not in St. Petersburg —
(*He turns to leave.*)

BIANCA: (*Anxiously to* MAX.) What's the matter with him? Have I insulted
him?

MAX: He's slinking away.
(*ANATOL has disappeared through the door upstage.*)

BIANCA: I don't understand.

MAX: Didn't you recognize him?

BIANCA: Yes, I recognized him — but — I don't know where or when.

MAX: But, Bibi, it was Anatol.

BIANCA: Anatol — ? Anatol — ?

MAX: Anatol. Piano. Red and green lamp. Here in the city. Three years ago.

BIANCA: (*Hands at her forehead.*) I must have been blind. Anatol! (*Going to
the door.*) I must call him back. (*Opening the door.*) Anatol! (*Runs out into
the hallway.*) Anatol! Anatol!

MAX: (*Standing at the door, smiling.*) Any luck?

BIANCA: (*Entering.*) He must be on the street by now. Excuse me. (*Rushing
to the window.*) There he is.

MAX: (*Behind her.*) Yes, there he is.

BIANCA: (*Calling.*) Anatol!

MAX: He can't hear you from here.

BIANCA: (*Stomping her foot lightly.*) What a pity! Please give him my apologies. I know I've hurt him. The dear, poor man.

MAX: Then you do remember him?

BIANCA: Well, of course. But — he looks exactly like someone I know in St. Petersburg.

MAX: (*Soothingly.*) I'll tell him.

BIANCA: And besides, when you haven't thought about someone in three years, and then suddenly he appears — well, one can't remember everything.

MAX: I'll close the window. There's a cold draft. (*Closes the window.*)

BIANCA: I *will* see him again while I'm here, won't I?

MAX: Perhaps. But I want to show you something. (*He takes an envelope from the writing-table and holds it out to her.*)

BIANCA: What is it?

MAX: It's the flower you wore on that evening. On that *particular* evening.

BIANCA: He kept it?

MAX: As you see.

BIANCA: You mean he loved me?

MAX: Passionately. Wildly. Eternally. Like all the others. (*He indicates the packets.*)

BIANCA: Like — all the others? What are these? All flowers?

MAX: Flowers. Letters. Locks of hair. Photographs. We were just in the middle of arranging them.

BIANCA: (*Piqued.*) Under different headings.

MAX: So it would seem.

BIANCA: And what file do *I* fit into?

MAX: In this one — I should think. (*He throws the envelope into the fireplace.*)

BIANCA: Oh!

MAX: (*To himself.*) I've avenged you as best I could, Anatol. (*Aloud.*) There. Now don't be angry. Sit down and tell me all about the last three years.

BIANCA: I'm not in the mood anymore. What a reception!

MAX: But I'm your friend. Come, Bianca. Tell me all about it.

BIANCA: (*Allows herself to be drawn into the armchair beside the fireplace.*) What do you want to hear?

MAX: Oh — about the man who looks exactly like him in St. Petersburg —

BIANCA: I can't stand you!

MAX: Well — ?

BIANCA: (*Angrily.*) What am I supposed to tell you?

MAX: Just begin. — Once upon a time — well? — there was a big, big city —

BIANCA: (*Peevishly.*) — and in the city was a big, big circus —

MAX: — and in the circus was a tiny little circus performer —

BIANCA: — who jumped through a big, big hoop — (*She laughs lightly.*)

MAX: And in a box — go on — in a box every evening there sat —

BIANCA: In a box every evening there sat a handsome, and very beautiful man. Ah!

MAX: And then? Hm?

(*The curtain has fallen.*)

IV. KEEPSAKE

Emilie's room, furnished in moderate elegance. Twilight. The window is open. The view is onto a park. The top of a tree, its leaves just bursting, nearly fills the window opening.

EMILIE: Oh! So here you are! At my desk? But — but what are you doing? What are you looking for? Anatol!

ANATOL: I had every right. Every right. And here's the proof.

EMILIE: But — what have you found? Your own letters.

ANATOL: And this? What's this?

EMILIE: This?

ANATOL: These two small stones? One of them a ruby, and this other, darker one? I don't recognize either. I didn't give them to you.

EMILIE: No, I — I forgot about them.

ANATOL: Forgot? But they were so carefully hidden away. In the back of the bottom drawer. Why not just confess? Don't lie like the others. Well? Nothing to say? No righteous indignation? How easy it is to be silent when you know you're guilty, and have been found out! Let's continue the search, shall we? Where have you stashed your other treasures?

EMILIE: I don't have any others.

ANATOL: Fine. (*He begins to tear open the drawers.*)

EMILIE: Why are you doing that? I've told you. I don't have any more.

ANATOL: And these? Why were these here?

EMILIE: It was wrong. Perhaps.

ANATOL: Perhaps! Emilie! This is the eve of our wedding day! I truly believed that we'd wiped out the past. Completely. That — that when the two of us sorted through your letters, and fans and the thousand and one little nothings that reminded me of the time before I knew you — and threw them into the fireplace — and then the bracelets, and rings, and earrings that we gave away, that we threw over the bridge into the river or out the window onto the street — and then you kneeling, swearing that it was all past — that you had discovered the meaning of true love only in my arms — and naturally I believed you — because we always believe what women tell us, from the first lie that transports us to paradise —

EMILIE: Shall I swear to it again?

ANATOL: What good would that do? I'm through. Through with you! Oh, how cleverly you played your part. Pretending you wanted to wash away all the stains of your past, you stood here in front of the fireplace watching the papers, and ribbons, and whatnots go up in flame. And how you sobbed in my arms the time we walked along the river and tossed the precious bracelet into the gray water and watched it sink. How you wept. Purifying tears. Tears of contrition. All of it a stupid farce. And for what. For nothing. I still mistrusted you. And here's the evidence. Why don't you say something? Why don't you defend yourself?

EMILIE: Because you're going to leave.

ANATOL: I still want to know what these two stones are doing here. Why you kept just *these* two?

EMILIE: You don't love me anymore.

ANATOL: The truth, Emilie! I want to know the truth!

EMILIE: Why? When you don't love me?

ANATOL: Because there may be something in the truth that —

EMILIE: That what?

ANATOL: That can make me — understand it all. Emilie. I don't want to think the worst of you.

EMILIE: You forgive me?

ANATOL: I want you to tell me. What do these stones mean?

EMILIE: And then you'll forgive me?

ANATOL: I want to know why you kept this ruby.

EMILIE: Will you listen to me? Quietly?

ANATOL: Yes. Just say something.

EMILIE: This ruby — was once set in a locket. It — it came loose.

ANATOL: Who gave you the locket?

EMILIE: That has nothing to do with it. I wore it on a — on a particular day — on a simple chain — around my neck.

ANATOL: Who gave you the locket!

EMILIE: That's not important. I think — my mother. You see? If I were as bad as you think I am, I'd have said at once that my mother gave it to me. And that's why I wanted to keep it. And you'd have believed me. But I kept this ruby because — because the day I wore the locket was — a very special day — that I want to remember.

ANATOL: What are you talking about?

EMILIE: And yet, there's something so sweet about the memory. A pain that seems to soothe. And then — that day is very special to me. Because on it I first felt the emotion that — that binds me to you. One needs to learn *how* to love, to love you as I do. If the two of us had met at a time when love was new to us, who knows? We might have passed each other by. Without knowing. Oh, Anatol. Don't shake your head. It's true. You said so yourself.

ANATOL: I?

EMILIE: You said it was good that we had to become mature to appreciate such passion.

ANATOL: Yes. Well. One always has such consolations in reserve when one loves a woman with a checkered past.

EMILIE: I'll be perfectly honest with you. This ruby reminds me of the day —

ANATOL: Go on. Say it.

EMILIE: You know what I mean, Anatol. The memory of that day. Oh, God! What a silly young thing I was. Sixteen years old.

ANATOL: And he was twenty. And tall. And dark.

EMILIE: (*Innocently.*) Oh, my dear. I don't remember. All I remember is the forest that rustled around us. The spring day that laughed above the tree-tops. And — and a ray of sunshine. That broke through the foliage. And sparkled on a bed of yellow flowers.

ANATOL: How can you not curse the day that took you from me. Before I ever *knew* you.

EMILIE: Perhaps that day gave us to each other. No, Anatol. No matter what, I'll never curse that day. And I'll never pretend to you that I ever did. Anatol, I love you. As I've never loved anyone. And as you've never been loved. And you know that. And even though every moment of my life was made meaningless by your first kiss, and every man I ever knew faded from my memory — I still can never forget that moment when I became a woman.

ANATOL: And you pretend to love me?

EMILIE: I can hardly remember his face anymore. Or how he looked at me.

ANATOL: But you can't forget that it was in his arms that you first felt love. That it was from his heart that love first streamed into yours. Ingrate! And you don't understand how this confession of yours drives me insane! How you've cruelly dredged up the sleeping past! And I realize all over again how you can dream of other men's kisses! And close your eyes and see other men's faces!

EMILIE: How *can* you misunderstand me like this! I think you're right. It might be better if we part.

ANATOL: And how am I to understand *that?*

EMILIE: Women who can lie are so fortunate. No. You men can't bear to deal with the truth. I want to know: Why did you always beg me to tell you? Oh, I can hear you say it: "I'll forgive you everything! Everything! But a lie!" And I! Who confessed everything to you! Who crawled at your feet like a kicked animal! And cried out to you: "Anatol, I'm not worthy of you, but I love you!" I gave you none of the silly excuses others give. No. I said it straight out: "Anatol, I've lived a dissolute life, I was hot-blooded, I lusted, I sold myself, I gave myself away. I'm not worthy of your love." And do you remember? I told you this before you kissed my hand for the first time. I wanted to escape you. Because I loved you so much. And you pursued me. You begged for my love. And I didn't want you. Because I didn't want to degrade the man I loved more, and differently than — oh, God, the first man I ever loved! And you took me. And I was yours! And you lifted me up so high. And gave me back everything, piece by piece, that they had taken from me. In your passionate arms I became what I had never been. Pure. Happy. You were so noble. You forgave me. And now?

ANATOL: And now?

EMILIE: And now you're turning me out again. Because I'm like all the others.

ANATOL: No. No. You're not.

EMILIE: (*Softly.*) What do you want me to do? Shall I throw the ruby away?

ANATOL: No. I'm not noble. I'm very petty. Throw it away. Throw the ruby away. (*Looks at it.*) It fell out of the locket. And it lay in the grass. Under the bed of yellow flowers. A ray of sunlight fell on it. And made it sparkle. (*Long pause.*) Come, Emilie. It's growing dark outside. Let's go for a walk in the park.

EMILIE: Won't it be too cold?

ANATOL: No. Spring's in the air.

EMILIE: Whatever you say, my love.

ANATOL: And what about *this* stone?

EMILIE: Oh. This.

ANATOL: Yes. This black one. What about this?

EMILIE: Do you know what it is?

ANATOL: Well?

EMILIE: (*With a look of greedy pride.*) A black diamond!

ANATOL: Ah!

EMILIE: (*Keeping her eyes on the stone.*) Very rare!

ANATOL: (*With suppressed rage.*) And why? Hm? Why did you — keep this one?

EMILIE: (*Still gazing at the stone.*) It's — it's worth a quarter of a million!

ANATOL: (*Crying out.*) Ah! (*Throws the stone into the fireplace.*)

EMILIE: (*Crying out.*) What are you doing! (*She kneels down, picks up the tongs and digs around in the coals for the stone.*)

ANATOL: (*Watches her rummage in the fireplace for a few moments, her face glowing, then says quietly.*) Whore! (*He leaves.*)

V. FAREWELL SUPPER

A private dining room at the Sacher Hotel. ANATOL stands at the door giving orders to the WAITER. MAX is leaning back in an armchair.

MAX: Well. Aren't you finished yet?

ANATOL: In a minute. In a minute. (*To the WAITER.*) Do you understand? (*The WAITER goes out.*)

MAX: (*As ANATOL returns to the center of the room.*) And what if she doesn't show up?

ANATOL: Why shouldn't she? It's — let's see — ten o'clock. She couldn't possibly be here yet.

MAX: The ballet's been over for —

ANATOL: Oh, really, Max. It takes time to take off the makeup. And change. I think I'll walk over and — wait for her.

MAX: Don't spoil her.

ANATOL: Spoil?! If you only knew.

MAX: I know! I know! You treat her brutally. But that's just another way of spoiling her.

ANATOL: That's not what I was going to say. As I was saying. If you only knew.

MAX: Well, say it.

ANATOL: How solemn I feel this evening.

MAX: You're not going to become engaged to her!

ANATOL: No, no. Even more solemn than that.

MAX: You're going to marry her! Tomorrow morning!

ANATOL: How superficial of you, Max. Can't there be a solemnity of the soul? That has nothing to do with all of this external nonsense?

MAX: I see. You've discovered a hitherto unknown corner in this world of your emotions? And you expect her to understand?!

ANATOL: You're a bad guesser today, Max. I'm celebrating — the end.

MAX: Ah.

ANATOL: A farewell supper.

MAX: And — you need *me* for that?

ANATOL: I want you to close the eyes of our deceased love.

MAX: That's in very bad taste, Anatol.

ANATOL: I've been postponing this supper for a week.

MAX: You must have quite an appetite by now.

ANATOL: No, no. We've had supper together every night. But — I haven't found the right words yet. I didn't dare. You have no idea how nervous it makes me.

MAX: But why do you need *me?!* Am I to whisper the words in your ear?

ANATOL: I need you here just in case. To support me, if need be. To calm things down. Smooth things over. To explain matters.

MAX: Care to tell me the reason for all this?

ANATOL: With pleasure. She bores me.

MAX: What you mean is, you're barking up another tree.

ANATOL: Yes.

MAX: I see. Well.

ANATOL: And what a catch!

MAX: Type?

ANATOL: None. Something new. Something unique.

MAX: Yes. Well. We only really discover the type toward the end.

ANATOL: Imagine a girl — how shall I describe her? In three-quarter time.

MAX: Too much ballet recently, Anatol.

ANATOL: Yes. Well. I can't help it. She reminds me of one of those slow Viennese waltzes. Sentimental gaiety. Smiling. Roguish melancholy. That's what she's like. A sweet, blonde little head. Well. You know how it goes. It's — it's not easy to describe. When I'm with her, I feel warm. Contented. When I bring her a bouquet of violets there's a tear in the corner of her eye.

MAX: Try a bracelet sometime.

ANATOL: Oh, my dear man. You're so wrong in this instance. It would never work. Believe me. I wouldn't even think of bringing her here to supper. Her style is more the cheap little restaurant. In the suburbs. With god-awful wallpaper. And civil servants at the next table. That's where I've spent every evening with her recently.

MAX: What? You just said you'd had supper with Annie.

ANATOL: Yes. And it's true. Last week I had supper twice each evening. With the girl I'm trying to win. And with the one I'm trying to lose. Unfortunately I've succeeded in neither.

MAX: I have a suggestion. Why not take Annie to one of those cheap restaurants, and bring the new blonde here to the Sacher. It just might work.

ANATOL: Since you don't know the new girl, your appraisal of the situation is a bit off. She's modesty itself. Oh, that girl! You should see her when I try to order a superior wine.

MAX: A tear in the corner of her eye? Hm?

ANATOL: She won't allow it. Under any circumstance. Simply won't allow it.

MAX: Then you've been drinking Markersdorfer lately?

ANATOL: Before ten. Yes. After that, of course, champagne. Such is life.

MAX: Excuse me. No. Such is *not* life.

ANATOL: You can imagine the contrast. But I've had enough of it now. This is another of those situations that makes me think that basically I'm really a rather honest individual.

MAX: Well, well.

ANATOL: But I can't handle this double-life anymore. I'm losing all self-respect.

MAX: Anatol, Anatol! It's me! Me! You don't have to put on an act with me!

ANATOL: Why not? You're here, aren't you? But seriously, Max. I can't pretend to love where I don't feel anything.

MAX: But you *can* pretend where you *do* feel something?

ANATOL: I told Annie very honestly at the start. At the very beginning. When we swore eternal love to each other. That if one fine day we feel that it's coming to an end — we should confess it openly.

MAX: Ah. So you agreed to that at the moment you swore eternal love. Very good, Anatol.

ANATOL: I've frequently told her that we have no obligation whatever to each other. That we're free. And when it's over, we simply part company. Calmly. With no deception. I abhor that sort of thing.

MAX: In that case, you should have smooth sailing this evening.

ANATOL: Smooth sailing. Now the time's come, I don't have the courage to say it. It's bound to hurt her. And I can't stand seeing women cry. I'll fall in love with her all over again if she cries. And then I'll be deceiving the other girl.

MAX: No, no. No deception. I abhor that sort of thing!

ANATOL: Your being here will make everything much easier. There's a sense of cool, sane cheerfulness about you that'll put a damper on the usual sentimentality of leave-taking. People don't cry in front of you.

MAX: Well, in any case, I'm here! But that's about all I can do for you. As for convincing her? I could never do such a thing. You're a far too likable man.

ANATOL: But, my dear Max! You could, up to a certain point? Couldn't you? I mean, you could tell her that I'm no great loss.

MAX: I suppose I could.

ANATOL: And that she'll find hundreds of other men who are — handsomer — richer —

MAX: More intelligent —

ANATOL: No, no, please. Don't exaggerate.

(*The WAITER opens the door. ANNIE enters in a rain cape and a white boa. She carries yellow gloves, and her hat is perched carelessly on her head.*)

ANNIE: Oh! Good evening!

ANATOL: Good evening, Annie. Forgive me.

ANNIE: You're so dependable, Anatol! (*She tosses off the rain cape.*) I looked all over for you. But there was no one!

ANATOL: Fortunately you didn't have far to go.

ANNIE: You must keep promises. Good evening, Max! (*To ANATOL.*) At least you might have let them start serving.

ANATOL: (*Embraces her.*) Nothing on underneath?

ANNIE: Well. Why dress up for you? I'm sorry!

ANATOL: It's quite all right. It's Max you should apologize to.

ANNIE: But why? He doesn't care one way or the other. He's not jealous. Well, then. Let's eat. (*The WAITER knocks.*) Come in. Today he knocks. Usually it never occurs to him.

(*The WAITER enters.*)

ANATOL: You may serve.

(*The WAITER goes off.*)

ANNIE: Weren't you at the opera this evening?

ANATOL: No. I had to —

ANNIE: You didn't miss much. It was so slow.

MAX: What was the opera?

ANNIE: I don't know. (*They sit at the table.*) I went to my dressing room.

Then on stage. I didn't care one way or the other. About anything. By the way. I have something to tell you, Anatol.

ANATOL: Have you? Anything important, my dear?

ANNIE: Rather. It may surprise you.

(*The WAITER enters and serves.*)

ANATOL: In that case, I'm curious. I, too, have —

ANNIE: Can't you wait! Do you want *him* to hear?

ANATOL: (*To the WAITER.*) You may go. We'll ring if we need you. Well?

(*The WAITER goes off.*)

ANNIE: Yes. My dear Anatol. It will surprise you. But why should it. It won't surprise you at all. It *mustn't* surprise you.

MAX: They've raised your salary?

ANATOL: Don't interrupt her.

ANNIE: Well, you see, Anatol — Oh, goodness! Are these Ostend or Whitestable?

ANATOL: What a time to talk about oysters! They're Ostend!

ANNIE: I thought so! I'm just wild about oysters! It's the only food one can eat every day.

MAX: Can?! Should! Must!

ANNIE: I know! I told you so!

ANATOL: You had something rather important to tell me?

ANNIE: Yes. Important it certainly is. Very important, in fact. Do you remember a certain remark you once made?

ANATOL: Which one? How should I know which remark you mean?

MAX: He's right.

ANNIE: Well. This one. Let's see. How did it go? Annie, you said — we must never deceive each other —

ANATOL: Yes. Yes. Well?

ANNIE: — never deceive each other. We should tell the truth at once —

ANATOL: Yes. I meant —

ANNIE: But what if it's too late?

ANATOL: What's that?

ANNIE: Oh! It's not too late! I'm telling you in time. But only *just* in time. Tomorrow might be too late.

ANATOL: Annie? Are you mad?!

MAX: What?

ANNIE: Anatol, you must eat your oysters. Otherwise I won't utter another word. Not a word!

ANATOL: What do you mean, I *must*?

ANNIE: Eat!

ANATOL: Tell me! At once! I don't like this kind of joke!

ANNIE: Well. We agreed that we should tell each other very calmly. When the time came. And — and now the time has come.

ANATOL: Meaning?

ANNIE: Meaning — that this is the last time we will have supper together.

ANATOL: Would you be so kind as to — explain yourself more fully.

ANNIE: It's over between us. It has to be over.

ANATOL: Yes. Well. Tell me —

MAX: Oh! This is choice!

ANNIE: Choice? Well, choice or not. That's the way it is.

ANATOL: My dear girl. I'm afraid I don't quite understand. Are you saying you've had a proposal of marriage?

ANNIE: If only! But that would be no reason for breaking with you.

ANATOL: Breaking with me?

ANNIE: Well, it has to come out sometime. I'm in love, Anatol. Madly in love!

ANATOL: May I ask with whom?

ANNIE: Max! Why are you laughing?

MAX: It's too amusing!

ANATOL: Ignore him! We two must have a talk, Annie. You have some explaining to do.

ANNIE: Well. But I'm explaining. I'm in love with someone else. And I'm telling you straight out. Because that's what we agreed on.

ANATOL: Yes. But who the hell with?

ANNIE: But, my dear, you needn't be so rude.

ANATOL: I demand! I absolutely demand —

ANNIE: Please, Max. Would you ring. I'm starving.

ANATOL: And now this! Hungry! Hungry!! At a time like this!

MAX: (*To ANATOL.*) Don't forget. This is only her *first* supper tonight.

(*The WAITER enters.*)

ANATOL: What is it?!

WAITER. You rang, sir.

MAX: Bring the next course.

(*The WAITER clears the table during the following.*)

ANNIE: Yes. Catalini's going to Germany. It's all settled.

MAX: Really? Letting her go just like that?

ANNIE: Well. No. Not just like that.

ANATOL: (*Rises and paces the room.*) Where's the wine?! You! Jean! Are you asleep?!

WAITER. Excuse me, sir. The wine —

ANATOL: I don't mean the wine on the table, for God's sake! The champagne! You know I always take it with the first course! (*The WAITER goes off.*) Would an explanation be out of order?

ANNIE: One shouldn't believe a word you men say. Not a word. I remember how beautifully you explained it to me. "When we feel that the end is coming, we should tell each other and part peacefully."

ANATOL: I want you to tell me.

ANNIE: He calls that "peacefully"!

ANATOL: But, my dear girl. You must understand. It is of some interest to me — who —

ANNIE: (*Slowly sipping the wine.*) Mmm!

ANATOL: Drink away, drink away!

ANNIE: You can wait a moment, can't you?

ANATOL: You usually drink it in one gulp!

ANNIE: But, Anatol dear, I'm taking leave of the Bordeaux, too. Who knows for how long.

ANATOL: What the hell are you talking about!

ANNIE: There won't be much Bordeaux in my future. And no oysters. No champagne. (*The WAITER enters with the next course.*) And no *filets aux truffes*. That's all past.

MAX: Good Lord, you have a sentimental stomach! (*As the WAITER serves.*) May I give you some?

ANNIE: Thanks.

(*ANATOL lights a cigarette.*)

MAX: Aren't you eating anything else?

ANATOL: Not just now. (*The WAITER goes off.*) Well now. If you don't mind, I should like to know who the lucky man is.

ANNIE: If I told you his name, it wouldn't mean a thing.

ANATOL: Well. What sort of person is he? How did you get to know him? What does he look like?

ANNIE: Beautiful. Beautiful as a picture. That's really all he —

ANATOL: Well. It appears to be enough for you.

ANNIE: Of course there won't be any oysters.

ANATOL: So we've heard.

ANNIE: And no champagne.

ANATOL: But damn it to hell! He must have some characteristics! Other than that he can't provide you with oysters and champagne!

MAX: He's right. You can't really call that a profession.

ANNIE: Well, what difference does it make? As long as I love him? I'm giving it all up. This is something new. Something I've never experienced.

MAX: Really now, Annie. In a pinch Anatol could have fed you badly, too.

ANATOL: What is he? A clerk? A chimney sweep? A traveling salesman?

ANNIE: I won't have that! I won't let you insult him!

MAX: Then tell us what he does.

ANNIE: He's an artiste.

ANATOL: What kind? A trapeze artiste, perhaps? Just what the doctor ordered. Or perhaps he's with the circus? Hm? A bareback rider?

ANNIE: Oh, will you stop this! He's a colleague of mine.

ANATOL: Ah! Well! An old acquaintance! Someone you've worked with daily for years! And someone you've been deceiving me with for sometime, too!

ANNIE: If I had, I'd never have told you. I trusted your word. That's why I'm telling you before it's too late.

ANATOL: But! You're already in love with him! For God knows how long! And you've deceived me in principle for God knows how long, too!

ANNIE: It's not against the law.

ANATOL: You are a —

MAX: Anatol!!

ANATOL: Do I know him?

ANNIE: Oh — I doubt you'd have noticed him. He dances in the chorus. But he'll be promoted. He'll make it.

ANATOL: Since when — have you been attracted to him?

ANNIE: Since this evening.

ANATOL: Don't lie to me!

ANNIE: It's the truth. This evening I felt that — that it was my destiny.

ANATOL: Her destiny! You hear that, Max? Her destiny!

ANNIE: Such things *are* destined.

ANATOL: Now you listen to me! I want to know everything! I have every right to know! As of this moment you are still my mistress! I want to know how long this has been going on — how it started — when he dared —

MAX: Yes. I really think you should tell us.

ANNIE: That's what you get for being honest. I should have played the game Fritzi plays with her baron. He still doesn't suspect. And for three months now she's been carrying on with a lieutenant from the Hussars.

ANATOL: He'll find out one of these days. Don't worry.

ANNIE: Probably. But you'd never have found out. Never. (*She pours herself a glass of wine.*)

ANATOL: Will you stop drinking!

ANNIE: Not tonight. I want to get tipsy. It'll be the last time.

MAX: For the next week!

ANNIE: For ever. I'm going to stay with Carl, because I really love him. Because he's fun. Even if he doesn't have any money. Because he won't pester me. Because he's a sweet, sweet — dear, lovely boy.

ANATOL: You didn't keep your word. You've been in love with him for a long time. That's a stupid lie, what you said about this evening!

ANNIE: So don't believe me.

MAX: Now, Annie. Tell us the whole story. You know. Everything. Or not at all. If you want to part friends, you at least owe it to Anatol to tell him.

ANATOL: Then I'll tell you something, too.

ANNIE: Well. It all began —

(*The WAITER enters.*)

ANATOL: Go on! Go on! (*Sits next to her.*)

ANNIE: It must have been about two weeks ago. Or maybe longer. He gave me a couple of roses. At the stage door. I laughed. He was so shy.

ANATOL: Why didn't you tell me about this?

ANNIE: Tell? What was there to tell?

ANATOL: All right! Go on! Go on!

ANNIE: And then at rehearsals he started hanging around me and — well — I began to notice. At first it bothered me. But later I was glad.

ANATOL: How simple.

ANNIE: Well. Then we started talking and — and I really began to like him.

ANATOL: What did you talk about?

ANNIE: Everything we could think of. How he was expelled from school. And how he was supposed to become an apprentice. And — and how he began to realize he was drawn to the theater.

ANATOL: I see! And you never mentioned this to me!

ANNIE: Well. And then we discovered that when we were children we grew up just two houses from each other. We were neighbors.

ANATOL: Ah! Neighbors! That's touching! Very touching!

ANNIE: Yes — yes — (*She drinks.*)

ANATOL: Go on!

ANNIE: What's there to go on with? I've told you everything. It's my destiny. And I can't deny — my destiny. And I — I can't deny my — my —

ANATOL: I want to know about this evening!

ANNIE: Well — what — (*Her head sinks down.*)

MAX: She's asleep.

ANATOL: Wake her up! Put the wine somewhere else! I must know what happened this evening! Annie! Annie!

ANNIE: This evening — he told me — that — that he — loves — me.

ANATOL: And you?

ANNIE: I told him — I was glad — and since I didn't want to deceive him — I'd break off with *you* —

ANATOL: Didn't want to deceive *him?!* Then it's not for *my* sake? But for *his!?*

ANNIE: Well? So what? I don't love you anymore.

ANATOL: Good! Fine! Fortunately this doesn't concern me any longer!

ANNIE: Oh!?

ANATOL: I, too, am in the enviable position of — of being able to deny myself your — your attention!

ANNIE: I see! I see!

ANATOL: Yes! Yes! I haven't loved you for a long while now. I love someone else!

ANNIE: Haha! Haha!

ANATOL: Not for a long while! Ask Max! Before you arrived, I told him the whole story!

ANNIE: I see. I see.

ANATOL: Not for a long while! And this other one is a thousand times better and more beautiful —

ANNIE: I see. I see.

ANATOL: I'd give up a thousand women like you for just one girl like her! Do you understand? (*ANNIE laughs.*) Don't laugh! Ask Max!

ANNIE: This is too funny for words. You're trying to make me believe —

ANATOL: It's true, I tell you! I swear it's true! I haven't loved you for a long time! Nor did I think about you when we were together! And when I kissed you I was thinking about her! About her! About her!

ANNIE: Well. Then we're quits.

ANATOL: Oh? You think so?

ANNIE: Yes. Quits. And I couldn't be happier.

ANATOL: No we're not quits! No, no! Not at all! These experiences of yours! And mine! Can't even be compared! My story is somewhat less — innocent!

ANNIE: (*Growing more serious.*) What?

ANATOL: That's right! My story sounds a bit different!

ANNIE: Different? How?

ANATOL: Well — I — I deceived you!

ANNIE: (*Rises.*) You what?!

ANATOL: Deceived you! As you deserved! Day after day! Night after night! I left her in order to meet you — and I left you in order to be able to return to her!

ANNIE: Infamous! This is — this is — infamous!! (*She goes to the coatrack and tosses her rain cape and her boa around her.*)

ANATOL: A man can't get rid of a woman like you fast enough! Or you beat him at his own game! Well! It's a good thing I have no illusions!

ANNIE: There you have it! Yes, indeed!

ANATOL: That's right! There you have it! There you have it!

ANNIE: Men are a hundred times more inconsiderate than women!

ANATOL: There you have it! That's right! That's how inconsiderate I was! You'd better believe it!

ANNIE: (*Has by now slung the boa around her neck, and is picking up her gloves and hat as she turns to him.*) Yes! Inconsiderate! I would never have told you — that! (*She turns to go.*)

ANATOL: What? (*Going after her.*)

MAX: Let her go. You can't stop her, anyway.

ANATOL: You didn't tell me *that?* What?! That you — that you — that —!

ANNIE: (*At the door.*) I would never have told you. Never. Only a man can be that inconsiderate.

WAITER: (*Enters with a cream dessert.*) Oh.

ANATOL: To hell with your dessert!

ANNIE: What?! Vanilla-creme!! Oh!

ANATOL: You dare!

MAX: Leave her alone. She's taking leave of the vanilla-creme. For ever.

ANNIE: Yes! With pleasure! From the Bordeaux! The champagne! The oysters! And especially from you, Anatol! (*With a derisive smile on her face, she suddenly leaves the doorway and walks to the cigarette box on a sideboard and stuffs a handful of cigarettes into her bag.*) They're not for me! I'm taking them — for him!

(*ANATOL goes after her, but stops at the door.*)

MAX: (*Calmly.*) There. You see? Smooth sailing all the way.

VI. AGONY

Anatol's room. Early twilight. The room is empty for a while, then ANATOL and MAX enter.

MAX: So there. I came up with you after all.

ANATOL: Stay a while.

MAX: But I don't want to disturb you.

ANATOL: Please stay. I don't want to be alone right now. And she might not even come.

MAX: Ah.

ANATOL: Seven times out of ten I wait and she doesn't come.

MAX: I wouldn't put up with it.

ANATOL: And at times you have to believe her excuses. Unfortunately they're true.

MAX: All seven times?

ANATOL: Oh, I don't know. What's worse than being the lover of a married woman.

MAX: Being her husband.

ANATOL: And this has been going on for — for how long now? Two years. Ah, God, no! Longer. It was two years at Carnival. And that was six months ago. This is the third "spring of our love."

MAX: What is it?

ANATOL: (*Without removing his topcoat, has thrown himself into the armchair beside the window.*) I'm so tired. And nervous. I don't know what I want.

MAX: Take a trip.

ANATOL: Why?

MAX: To hasten the end.

ANATOL: The end!?

MAX: I've seen you like this before. The *last* time, in fact. When you couldn't make up your mind to break it off with some silly little thing who wasn't worth the pain she caused.

ANATOL: You're saying I don't love her anymore?

MAX: That would be wonderful. By that time the suffering's over. But now you're going through something a lot worse than death. You're dying.

ANATOL: You have a knack for saying such pleasant things. But you're right. It's unmitigated agony.

MAX: At least it's comforting to talk about it. And we don't even need a philosophy. We can avoid the larger generalities and simply deal with the particular.

ANATOL: I'm not overwhelmed by the suggestion.

MAX: I was just talking. But I noticed you were pale and tired this afternoon in the Prater.

ANATOL: She was to take a drive there today.

MAX: I think you were relieved when she didn't show up. You don't have the smile you had two years ago. When you first met her.

ANATOL: (*Rises.*) Why does it happen? Tell me. Why does it happen? Why do I have to go through this again? This slow, tedious, melancholy fading away of love. Gives me the shivers.

MAX: Take a trip. Or have the courage to tell her the truth.

ANATOL: What are you talking about. How can I?

MAX: Simple. Tell her it's over.

ANATOL: It's a kind of truth I'm not terribly proud of. The brutal honesty of tired liars.

MAX: Of course. You prefer hiding it to telling her you've made the decision. Why?

ANATOL: Because we don't believe it's really over. Because in the middle of this agony there are moments when it all seems more beautiful than ever. We long for happiness more in the dying days of a love than at any other time. And when the illusion of happiness comes, we rush headlong toward it, rather than look behind its mask. And then there are moments when we're ashamed for thinking that all that sweetness is gone. And we forgive. In silence. We exhaust ourselves with the fear of dying. And then all of a sudden life is there again. Hotter and more glowing than ever. And more deceptive.

MAX: Just don't forget. The end often begins sooner than we imagine. There's a happiness that starts to die with the first kiss. Some incurably ill people believe themselves healthy until the last moment.

ANATOL: Unfortunately I'm not one of them. That's for sure. I've always been a hypochondriac where love is concerned. Perhaps my emotions weren't always as sick as I believed them to be. Worse luck. At times I believe in the Evil Eye. In my case it's true. But it's turned inward. And my best emotions sicken under its glance.

MAX: If you've got it, use it.

ANATOL: I can't. Because I envy those happy people whose every step is a new conquest in life. I have to force myself to finish anything. I stop along the way. I think about it. I rest. I drag along. While the others play at conquest like a game, in the very midst of experience. It's all the same to them.

MAX: Don't envy them, Anatol. They don't conquer. They merely pass by.

ANATOL: Isn't that happiness, too? At least they aren't plagued with this painful guilt we feel when love ends.

MAX: What guilt?

ANATOL: We're expected to put the eternal love we promise into the few years or hours we actually love them. But we can't. Never. With every woman we leave behind, we suffer the same guilt. And our melancholy is our secret confession of it. Our last vestige of honesty.

MAX: Sometimes our first.

ANATOL: And it brings so much pain.

MAX: These long affairs aren't good for you. You have too fine a nose.

ANATOL: What are you talking about?

MAX: Escape the past. Don't drag it around like a ball and chain. When the first years of a love begin to decay — as they're doing now — be strong enough to walk away. But you don't. And where does it get you? It poisons whatever healthy, glorious love you have in the present.

ANATOL: You may be right.

MAX: That's why you always confuse the Then, the Now and the Later. Their outlines are always blurred where you're concerned. For you the past is never a simple, static fact. It's weighted down with the emotions that were a part of it. They're like a dense cloud that obscures the facts. They only become dimmer and wither and finally die.

ANATOL: Very true. And this decay gives birth to the pain that destroys my finest moments. And that's what I want to escape from.

MAX: We all say something really first-class from time to time. And the tip of my tongue is dying to say: "Be strong, Anatol, and recover."

ANATOL: You're laughing even while you say it. Yes. It's possible. Except that I lack one important factor. The desire. Think of what I'd lose if one fine day I suddenly became "strong." There are many illnesses. But only one health. When you're healthy you're like everyone else. But when you're sick, you're sick in your own way.

MAX: Is that some kind of vanity?

ANATOL: And what if it is? Is vanity a fault?

MAX: I gather, then, you're not taking the trip.

ANATOL: Who knows. I might. But it must come as a surprise. No planning. Planning would destroy it. That's what's so dreadful. You pack your bags, call a cab and say: "To the station!"

MAX: I can see to that. (*ANATOL has rushed to the window to look out.*) What is it?

ANATOL: Nothing.

MAX: Of course. I forgot. I'll be going.

ANATOL: There, you see. At this very moment I feel —

MAX: Well?

ANATOL: That I adore her.

MAX: And there is a very simple explanation. At this very moment you *do* adore her.

ANATOL: Good-bye, then. And don't order the cab just yet.

MAX: Don't be so presumptuous. The express train to Trieste doesn't leave for four hours. And your baggage can be sent on.

ANATOL: Thanks a lot.

MAX: (*At the door.*) I can't possibly leave without an aphorism.

ANATOL: I'm waiting.

MAX: Woman is an enigma!

ANATOL: Oh, God!!

MAX: Let me finish. Woman is an enigma — as we say. But what sort of enigma would we be for women if they had the intelligence to think about us?

ANATOL: Bravo! Bravo!

(*MAX bows and goes out. ANATOL, alone for a while, paces the room several times, then sits beside the window and smokes a cigarette. The sounds of a violin drift down from an upper floor. Pause. Then steps are heard in the hallway. ANATOL listens to them, rises, puts the cigarette in an ashtray and goes to meet ELSA who has just entered, thickly veiled.*)

ANATOL: At last!

ELSA: Yes, yes. I know it's late! (*She takes off her hat and veils.*) I couldn't get here earlier. It was impossible!

ANATOL: Couldn't you have let me know? I get nervous when I wait. But — you're staying?

ELSA: Not for long, angel. My husband — (*ANATOL turns away in bad humor.*) There you go again. I couldn't help it.

ANATOL: Yes. I guess you're right. That's just the way he is. And — we have to put up with it. Come, my sweet. Come here.

(*They walk to the window.*)

ELSA: Someone could see me.

ANATOL: It's dark. And the curtain hides us. I wish you could stay longer. I haven't seen you for two days. And the last time for only a few minutes.

ELSA: Do you love me?

ANATOL: You know I do. You're everything to me. Everything. I want to be with you always.

ELSA: And I like being with you.

ANATOL: Come. (*He pulls her down into the armchair beside him.*) Your hand! (*He puts her hand to his lips.*) Do you hear the old man playing upstairs? Beautiful, isn't it?

ELSA: My precious!

ANATOL: I wish we were on Lake Como now. Or in Venice.

ELSA: That's where I spent my honeymoon.

ANATOL: (*With suppressed anger.*) Did you have to say that?

ELSA: But I love only you. I've never loved anyone — anyone but you. And certainly not my husband.

ANATOL: (*Folding his hands.*) Please. Forget you're married. For a few seconds at least. Enjoy the moment. Imagine that we two are alone in the world.

(*A clock strikes.*)

ELSA: What time is it?

ANATOL: Elsa, Elsa. Don't ask. Forget that there are others. You're with *me* now.

ELSA: (*Tenderly.*) Haven't I forgotten enough for you?

ANATOL: My sweet. (*Kissing her hand.*)

ELSA: My dear Anatol.

ANATOL: (*Softly.*) What, Elsa? (*ELSA, smiling, indicates with a gesture that she has to leave.*) You mean?

ELSA: I must go.

ANATOL: Really?

ELSA: Yes.

ANATOL: You really have to go? Now? Now? All right. Go.

ELSA: You're impossible to talk to.

ANATOL: Impossible to talk to! (*Pacing the room.*) Can't you understand that this life is driving me mad?

ELSA: Is that the thanks I get?

ANATOL: Thanks! Thanks! Thanks for what? Haven't I given you as much as you've given me? Do I love you any less than you love me? Do I make you any less happy than you make me? Love. Madness. Pain. Perhaps. But thanks? Where did you get that stupid word?

ELSA: So, then. I don't deserve even a little thanks. I who sacrificed everything for you?

ANATOL: Sacrifice? I don't want sacrifice. And if it *was* sacrifice, then you never loved me.

ELSA: Oh, that too now! I don't love you. I, I who deceived my husband for you. I, I — I don't love you!

ANATOL: I didn't say that.

ELSA: Oh, what have I done!

ANATOL: (*Standing in front of her.*) "Oh, what have I done!" This brilliant remark is all I needed! What have you done? I'll tell you! You were a stupid, silly little flapper seven years ago. And then you got married. Because getting married was the thing to do. And you went on a honeymoon. You were happy. In Venice.

ELSA: Never!

ANATOL: Happy. In Venice. On Lake Como. It had to be love. At certain moments at any rate.

ELSA: Never!

ANATOL: What? Didn't he kiss you? Embrace you? Weren't you his wife? And then you returned. And you grew bored. Naturally. Because you're beautiful. And elegant. And a woman! And he's a stupid ass! And then came your years of flirtation. You said you never loved anyone before me. Well. I can't prove that. But I'll take it for granted. Rather than believe the other.

ELSA: Anatol. How can you? Flirtation!

ANATOL: Yes. Flirtation! And what does it mean to be a flirt? It means to be lascivious and a liar at the same time.

ELSA: And I was that?

ANATOL: Yes. You. And then came your years of struggle. You wavered. "Shall I never have a romantic adventure?" You became more and more beautiful. And your husband more tedious. Stupider and uglier. Finally it had to happen. And you took a lover. And I happened to be that lover. Just by chance.

ELSA: By chance? You?

ANATOL: Yes. By chance. Me. Because if I hadn't been available — someone else would have been. You were either unhappy in your marriage or not happy enough. And you wanted to be loved. You flirted with me a bit. Raved on about the Grand Passion. And one fine day as you saw one of your friends driving by in her carriage, or maybe a coquette sitting in a box next to you in a theater, you thought to yourself: "Why shouldn't I enjoy myself, too!" And so you became my mistress. *That's* what you've done. That and nothing more. And I don't see why you need to use such big phrases for such a little adventure.

ELSA: Anatol. Anatol! Adventure?!

ANATOL: Yes.

ELSA: Take back what you just said. Please.

ANATOL: What's there to take back? What else was it for you?

ELSA: You really believe that?

ANATOL: Yes.

ELSA: Very well then. I must go.

ANATOL: Go. I'm not holding you back.

(*Pause.*)

ELSA: You're sending me away?

ANATOL: Sending you away? I? Just a moment ago you said: "I must go!"

ELSA: Anatol. I *do* have to. Don't you understand?

ANATOL: (*Decisively.*) Elsa.

ELSA: What is it?

ANATOL: Elsa. Do you love me? That's what you say, but —

ELSA: Of course that's what I say. For God's sake! What proof do you want?

ANATOL: Do you really want to know? Good. Maybe I'll know you love me after all.

ELSA: Maybe? That's what you say today.

ANATOL: Do you love me?

ELSA: I adore you.

ANATOL: Then — stay with me.

ELSA: What?

ANATOL: Let's escape this place. Together. Will you? Go to another city. To another world. I want to be alone with you.

ELSA: What can you be thinking of?

ANATOL: What can I be thinking of? The only natural thing there is. How can I let you get away? To him? How could I ever let you do that? How can you do it to yourself? You, who say you adore me. How? Out of my arms? Away from my kisses? Back to a house that's become strange to you since you became mine? No, no. We got used to all this. That's all. We never realized how monstrous it is. It's impossible to go on living like this. Elsa. Elsa. You're coming with me. Well? Answer me? Elsa! We'll go to Sicily. Wherever you like. Across the ocean, for all I care. Elsa!

ELSA: Do you know what you're saying?

ANATOL: No one to stand between us ever again. Across the ocean, Elsa. And we'll be alone.

ELSA: Across the ocean?

ANATOL: Wherever you like.

ELSA: My dear, sweet — child —

ANATOL: Why are you hesitating?

ELSA: But, my sweet. Why do we need that?

ANATOL: What?

ELSA: To go away. There's no need. We can see each other in Vienna almost as often as we like.

ANATOL: Almost as often as we like. Yes, that's right. There's no need to —

ELSA: These are fantasies.

ANATOL: You're right.

(*Pause.*)

ELSA: Angry?

(*Bells are heard.*)

ANATOL: You must go.

ELSA: Oh, God! Look how late it is!

ANATOL: Well. Go. Go.

ELSA: Tomorrow, then — I'll see you at six o'clock.

ANATOL: Whatever you say.

ELSA: Aren't you going to kiss me?

ANATOL: Oh — yes —

ELSA: I'll make it up to you. Tomorrow.

ANATOL: (*Accompanies her to the door.*) Good-bye.

ELSA: (*At the door.*) One more kiss.

ANATOL: Why not. There. (*He kisses her. She goes out. ANATOL comes back into the room.*) With that kiss I made her into what she deserves to be. Just one more! (*He shudders.*) Stupid! Stupid!

VII. ANATOL'S WEDDING MORNING

A tastefully appointed bachelor apartment. The door on the right leads into the hallway; the door on the left, with curtains at the sides, leads into the bedroom. ANATOL, dressed in a house jacket, enters from the door on the left, closing it quietly behind him. He sits down on a couch and presses a button; a bell rings. FRANZ, a servant, enters from the right and, without noticing ANATOL, goes to the door on the left. ANATOL, who at first does not see him, runs after him and prevents him from opening the door.

ANATOL: Why are you creeping along like that? I didn't even hear you.

FRANZ: What do you wish, sir?

ANATOL: The samovar.

FRANZ: Yes, sir. (*Goes off.*)

ANATOL: Quiet, you fool! Can't you be less noisy? (*He tiptoes to the door on the left and opens it slightly.*) She's sleeping. She's still sleeping. (*Closes the door.*)

FRANZ: (*Enters with the samovar.*) Two cups, sir?

ANATOL: Yes. (*The bell rings.*) See who it is. (*FRANZ goes off.*) I'm certainly not in the mood to get married today. I wish I could call it off.

(*FRANZ opens the door on the right and MAX enters.*)

MAX: (*Affectionately.*) My dear Anatol.

ANATOL: Shh! Quiet! Another cup, Franz.

MAX: There are two cups here already.

ANATOL: Another cup, Franz. And you may go. (*FRANZ goes off.*) There now. Well, old boy. What brings you here at eight in the morning?

MAX: Ten.

ANATOL: Very well. What brings you here at ten in the morning?

MAX: My poor memory.

ANATOL: Not so loud.

MAX: Why? Nervous?

ANATOL: Very.

MAX: You shouldn't be nervous today.

ANATOL: What do you want?

MAX: As you may recall, I'm best man at your wedding this afternoon. And your charming cousin Alma is the bridesmaid.

ANATOL: (*Flatly.*) Come to the point.

MAX: Well. I forgot to order the bouquet. And for the life of me I can't remember what color dress she's wearing. Will it be white, pink, blue or green?

ANATOL: (*Peevishly.*) Certainly not green!

MAX: Why certainly not green?

ANATOL: My cousin never wears green

MAX: (*Piqued.*) How am I to know that?

ANATOL: (*As above.*) Don't scream. Can't we settle this quietly?

MAX: Then you don't know what color she'll be wearing?

ANATOL: Pink or blue!

MAX: Those are two different propositions.

ANATOL: Oh, pink or blue! What does it matter!

MAX: It matters a great deal for the bouquet I'm to order.

ANATOL: Order two. You can put one in your buttonhole.

MAX: I didn't come to hear you crack miserable jokes.

ANATOL: At two this afternoon I'll crack an even worse one.

MAX: What a fine mood for your wedding morning.

ANATOL: I'm nervous.

MAX: You're hiding something from me.

ANATOL: I'm not.

ILONA'S VOICE: (*From the bedroom.*) Anatol!

    (*MAX looks at ANATOL in surprise.*)

ANATOL: Excuse me for a moment.

    (*ANATOL goes to the door and disappears. MAX looks after him in astonishment. ANATOL kisses ILONA at the door, without MAX seeing, closes the door and re-enters the room.*)

MAX: (*Exasperated.*) What a hell of a way to start!

ANATOL: Hear me out first, Max. And then judge.

MAX: I hear a female voice from the bedroom and I judge that you're getting a head start on deceiving your wife.

ANATOL: Just sit down and listen. You'll understand.

MAX: No. I'm no paragon of virtue. But this!

ANATOL: And you refuse to listen?

MAX: All right. Tell me. But hurry. I'm invited to your wedding.

(*MAX and ANATOL sit.*)

ANATOL: (*Sadly.*) Yes. Well.

MAX: (*Impatiently.*) I'm waiting.

ANATOL: Well — well, there was a party last night. At my future parents-in-law.

MAX: I know. I was there.

ANATOL: That's right. You were. There were hordes of people. It was a very lively group. Champagne. Toasts.

MAX: I made one, too. To your happiness.

ANATOL: Yes, so you did. To my happiness. (*Shakes MAX's hand.*) Thank you.

MAX: You thanked me last night.

ANATOL: Spirits were very high until midnight.

MAX: I know.

ANATOL: For a moment there, I thought I was happy.

MAX: After your fourth glass of champagne.

ANATOL: (*Sadly.*) Wrong. After my sixth. It's sad. I can hardly believe it.

MAX: We've discussed it often enough.

ANATOL: And that young man was there. Who I'm sure was my bride's childhood sweetheart.

MAX: Young Ralman. Yes.

ANATOL: Yes. Some kind of poet, I think. One of those men who are destined to be the first love of many women, but the last love of none.

MAX: Would you come to the point?

ANATOL: I didn't care one way or the other. I just smiled when I thought about him. The party broke up at midnight. I bade my bride-to-be farewell with a kiss. And she kissed me. Very coldly, I might add. I shivered as I walked down the steps.

MAX: Aha.

ANATOL: At the gate a few others congratulated me. Uncle Edward was drunk and embraced me. A doctor of law struck up a student song. The childhood sweetheart — the poet, I mean, disappeared down a side street with his collar turned up. Someone teased me about surely spending the night pacing beneath my beloved's window. I smiled scornfully. It had begun to snow. People gradually dispersed. I stood alone.

MAX: (*Sympathetically.*) Hm.

ANATOL: (*Warming up.*) Yes. I stood alone in the street. In the cold winter night. While the snow came down in enormous flakes and swirled around me. It was really quite — gruesome.

MAX: Excuse me. But where did you finally end up?

ANATOL: (*Grandly.*) I needed to go — to the masquerade.

MAX: Ah.

ANATOL: Surprised?

MAX: I can imagine the rest of it.

ANATOL: Not at all, friend Max. As I stood there in the cold winter night —

MAX: Shivering!

ANATOL: Freezing! Suddenly the painful realization hit me. That I would no longer be a free man. That I had to bid farewell to the sweet, wild days of bachelorhood. The last night, I said to myself, that you'll be able to come home without being asked where you've been. The last night of freedom. Of adventure. And maybe even of love.

MAX: Oh.

ANATOL: And then suddenly I found myself in the middle of the crowd. Satin and silk garments rustled about me. Eyes glowed. Masks nodded seductively. White gleaming shoulders exhaled their fragrances. The Carnival breathed and tumbled around me. I plunged myself into the swirling madness and let it batter against me. I wanted to soak it in. I wanted to bathe in it.

MAX: Get to the point. We don't have time.

ANATOL: The force of the crowd pushed me forward. Intoxicated me with its perfume. Just as earlier I had been intoxicated with alcohol. It surged over me as never before. I felt the Carnival was giving me my own personal farewell celebration.

MAX: I'm waiting for the third intoxication.

ANATOL: It came. The intoxication of the heart.

MAX: The senses.

ANATOL: The heart! All right! The senses! Do you remember Katherine?

MAX: (*Loudly.*) Oh, Katherine.

ANATOL: Shh!

MAX: (*Indicating the bedroom door.*) Is it?

ANATOL: No, it isn't. But she was there, too. Along with a charming brunette.

Whose name I won't mention. And Theodore's little blonde Lizzie. Except that Theodore wasn't there. And so on. I recognized them all behind their masks. By their voices. By their walk. By some gesture or other. But strangely enough, there was one I didn't recognize. Not at first. I followed her. Or she me. I recognized her bearing. In any case, we were always running into each other. At the fountain. At the buffet. Beside the proscenium box. Constantly. Finally she took my arm. And I knew who she was. (*Indicating the bedroom door.*)

MAX: An old acquaintance?

ANATOL: Can't you guess? Don't you remember what I told her six weeks ago? When I became engaged? Same old story. "I'm leaving on a trip. I'll be back soon. I'll love you forever."

MAX: Ilona?

ANATOL: Shh!

MAX: It's not Ilona?

ANATOL: Yes. Just keep quiet! "You're back," she whispered in my ear. "Yes," I said, quick on the draw. "When did you arrive?" "This evening." "Why didn't you write?" "No postal connections." "Where, for heaven's sake?" "Some ungodly village!" "And now?" "Happy. Back again. And faithful as ever." "Me, too, me, too." Bliss, champagne, and more bliss!

MAX: And more champagne.

ANATOL: No. No more champagne. And then as we rode home in the cab, like we used to, she leaned against my chest. "We must never part again," she said.

MAX: (*Rises.*) Wake up, Anatol, and let's get this over with.

ANATOL: "Never part again." (*Rising.*) And at two this afternoon I'll be married.

MAX: To someone else.

ANATOL: Well, of course. One always marries someone else.

MAX: (*Looking at the clock.*) It's high time. (*He gestures that ANATOL should get rid of ILONA.*)

ANATOL: Yes. All right. I'll see if she's ready. (*Goes to the door, but stops and turns to MAX:*) Isn't it sad?

MAX: It's immoral.

ANATOL: Yes. But sad, too.

MAX: Go on, for God's sake!

(*ANATOL goes to the bedroom door.*)

ILONA: (*Sticks her head around the door and enters dressed in an elegant domino.*) Oh! It's only Max!

MAX: (*Bowing.*) Only Max.

ILONA: (*To ANATOL.*) Why didn't you tell me? I thought it was a stranger. I'd have come out long ago. How are you, Max? What do you think about this rascal?

MAX: That's what he is, all right.

ILONA: I cried my eyes out over him for six weeks. And he was — where were you?

ANATOL: (*With a large gesture.*) Oh, somewhere that —

ILONA: Didn't he write you, either? But now I have him back. (*Taking his arm.*) And there'll be no more trips. And no more partings. Kiss me!

ANATOL: But —

ILONA: Oh, Max doesn't mind! (*Kisses ANATOL.*) What a face! Now I'll pour some tea for us, if you don't mind.

ANATOL: Please.

MAX: Ilona dear, I'm afraid I can't breakfast with you this morning. And I can't understand —

ILONA: (*Busies herself at the samovar.*) What can't you understand?

MAX: Anatol really ought to —

ILONA: Really ought to what?

MAX: (*To ANATOL.*) Ought to be dressed.

ILONA: Don't be silly, Max. We're staying at home today. We're not budging an inch.

ANATOL: Unfortunately, my dear, that won't be possible.

ILONA: Oh, but it *will* be possible.

ANATOL: I've been invited —

ILONA: (*Pouring the tea.*) Turn it down.

MAX: He *can't* turn it down.

ANATOL: I've been invited to a wedding.

(*MAX makes encouraging gestures at ANATOL.*)

ILONA: Oh, that's not important.

ANATOL: I'm the best man.

ILONA: Is the bridesmaid in love with you?

MAX: That's quite beside the point.

ILONA: But I *love* him. And that *is* the point. And I wish you wouldn't interrupt.

ANATOL: My dear. I do have to go.

MAX: Yes. He means it. He really does.

ANATOL: You'll have to give me a few hours leave.

ILONA: Please sit down. How many lumps, Max?

MAX: Three.

ILONA: (*To ANATOL.*) You?

ANATOL: It's time to go.

ILONA: How many lumps?

ANATOL: You should know by now. Two.

ILONA: Cream? Rum?

ANATOL: Rum. You should know that, too.

ILONA: Rum and two lumps of sugar. (*To MAX.*) The man has principles.

MAX: I have to go.

ANATOL: (*Softly.*) You're leaving me?

ILONA: At least drink your tea, Max.

ANATOL: My dear, I'm afraid I have to change now.

ILONA: For God's sake! When is this miserable wedding?

MAX: Two hours.

ILONA: Are you invited, too?

MAX: Yes.

ILONA: Are you the best man, too?

ANATOL: Yes, he is.

ILONA: Who's getting married?

ANATOL: You don't know him.

ILONA: What's his name? It's no secret, is it?

ANATOL: It's a secret.

ILONA: What?

ANATOL: The wedding's taking place in secret.

ILONA: With best men and bridesmaids? That's ridiculous.

MAX: Only the parents mustn't know.

ILONA: (*Sipping her tea; quietly.*) I think you're lying to me.

MAX: Oh, come on.

ILONA: God knows where you two are going today. But you can forget it.
You, dear Max, can go anywhere you like. But he stays here.

ANATOL: I'm sorry. That's quite impossible. I can't miss my best friend's wedding.

ILONA: (*To MAX.*) Shall I let him go?

MAX: Dear, dear Ilona. You must —

ILONA: What church?

ANATOL: (*Calmly.*) Why do you ask?

ILONA: I thought I might drop by.

MAX: That's impossible.

ILONA: Why?

ANATOL: Because the wedding's taking place in a — in an underground chapel.

ILONA: There's got to be a way to get there.

ANATOL: No. What I mean is. Of course there's a way to get there.

ILONA: I want to see your bridesmaid, Anatol. I'm jealous of her. There are tales of best men who go on to marry their bridesmaids. And I assure you, I don't want you getting married.

MAX: What would you do if he — did get married?

ILONA: (*Very calmly.*) Interrupt the ceremony.

ANATOL: Would you?

MAX: And how would you manage that?

ILONA: Haven't made up my mind yet. Probably some big scandal at the church door.

MAX: That's nothing.

ILONA: Oh, I'd find a new touch.

MAX: For example?

ILONA: I'd drive up dressed as a bride. With a wreath and a veil. Wouldn't *that* be original!

MAX: Most! (*Rises.*) I have to go now. Good-bye, Anatol.

ANATOL: (*Rises with determination.*) Excuse me, my dear. But I have to change. It's getting late.

FRANZ: (*Enters with a bouquet.*) The flowers, sir.

ILONA: What flowers?

FRANZ: (*Looks at ILONA with surprise and a somewhat confidential expression.*) The flowers, sir.

ILONA: You still have Franz with you, I see. (*FRANZ goes off.*) I thought you were getting rid of him.

MAX: Easier said than done.

(*ANATOL stands with the tissue paper–wrapped bouquet in his hand.*)

ILONA: Let's see what kind of taste you have in flowers.

MAX: The bridesmaid's bouquet?

ILONA: (*Pulling back the tissue paper.*) This is the bride's bouquet!

ANATOL: Good God! They've sent me the wrong one! Franz! Franz! (*He hurries off with the bouquet.*)

MAX: The poor bridegroom probably has Anatol's.

ANATOL: (*Re-entering.*) Franz has gone after him.

MAX: You'll have to excuse me. I must go.

ANATOL: (*Walking him to the door.*) What shall I do?

MAX: Confess.

ANATOL: That's impossible!

MAX: I'll come back as soon as I can.

ANATOL: Please do!

MAX: What about the color I came for?

ANATOL: Blue or red. I have a feeling it will be one or the other. Bye.

MAX: Good-bye, Ilona. (*Softly.*) I'll be back in an hour.

(*ANATOL comes back into the room.*)

ILONA: (*Runs into his arms.*) At last! Oh, how happy I am!

ANATOL: (*Mechanically.*) Angel!

ILONA: You're so cold.

ANATOL: I just called you my angel.

ILONA: Must you really go to that stupid wedding?

ANATOL: In all seriousness, yes.

ILONA: Would you mind if I drove with you in the carriage as far as the lady's house?

ANATOL: Don't be silly. I'll see you again this evening. You'll be at the theater.

ILONA: I'll cancel tonight.

ANATOL: No, no, I'll pick you up. But now I have to change into my morning suit. (*Looks at the clock.*) How time flies. Franz! Franz!

ILONA: What do you want?

ANATOL: (*To FRANZ, entering.*) Have you laid out my clothes?

FRANZ: You mean the morning suit, the white cravat, sir —

ANATOL: Of course.

FRANZ: I'll do it at once, sir.

ANATOL: (*Pacing.*) So! Ilona! This evening? After the theater?

ILONA: I wish I could stay with you all day today.

ANATOL: Don't be childish. I have certain obligations. You can understand that.

ILONA: All I understand is that I love you.

ANATOL: It's absolutely essential.

FRANZ: (*Enters from the bedroom.*) Everything is laid out, sir. (*He goes off.*)

ANATOL: Good. (*Goes into the bedroom and speaks from behind the door while ILONA remains onstage.*) I mean, it's absolutely essential you understand that.

ILONA: Are you really changing?

ANATOL: I can't go to a wedding looking like this.

ILONA: But why are you going?

ANATOL: Are you starting in again? I have no choice.

ILONA: Tonight, then.

ANATOL: Yes. I'll wait for you at the stage door.

ILONA: And be on time.

ANATOL: Of course. Why shouldn't I be?

ILONA: Oh, you remember. I once waited for you for a whole hour.

ANATOL: Really? I don't recall.

    (*Pause.*)

ILONA: (*Walks about the room looking at the ceiling and walls.*) Anatol, you've bought a new picture!

ANATOL: Do you like it?

ILONA: I don't know anything about pictures.

ANATOL: It's a very beautiful picture.

ILONA: Did you bring it back with you?

ANATOL: Back? From where?

ILONA: From your trip, of course.

ANATOL: Yes. Of course. From my trip. No, actually. It was a gift.

    (*Pause.*)

ILONA: Anatol?

ANATOL: (*Nervously.*) Yes?

ILONA: Where were you exactly?

ANATOL: I've already told you.

ILONA: No, not a word.

ANATOL: I told you yesterday evening.

ILONA: Then I've forgotten again.

ANATOL: I was in the neighborhood of Bohemia.

ILONA: What were you doing in Bohemia?

ANATOL: I wasn't *in* Bohemia. I was in the neighborhood *of*.

ILONA: Ah. You had an invitation to go hunting.

ANATOL: Yes. We hunted rabbits.

ILONA: For six whole weeks?

ANATOL: Yes. Without interruption.

ILONA: Why didn't you say good-bye to me?

ANATOL: I didn't want to depress you.

ILONA: You wanted to leave me, Anatol.

ANATOL: That's ridiculous.

ILONA: Well, you tried it once before.

ANATOL: Yes I did. It didn't work.

ILONA: What? What did you say?

ANATOL: I said, yes, I wanted to tear myself away from you. You know that.

ILONA: That's nonsense. You know you can't tear yourself away from me.

ANATOL: Haha!

ILONA: What did you say?

ANATOL: I said haha!

ILONA: Don't laugh, my precious. You came back to me that time, too.

ANATOL: Well, yes. That time.

ILONA: And this time, too. You love me.

ANATOL: Unfortunately.

ILONA: What?

ANATOL: Unfortunately.

ILONA: You're very brave from another room. You wouldn't dare say that to my face.

ANATOL: (*Opens the door and sticks his head out.*) Unfortunately.

ILONA: (*Goes to the door.*) What does this mean, Anatol?

ANATOL: (*Behind the door again.*) It means that this can't go on forever.

ILONA: What?

ANATOL: It can't go on like this, I said. It can't last forever.

ILONA: Now it's my turn. Haha!

ANATOL: What?

ILONA: (*Tears open the door.*) Haha!

ANATOL: Close it. (*She shuts the door.*)

ILONA: No, no, my little precious. You love me and you'll never be able to leave me.

ANATOL: You think so?

ILONA: I know so.

ANATOL: You know so?

ILONA: I feel it.

ANATOL: What you mean is, I will lie at your feet for all eternity.

ILONA: You'll never marry. I know that.

ANATOL: And you, my dear, are insane. I love you. That's fine. But we're not bound together for eternity.

ILONA: Do you really think I'll give you up?

ANATOL: You'll have to one day.

ILONA: Have to? When?

ANATOL: When I get married.

ILONA: (*Pounding on the door.*) And when will that be, my precious?

ANATOL: (*Scornfully.*) Soon, my precious.

ILONA: (*Growing more excited.*) But when?

ANATOL: Stop that pounding! In a year I'll be an old married man.

ILONA: You fool.

ANATOL: I could even be married in two months.

ILONA: I suppose you have someone waiting.

ANATOL: Yes. Right now. This very moment.

ILONA: In two months?

ANATOL: You seem to have doubts. (*ILONA laughs.*) Don't laugh. I'm getting married in a week. (*ILONA laughs more loudly.*) Don't laugh, Ilona. (*ILONA falls laughing onto the divan. ANATOL enters dressed in a morning suit.*) Don't laugh.

ILONA: (*Laughing.*) When are you getting married?

ANATOL: Today.

ILONA: (*Looking at him.*) When?

ANATOL: Today, my precious.

ILONA: (*Rises.*) Anatol. Stop making jokes.

ANATOL: I'm serious, my dear. I'm getting married today.

ILONA: You've lost your mind, haven't you?

ANATOL: Franz!

FRANZ: (*Entering.*) Sir?

ANATOL: The bouquet!

(*FRANZ goes off.*)

ILONA: (*Stands threateningly in front of ANATOL.*) Anatol — (*FRANZ brings the bouquet. ILONA turns around and rushes at the bouquet with a scream. ANATOL quickly takes it from FRANZ. FRANZ goes off, smiling.*) Ah!!! Then it's true!

ANATOL: As you can see. (*ILONA tries to tear the bouquet from his hands.*) What are you doing?

(*ANATOL has to escape from her. She runs around the room after him.*)

ILONA: You miserable, miserable — !

(*MAX enters carrying a bouquet of roses, but stands stunned at the door.*)

ANATOL: (*Has taken refuge on an armchair, and holds his bouquet out of reach.*) Max! Help me!

(*MAX rushes at ILONA, trying to hold her back. ILONA turns to him, wrenches the bouquet out of his hand, throws it to the floor and stomps on it.*)

MAX: Ilona! She's gone mad! My bouquet! What will I do!

(*ILONA falls sobbing to a chair.*)

ANATOL: (*Embarrassed, from the easy chair.*) She antagonized me. Yes. You're crying now. Aren't you, Ilona. Of course. Why did you laugh at me? She was mocking me, Max. She said I wouldn't dare get married. So now I'm getting married. Just to spite her. (*Starts to climb down from the chair.*)

ILONA: Hypocrite! Deceiver!

(*ANATOL climbs back up onto the chair.*)

MAX: (*Has picked up his bouquet.*) My bouquet!

ILONA: I meant to spoil *his!* But you don't deserve any better! You're guilty, too!

ANATOL: (*Still on the chair.*) Be reasonable!

ILONA: Yes, that's what you all say when you've driven a woman mad. But you just wait and see. We'll just have ourselves a nice little wedding. Just you wait. (*She rises.*) I'll see you later.

ANATOL: (*Jumping from the chair.*) Where?

ILONA: You'll find out.

ANATOL: Where?

MAX: Where?

ILONA: Just leave me alone.

MAX and ANATOL: (*Blocking her exit.*) Ilona! What do you want? Ilona! What do you want?

ILONA: Leave me! Let me go!

ANATOL: Be sensible! Calm down!

ILONA: So you won't let me leave! Is that right? (*She runs around the room, and in a rage tosses the tea service to the floor.*)

(*ANATOL and MAX stand there helplessly.*)

ANATOL: Now I ask you! Does a man have to get married when he's loved like that! (*ILONA, broken, sinks onto the divan. She cries. Pause.*) The calm after the storm.

MAX: We have to go. And here I am — without a bouquet.

FRANZ: (*Enters.*) The carriage is ready, sir. (*Goes off.*)

ANATOL: The carriage! The carriage! What am I to do! (*To ILONA, moving behind her, kissing her hair.*) Ilona!

MAX: (*On the other side.*) Ilona — (*ILONA continues to cry, her handkerchief at her face.*) You go on. I'll take care of this.

ANATOL: I really have to go. But how can I —

MAX: Go!

ANATOL: Can you get rid of her?

MAX: I'll whisper it to you during the ceremony.

ANATOL: I'm afraid!

MAX: Will you go!

ANATOL: Oh, God! (*He turns to go, then returns on tiptoe, softly presses a kiss on ILONA's hair and goes out quickly.*)

(*MAX sits opposite ILONA, who still cries into the handkerchief at her face. He looks at the clock.*)

MAX: Hm. Hm.

ILONA (*Looks around as if waking from a dream.*) Where is he?

MAX: (*Takes her hands in his.*) Ilona.

ILONA: (*Rising.*) Where is he?

MAX: (*Keeping hold of her hands.*) You'd never find him.

ILONA: But I will.

MAX: You're not being sensible, Ilona. You don't want a scandal.

ILONA: Let me go.

MAX: Ilona.

ILONA: Where does the wedding take place?

MAX: That's beside the point.

ILONA: I want to *go* there. I *have* to go.

MAX: You can't. What are you thinking of.

ILONA: Oh, this hypocrisy! This deception!

MAX: It's neither one nor the other. It's life.

ILONA: Don't talk to me — you — you with your fine phrases!

MAX: You're being childish, Ilona. Or you'd see that all this is useless.

ILONA: Useless?!

MAX: It's absurd.

ILONA: Absurd!?

MAX: You'd make a laughingstock of yourself is all.

ILONA: You're insulting me, too, now!

MAX: You'll recover.

ILONA: How little you know me.

MAX: It's not as if he were going to America.

ILONA: What are you talking about?

MAX: As though he were really lost to you.

ILONA: What do you mean?

MAX: The main point is that — it's not you who are being deceived.

ILONA: — ?

MAX: He can always come back to you. When he's through with her.

ILONA: Oh! If only! (*She looks up with an expression of wild joy.*)

MAX: How noble you are. (*Presses her hand.*)

ILONA: I want my revenge. That's why I'm so happy with what you've said.

MAX: You're one of those women who bite when they make love.

ILONA: Yes. I'm one of them.

MAX: Suddenly you're larger than life! A woman who would avenge her whole sex on us!

ILONA: Yes! That's what I'll do!

MAX: (*Rises.*) I still have time to drive you home. (*To himself.*) To avert another disaster. (*Extending her his arm.*) Say farewell to these rooms.

ILONA: No, my dear friend. Not farewell. I'll be back!

MAX: You think you're a demon — but all you are is a woman. (*As ILONA registers irritation.*) And that's quite enough. (*Opening the door for her.*) If you please, fair lady!

ILONA (*Turns around once again on leaving, with affected grandness.*) I'll be
back!
(*ILONA and MAX go off.*)

END OF PLAY

THE GREEN COCKATOO

A Grotesquery in One Act

Émile *Duke de Cadignan*
François *Vicomte de Nogeant*
Albin *Chevalier de la Tremouille*
Marquis de Lansac
Séverine *his wife*
Rollin *a poet*
Prospère *host of* The Green Cockatoo *and former theater director*

MEMBERS OF PROSPÈRE'S TROUPE

Henri
Balthasar
Guillaume
Scaevola
Jules
Étienne
Mauice
Georgette
Michette
Flipotte

Léocadie *an actress and Henri's wife*
Grasset *a philosopher*
Lebrêt *a tailor*
Grain *a tramp*
Police Sergeant
Aristocrats
Actors and Actresses
Citizens of Paris

TIME AND PLACE

Paris, the Wine Room of Prospère's The Green Cockatoo; the evening of July 14, 1789

The Green Cockatoo

Wine room of The Green Cockatoo. A moderate-sized room in a cellar. Seven steps lead down from upstage right, terminated at the top by a door. A second floor, scarcely visible, is situated upstage left. Almost the entire room is occupied by a number of simple wooden tables surrounded by chairs. The bar is at left center; behind it a number of barrels with taps. The room is lighted by oil-lamps hanging from the ceiling. PROSPÈRE, the host, is sitting behind the bar. Citizens LEBRÊT and GRASSET enter.

GRASSET: (*Still on the stairs.*) In here, Lebrêt. I know the place. My old friend Prospère always has a barrel of wine. Even when the rest of Paris is dry as a bone.

PROSPÈRE: Evening, Grasset. Back again, I see. Given up on philosophy, eh? Or dreaming of another hitch with my troupe?

GRASSET: Oh, God! Wine, Prospère! You're the host. I'm the guest.

PROSPÈRE: Wine? You must be joking. Where would I get wine? Last night every wine shop in Paris was plundered. Probably at your instigation.

GRASSET: Wine, Prospère! Wine! For the rabble that's coming. (*Listening.*) Hear anything, Lebrêt?

LEBRÊT: Sounds like distant thunder.

GRASSET: Well done, Citizens of Paris! (*To PROSPÈRE.*) You've always got a barrel of wine hidden somewhere, Prospère. Let's see it. My friend, Citizen Lebrêt, tailor from the Rue St. Honore'll foot the bill. Eh, Lebrêt?

LEBRÊT: You bet.

(*PROSPÈRE hesitates.*)

GRASSET: Show him your money, Lebrêt.

(*LEBRÊT pulls out his purse.*)

PROSPÈRE: Well. I'll see if I — (*He turns the tap on one of the barrels and fills two glasses.*) Where've you been, Grasset? Palais Royale?

GRASSET: Delivered a speech there, too, I might add. My turn now. Guess who spoke just ahead of me.

PROSPÈRE: No idea.

GRASSET: Camille Desmoulins. I actually had the nerve. Tell him, Lebrêt. Who got the most applause? The truth.

LEBRÊT: You. Hands down.

GRASSET: And how'd I do, eh?

LEBRÊT: Stupendous.

GRASSET: Hear that, Prospère? I stood on a table like a statue on a public monument. Damn right. And a thousand. Five thousand. Ten thousand pushed in around me. Same as for Desmoulins. And they cheered me, too.

LEBRÊT: Louder.

GRASSET: Right. Not *much* louder, maybe. But enough. They're headed for the Bastille. And all because of me. Before the night's out, the Bastille will be ours.

PROSPÈRE: If speeches can crumble walls — maybe —

GRASSET: Speeches! Hell! Guns! The soldiers are with us. They hate that filthy prison. Same as us. They had fathers holed up there. Brothers. But they wouldn't've lifted a gun. Not if we hadn't opened our mouths. Never belittle the power of the mind. (*To LEBRÊT.*) Where're the papers?

LEBRÊT: Here — (*Pulls a number of pamphlets from his pockets.*)

GRASSET: Pamphlets. The latest. Handin' 'em out at the Palais Royale right now. Here's one. By my friend Cerutti. *Memorandum for the French People.* And another. By Desmoulins. Talks better than he writes. *Freedom for France.*

PROSPÈRE: When's yours coming out? The one you're always running off at the mouth about.

GRASSET: Words! Hell! It's time to act! The man who sits at home's a coward. A real man's on the streets.

LEBRÊT: Bravo, Grasset! Bravo!

GRASSET: In Toulon they killed their mayor. And they plundered a dozen houses in Brignolles. Only we Parisians are stupid enough to still swallow that crud.

PROSPÈRE: Not anymore.

LEBRÊT: (*Who has been drinking steadily.*) Arise! Citizens! Arise!

PROSPÈRE: When the time's right, I'll be there.

GRASSET: When it's safe, you mean.

PROSPÈRE: You calling me a coward? What's important now is my business.

GRASSET: A Citizen of Paris has only *one* business. Freedom for his brothers.

PROSPÈRE: Unless he's got something else to —

LEBRÊT: Looks to me like he's pulling our leg.

PROSPÈRE: Wouldn't think of it. But you better get going. The performance starts soon. You're the *last* one I need around.

LEBRÊT: Performance? This a theater?

PROSPÈRE: What else? Grasset here acted with us a few weeks ago.

LEBRÊT: Grasset? You standing for that?

GRASSET: Slow down. It's true. I did. This is no ordinary tavern. It's a den of thieves. Come on.

PROSPÈRE: Gentlemen, the bill.

LEBRÊT: In a den of thieves like this?

PROSPÈR: (*To GRASSET.*) Tell him.

GRASSET: A strange place this. Take my word. People come here who *play* the criminal, while others *are* criminals without knowing it.

LEBRÊT: (*Befuddled.*) I don't —

GRASSET: I told you. Prospère was my manager once. He still acts with his troupe. But not like before. My former fellow actors sit around here acting the role of criminals. Understand? Telling about hair-raising experiences they never had. Crimes they never committed. And the audience eats it up. Think they're rubbing elbows with the scum of the Parisian gutters. Swindlers. Thieves. Murderers —

LEBRÊT: Who's your audience?

PROSPÈRE: Cream of the crop.

GRASSET: Nobles.

PROSPÈRE: Gentlemen of the Court.

LEBRÊT: They can go to hell!

GRASSET: It excites them. Satisfies them. Rouses their jaded senses. I got my start right here. My first speech. Only I pretended it was a joke. Here's where I learned to hate those bastards that sit with us in their fine clothes and perfume and stuffed bellies. (*To LEBRÊT.*) This is where I got my start. So now you've seen it. And from there I went on to greater things. (*In another tone of voice.*) Prospère? What if something goes wrong?

PROSPÈRE: Wrong? What?

GRASSET: With my career. My political career. Would you hire me again?

PROSPÈRE: You couldn't *buy* your way back.

GRASSET: (*Lightly.*) Why? Afraid your old friend Henri might be upstaged?

PROSPÈRE: Not really. But one day you might attack one of my paying customers and mean it.

GRASSET: (*Flattered.*) And you might be right.

PROSPÈRE: As for me, I can control myself.

GRASSET: I'd admire your self-control, Prospère, if I didn't know you were a coward.

PROSPÈRE: If I do what I do well, I'm happy. If I can tell those bastards to their faces what I think of them, I'm happy. And they sit here and think it's all a joke. Just another way of letting off steam. (*He draws a dagger and lets it glitter in the light.*)

LEBRÊT: Citizen Prospère, I don't understand.

GRASSET: Don't worry. The dagger's probably not even sharp.

PROSPÈRE: Don't count on it. One day the joke will be serious. And I'll be ready.

GRASSET: There's not long to wait, Prospère. It's a great time we live in. Come, Citizen Lebrêt. Let's join the crowd. Good-bye, Prospère. The next time we meet, I'll be a great man. Or dead.

LEBRÊT: (*Staggering.*) A great man — or dead — !

(*They go off.*)

PROSPÈRE: (*Sits on one side of the tables, opens a pamphlet and reads.*) "The beast is now in the noose; let us strangle it!" Not a bad writer, our little Desmoulins. "Never has greater booty awaited a conqueror! Forty thousand palaces and castles, two-fifths of all the wealth of France will be the reward of valor! They who think themselves the conqueror will be conquered; the nation will be purged!"

(*The POLICE SERGEANT enters. PROSPÈRE looks hard at him.*)

PROSPÈRE: Looks like the rabble's arriving early tonight.

SERGEANT: Don't joke with your district police sergeant, Prospère.

PROSPÈRE: What can I do for you?

SERGEANT: My orders are to attend your performance this evening.

PROSPÈRE: I am honored, sir.

SERGEANT: That's not the point. The authorities are curious to know what goes on here. These last few weeks —

PROSPÈRE: It's a place of amusement, Sergeant. Nothing more.

SERGEANT: May I finish? Rumor has it there have been orgies here the last few —

PROSPÈRE: Rumor has misinformed you, Sergeant. People come here to be amused. Nothing more.

SERGEANT: That may be how it begins, but how does it end? You were once an actor?

PROSPÈRE: A theatrical manager, Sergeant. Of an excellent company that last played in Saint-Denis.

SERGEANT: That's immaterial. You then came into a small inheritance?

PROSPÈRE: Scarcely worth the mention, Sergeant.

SERGEANT: And your company disbanded?

PROSPÈRE: Along with the money. Yes.

SERGEANT: (*Smiling.*) Excellent.

(*They both smile.*)

SERGEANT: (*Suddenly serious.*) At which time you opened this tavern.

PROSPÈRE: Which did miserable business.

SERGEANT: You then hit upon an ingenious idea.

PROSPÈRE: You flatter me, Sergeant.

SERGEANT: You reassembled your troupe, and now you give somewhat ambiguous performances, as I hear.

PROSPÈRE: Ambiguous, Sergeant? If so, I'd have no audience. Which, if I may say so, is the most distinguished in Paris. The Vicomte de Nogeant is my daily guest. The Marquis de Lansac comes frequently. And the Duke de Cadignan, Sergeant, is a most enthusiastic admirer of my leading actor, the famous Henri Baston.

SERGEANT: As well as an admirer of the art — or should I say arts — of your actresses?

PROSPÈRE: If you knew my actresses, Sergeant, you would blame no one for admiring them.

SERGEANT: Enough of this. It has been reported to the authorities that the entertainment offered by your — what shall I call them — ?

PROSPÈRE: May I suggest "artists," Sergeant?

SERGEANT: I'd suggest hirelings. That the entertainment offered by your "hirelings" goes far beyond what's allowed. We are given to believe that certain speeches are delivered here by your "make-believe" criminals, which — let me see how my report puts it — (*Reads, as earlier, from his notebook.*) which are not only immoral — which would scarcely trouble us — but which at the same time are said to be highly seditious. And considering the troubled times we live in, the authorities can scarcely remain indifferent.

PROSPÈRE: My dear Sergeant. My reply to these accusations is an invitation to attend the performance and discover for yourself. You'll find nothing seditious here. My audience isn't susceptible to sedition. This is a theater. We perform. Nothing more.

SERGEANT: I won't, of course, accept your invitation. Though I will stay by virtue of my official capacity.

PROSPÈRE: I promise you, Sergeant. You have an enjoyable evening in store. But I suggest you come dressed as a civilian. Your uniform might not sit too well with my actors. Not to mention my audience. Spontaneity is essential.

SERGEANT: Exactly. I shall return as a young gentleman of fashion.

PROSPÈRE: Ah. No problem. Or perhaps a tramp? That would be equally innocuous. Just not as a police official.

SERGEANT: Good-bye. (*He begins to leave.*)

PROSPÈRE: (*Bows.*) I trust the day's not far off when —

(*The SERGEANT meets GRAIN in the doorway. GRAIN is extremely ragged and dirty, and starts when he sees the SERGEANT. The SERGEANT looks him over sharply, then smiles and finally turns to PROSPÈRE.*)

SERGEANT: One of your "artists"? (*Goes off.*)

GRAIN: (*Speaks with a pathetic whine.*) Good evening —

PROSPÈRE (*Who has studied him for a long while.*) If you're a member of my company, congratulations. I don't recognize you.

GRAIN: Sorry?

PROSPÈRE: Stop this nonsense! Take off your wig. Who are you? (*He pulls at GRAIN's hair.*)

GRAIN: Ouch!

PROSPÈRE: Damn! It's real! Who are you? You certainly *look* real enough to be a tramp.

GRAIN: I am.

PROSPÈRE: What do you want?

GRAIN: Have I the honor of addressing Citizen Prospère? Host of The Green Cockatoo?

PROSPÈRE: You have.

GRAIN: The name's Grain. Though at times it's Carniche. Not to mention The Bellowing Brimstone. And yet, Citizen Prospère, I was imprisoned under the name of Grain. And that, after all, is the main point.

PROSPÈRE: Yes. I understand. You come here looking for a job and you're demonstrating your craft. All right. Continue.

GRAIN: Citizen Prospère. You mustn't take me for a swindler. I'm a man of honor. I told you I had been in prison. That was the truth.

(*PROSPÈRE looks at him suspiciously. GRAIN pulls a paper from his coat.*)

GRAIN: Here you are, Citizen Prospère. By this you will know that I was released yesterday at four o'clock.

PROSPÈRE: Two years in prison. Hm. I'll be damned. It's real.

GRAIN: Do you doubt me, Citizen Prospère?

PROSPÈRE: In jail for two years, eh? Why?

GRAIN: Normally they'd have hanged me. But I was fortunate enough to be an only child when I murdered my poor aunty.

PROSPÈRE: Murdered your aunt?

GRAIN: Yes. She was a bit closer to me than most aunts are to their nephews. Our family relationships were a bit peculiar. You might say I became embittered. Mind if I tell you about it?

PROSPÈRE: Do. Perhaps we can do business.

GRAIN: I had a sister. She, too, was a child when she ran away from home. And who with, do you think?

PROSPÈRE: I don't dare guess.

GRAIN: Her uncle. And then he deserted her. *With* child.

PROSPÈRE: Now listen here, Bellowing Brimstone, or whatever you're called! I have other matters to attend to than listen to a tramp tell me about his family murders. What's this got to do with me? Except that you're trying to worm something out of me.

GRAIN: Yes, Citizen Prospère. I've come to ask you for employment.

PROSPÈRE: (*Sneering.*) This, let me remind you, is a place of entertainment. Not a haven for murderers.

GRAIN: Oh, I've had my fill of that, thank you. I now want to become an honest man. I was directed to you.

PROSPÈRE: By whom?

GRAIN: By an amiable young man who was thrown into my cell a few days ago. Now he's there all alone. Name of Gaston. I believe you know him.

PROSPÈRE: Gaston?! So that's where he's been these last few nights. One of my crack pickpockets. He lays the audience in the aisles with his stories.

GRAIN: Except now they've caught up with him.

PROSPÈRE: Caught up with him? But he never *really* stole.

GRAIN: Ah, but he did. Must have been a novice. Terribly clumsy. Imagine! (*Confidentially.*) Stuck his hand directly into a woman's pocket! On the Boulevard des Capucines! And pulled out her purse! Now that's an amateur! Citizen Prospère. You're a person who inspires confidence. I will therefore confess to you that I have been guilty of similar behavior. But never without my dear father. Ah! When I was still a child, when all of us lived together, and my poor aunt was still alive — !

PROSPÈRE: Stop sniveling. It's in bad taste. You shouldn't have killed her.

GRAIN: Good advice. But too late. But as I was saying. Please take me into your service. I want to do the opposite of Gaston. He began by *acting* the criminal and then *became* one. I, on the other hand —

PROSPÈRE: All right, all right. I'll audition you. Can't hurt. When the time's right, you tell the story of your aunt. Just like it happened. Someone will start you off with a question.

GRAIN: Thank you, Citizen Prospère. And my salary?

PROSPÈRE: I don't pay auditioners. But you'll eat and drink well. Plus a few francs for a lodging, if you need it.

GRAIN: Thank you. You may introduce me to your other actors as a guest from the provinces.

PROSPÈRE: On the contrary. I'll tell them you're a murderer. More interesting that way.

GRAIN: Why discredit me all at once? I don't understand.

PROSPÈRE: A little stage experience and you will.

(*SCAEVOLA and JULES enter.*)

SCAEVOLA: Good evening, Master Manager.

PROSPÈRE: *Host*, gentlemen. *Host*. Call me manager and you crack the illusion wide open.

SCAEVOLA: Whatever — I doubt there will be a show tonight.

PROSPÈRE: What?!

SCAEVOLA: Who'll be in the mood? It's a madhouse out there. The mob at the Bastille is out for blood.

PROSPÈRE: So? It's been going on for months. They *still* come. People want to enjoy themselves.

SCAEVOLA: Right. The enjoyment of those about to be hanged.

PROSPÈRE: I hope I live to see it.

SCAEVOLA: Wine, Prospère! Get us in the mood. I don't feel inspired today.

PROSPÈRE: *Today?!* What about last night?!

SCAEVOLA: I beg — !

PROSPÈRE: That burglary story of yours was ridiculous.

SCAEVOLA: Ridiculous?

PROSPÈRE: Unconvincing. Totally. Why do you yell all the time?

SCAEVOLA: I do not yell.

PROSPÈRE: You *always* yell! I need to rehearse you. You don't have an idea in your head. Why can't you be like Henri?

SCAEVOLA: Henri! Henri! That's all I hear! Henri is a *ham!* My burglary story was a *masterpiece.* Henri couldn't have carried it off to save his life. But all right. All right. If you're not satisfied, my dear Prospère, I can go elsewhere. There are *other* theaters. All you have here is a bunch of bums. (*Noticing GRAIN.*) And who's this? Not one of us, for sure. Hired a new man? What's the makeup he's using?

PROSPÈRE: Calm down. He's not an actor. He's a murderer.

SCAEVOLA: I see — (*Goes to GRAIN.*) Delighted to make your acquaintance. Name's Scaevola.

GRAIN: Pleased. Mine's Grain.

(*JULES has paced back and forth the whole time, pausing occasionally, like an inwardly tormented man.*)

PROSPÈRE: What's your problem, Jules?

JULES: Rehearsing.

PROSPÈRE: Rehearsing what?

JULES: Pangs of conscience. Tonight I'm a conscience-stricken sinner. How's my frown? Tormented enough? (*He rages back and forth.*) Do I —

SCAEVOLA: (*Bellows.*) Wine! Some wine here!

PROSPÈRE: Stop acting. Wait for the audience.

(*HENRI and LÉOCADIE enter.*)

HENRI: Good evening. (*He greets those seated in the rear with a light gesture of his hand.*) Good evening, gentlemen.

PROSPÈRE: Good evening, Henri. What's this! You and Léocadie together?

GRAIN: (*Has looked attentively at LÉOCADIE; to SCAEVOLA.*) I know that woman. (*Continues speaking softly to SCAEVOLA.*)

LÉOCADIE: Yes, dear Prospère. It's Léocadie.

PROSPÈRE: I haven't seen you for a year. Permit me — (*He is about to kiss her.*)

HENRI: That will do, Prospère. (*He frequently glances at her with pride and passion, but also with a certain anxiety.*)

PROSPÈRE: But, Henri. We're old friends. And your former manager, Léocadie.

LÉOCADIE: Ah, those were lovely days, Prospère.

PROSPÈRE: Why the sighs? If any of us made a career, it's you. But it's always easier for a lovely young woman than for —

HENRI: (*Raging.*) I said that will do.

PROSPÈRE: Why are you always shouting at me? — But what are you two doing together?

HENRI: Shut up. She's my wife. Since yesterday.

PROSPÈRE: Your wife? (*To LÉOCADIE.*) He's joking.

LÉOCADIE: It's true. He married me.

PROSPÈRE: Congratulations. Hey, Jules! Scaevola! Henri's got himself married.

SCAEVOLA: (*Comes forward.*) Congratulations, Henri! (*He winks at LÉOCADIE.*)

(*JULES shakes hands with both of them.*)

GRAIN: (*To PROSPÈRE.*) Strange. I saw that woman right after I got out of prison.

PROSPÈRE: How's that?

GRAIN: She was the first beautiful woman I'd seen in two years. I was — moved. But she was with another man, not with — (*Continues talking with PROSPÈRE.*)

HENRI: (*In a high-pitched, inspired voice, but without being declamatory.*) Léocadie! My beloved! My wife! All that once was is no more. A moment like this wipes away all the past.

(*SCAEVOLA and JULES have gone toward the rear. PROSPÈRE comes forward again.*)

PROSPÈRE: What moment, Henri?

HENRI: We're joined now by a holy sacrament. Which is more by far than any human vow. With the eye of God watching over us, we may now forget our former lives. Ah, Léocadie! Our life is sacred now. However wild our kisses, they will always be sacred. Léocadie! My beloved! My wife! (*He looks passionately at her.*) Hasn't she changed, Prospère? I mean, since the last time you saw her. Her eyes are so bright. And her clear forehead. All that was is no more. Isn't that true, Léocadie?

LÉOCADIE: Of course, Henri.

HENRI: And all's well. We leave Paris tomorrow. Tonight Léocadie will appear for the last time at the Théâtre Porte St. Martin. And this evening is my final performance here.

PROSPÈRE: (*Startled.*) Henri! You're insane! You're deserting me? And the director of the Porte St. Martin would never think of letting Léocadie go. He'd have no customers without her. She draws the young gentlemen like flies.

HENRI: Shut up! Léocadie goes with *me*. She'll never leave me. Tell me that you'll never leave me, Léocadie. (*Brutally.*) Tell me!

LÉOCADIE: I'll never leave you, Henri.

HENRI: Because if you ever do, I'll — (*Pause.*) I'm sick and tired of this life. I want peace. Peace and quiet.

PROSPÈRE: But what will you do, Henri? It's ridiculous. Listen. I have a suggestion. Take Léocadie from the Porte St. Martin. But bring her here. I'll hire her. I need a talented actress.

HENRI: I've decided, Prospère. We're leaving the city. We'll live in the country.

PROSPÈRE: The country? But where in the country?

HENRI: With my poor father. Who lives all alone in his little village. Haven't seen him in seven years. And he never hoped to see his son again. He'll be glad to see us.

PROSPÈRE: But what will you *do* in the country? People starve out there. It's a thousand times worse than in Paris. What will you *do* there? You're not a man to till the fields.

HENRI: You'll see. I'll prove it to you.

PROSPÈRE: Soon there'll be no more grain growing in France. You're damning yourself to a life of misery.

HENRI: To a life of happiness, Prospère! Right, Léocadie? We often dreamt of it. I long for the peace of the open countryside. In my dreams I see the two of us. Walking through the fields in the evening. Infinite peace surrounding us. Beneath a wonderful, comforting sky. We escape the dreadful, dangerous city, and a great peace descends on us. Right, Léocadie? We often dreamt about it.

LÉOCADIE: Yes. We often dreamt about it.

PROSPÈRE: Think it over, Henri. I'll even raise your salary. And pay Léocadie the same as you.

LÉOCADIE: Did you hear that, Henri?

PROSPÈRE: There's no one to take your place. No one has ideas like yours. Clever ideas. And you're popular. No one can match you. Don't go.

HENRI: You're right. You won't be able to replace me.

PROSPÈRE: Please stay, Henri. (*He looks at LÉOCADIE, who intimates that she will arrange it all.*)

HENRI: And my parting won't be easy. For my audience or for me. For my final performance, I've prepared something to make them tremble. They will have a presentiment of the end of their world. Because the end of their world is near. But I won't be here to experience it. We'll be in the country, Léocadie, many days after it's happened. But tonight! They'll tremble! I promise you. And even you, Prospère, will see that Henri has never performed so well before.

PROSPÈRE: What? Tell me. What do you know about this, Léocadie?

LÉOCADIE: Nothing.

HENRI: No one knows the artist that lives in me.

PROSPÈRE: We know, Henri. We know. Don't bury such talent in the country. You wrong yourself. You wrong the cause of art.

HENRI: To hell with art! I want peace. Can't you understand, Prospère? You've never loved —

PROSPÈRE: Oh?

HENRI: Not like me. I want to be alone with her. That's all there is for me. The only way, Léocadie. And we can forget everything. We'll be happier than humans ever were. We'll have children. You'll be a good mother, Léocadie. And a wonderful wife. And everything, everything will be wiped away forever.

(*Long pause.*)

LÉOCADIE: It's late, Henri. I have to get to the theater. Good-bye, Prospère.

I'm glad to have finally seen your famous establishment where Henri has had such success.

PROSPÈRE: Why didn't you come sooner?

LÉOCADIE: Henri wouldn't let me. All the young nobles I'd have to sit with. You know —

HENRI: (*Has gone to the rear.*) Give me a drink, Scaevola. (*He drinks.*)

PROSPÈRE: (*To LÉOCADIE so that HENRI can't hear.*) What a fool Henri is. You've done worse things than that.

LÉOCADIE: That's enough of that, Prospère.

PROSPÈRE: You're a silly child. Let me warn you. He'll murder you one day.

LÉOCADIE: Really!

PROSPÈRE: You were seen with one of your "gentlemen" only yesterday.

LÉOCADIE: Idiot! Do you know who that was?

HENRI (*Suddenly turns around.*) What's going on over there! No joking around with her! No whispering! She has no more secrets from me. She's my wife now.

PROSPÈRE: What did he give you for a wedding present?

LÉOCADIE: Oh, he never thinks of such things.

HENRI: You'll have your present this evening.

LÉOCADIE: What?

HENRI: (*Completely serious.*) When you finish your scene at the Porte St. Martin, you'll come here and watch me act. (*Laughter.*) The best wedding present a woman ever had. Come, Léocadie. Good-bye, Prospère. I'll be back shortly.

(*HENRI and LÉOCADIE go off. FRANÇOIS, VICOMTE DE NOGEANT and ALBIN, CHEVALIER DE LA TREMOUILLE enter together.*)

SCAEVOLA: What a braggart.

PROSPÈRE: Good evening, pigs!

(*ALBIN recoils in fright.*)

FRANÇOIS: (*Paying no attention.*) Wasn't that Léocadie? From the Porte St. Martin? And with Henri?

PROSPÈRE: Any objections? If she set her mind to it, she could get a rise even out of *you*.

FRANÇOIS: (*Laughing.*) Nothing's impossible. Looks like we're a bit early this evening.

PROSPÈRE: In the meantime amuse yourself with your mignon.

(*ALBIN starts angrily.*)

FRANÇOIS: Control yourself. I warned you what to expect. Wine here!

PROSPÈRE: One of these days you'll be drinking water from the Seine.

FRANÇOIS: Very likely. But tonight it will be wine. Your best.

(*PROSPÈRE goes to the bar.*)

ALBIN: Dreadful man.

FRANÇOIS: Not at all. It's a joke. At least here it is. But there are places around where they mean it.

ALBIN: It's against the law.

FRANÇOIS: (*Laughs.*) How fresh from the provinces you are, my boy.

ALBIN: Things are the same down our way. Insolent peasants we don't know how to handle.

FRANÇOIS: Well? They're hungry, poor devils. That's the point.

ALBIN: Is that *my* fault? Or my great-uncle's?

FRANÇOIS: Great-uncle?

ALBIN: The peasants held an open meeting in our village recently. They called my great-uncle, the Comte de la Tremouille, a usurer in grain.

FRANÇOIS: Is that all?

ALBIN: *Really!*

FRANÇOIS: Tomorrow when we go to the Palais Royale, you'll hear monstrous speeches. But what of it? It lets off steam. They're good souls at heart. They need a vent to their anger.

ALBIN: (*Indicating SCAEVOLA and the others.*) Why are they staring at us? (*Reaches for his dagger.*)

FRANÇOIS: (*Pulls ALBIN's hand away.*) Don't make a fool of yourself. (*To the ACTORS.*) You needn't begin yet. Wait till you have a larger audience. (*To ALBIN.*) Actors are the most respectable people in the world. And I know you've sat around with far more disreputable creatures.

ALBIN: But they were better dressed.

(*PROSPÈRE brings the wine. MICHETTE and FLIPOTTE enter.*)

FRANÇOIS: Evening, girls. Sit with us.

MICHETTE: We're here! Come on, Flipotte. She's still so shy.

FLIPOTTE: Good evening, gentlemen.

ALBIN: Good evening, ladies.

MICHETTE: Such a nice boy. (*Sits on ALBIN's lap.*)

ALBIN: François? Are these respectable women?

MICHETTE: What!

FRANÇOIS: Respectable? How stupid, Albin!

PROSPÈRE: What may I bring the duchesses?

MICHETTE: Sweet wine.

FRANÇOIS: (*Indicating FLIPOTTE.*) A friends of yours?

MICHETTE: We live together. Even share the same bed.

FLIPOTTE: (*Blushing.*) Will that embarrass you when you visit her? (*She sits on FRANÇOIS's lap.*)

ALBIN: You said she was shy.

SCAEVOLA: (*Rises, comes to the table, and speaks darkly.*) So you're the one. (*To ALBIN.*) Seducer! She's mine!

(*PROSPÈRE watches them.*)

FRANÇOIS: (*To ALBIN.*) It's a joke. It's a joke.

ALBIN: You mean she *isn't* his?

MICHETTE: Get away! I sit where I want.

(*SCAEVOLA stands there with clenched fists.*)

PROSPÈRE (*Behind him.*) Well? Well?

SCAEVOLA: Ha! Ha!

PROSPÈRE: (*Takes him by the collar.*) Ha! Ha! (*Aside to SCAEVOLA.*) If that's the best you can do, you have less talent than I thought. You yell too much!

MICHETTE: (*To FRANÇOIS.*) He was better the other evening.

SCAEVOLA: (*To PROSPÈRE.*) I have to get in the mood, damn it! I'll wait till there are more people. I need an audience, Prospère!

DUKE DE CADIGNAN: (*Enters.*) In full swing, I see.

(*MICHETTE and FLIPOTTE run to him.*)

MICHETTE: My sweet little Dukey!

FRANÇOIS: Good evening, Émile. (*Introducing.*) This is my young friend Albin, Chevalier de la Tremouille. The Duke de Cadignan.

DUKE: Pleased to know you. (*To MICHETTE and FLIPOTTE, still clinging to him.*) Girls, girls! Not all at once! (*To ALBIN.*) Giving our bizarre little tavern a look-see, eh?

ALBIN: I'm a bit confused.

FRANÇOIS: The Chevalier arrived in Paris a few days ago.

DUKE: (*Laughing.*) You chose your time well.

ALBIN: Why?

MICHETTE: Smell the new perfume. He's the best-smelling man in Paris.

DUKE: And she should know.

FLIPOTTE: Can I play with your sword? (*She pulls the sword from its scabbard and lets it catch the light.*)

GRAIN: (*To PROSPÈRE.*) That was the man! (*He continues whispering to* PROSPÈRE, *who appears astonished.*)

DUKE: Where's Henri? (*To ALBIN.*) When you see Henri, you'll know why you've come.

PROSPÈRE: Back again, eh? You won't have that pleasure much longer.

DUKE: Why? I like it here.

PROSPÈRE: I know. But you'll probably be one of the first.

ALBIN: I don't understand.

PROSPÈRE: Oh, I think you do. The first ones to fall are the lucky ones. (*He goes to the back.*)

DUKE: (*After a moment of thought.*) If I were king, he'd be my court fool. Of course, I'd have a number of them. But he'd be one.

ALBIN: What did he mean? The lucky ones?

DUKE: He means, Chevalier —

ALBIN: Please. Not Chevalier. Everyone calls me Albin.

DUKE: Gladly. But you must call me Émile. Agreed?

ALBIN: With your permission — Émile.

DUKE: These people have a sinister wit about them.

FRANÇOIS: Sinister? I find it reassuring. As long as the mob is in the mood for joking, nothing very serious can happen.

DUKE: But at times the jokes are a bit strange. I heard something today that set me thinking.

FRANÇOIS: What?

FLIPOTTE and MICHETTE: Yes. Tell us.

DUKE: Do you know Lelange?

FRANÇOIS: Of course. The village. The Marquis de Montfarrat has one of his finest hunting preserves there.

DUKE: Exactly. My brother's visiting him at his castle. He's just written me about the whole affair. They have a most unpopular mayor in Lelange —

FRANÇOIS: Name me one who isn't.

DUKE: And the women of the village marched to the mayor's residence — with a coffin.

FLIPOTTE: What? A coffin? Never catch *me* carrying a coffin!

FRANÇOIS: Quiet, my dears. No one's asking you to — (*To the DUKE.*) Well?

DUKE: Well. A couple of women went into the mayor's house and told him that he would die soon. But that they'd do him the honor of burying him.

FRANÇOIS: And *did* they?

DUKE: My brother didn't say.

FRANÇOIS: You see! Braggarts! Show-offs! Clowns! That's all they are! Today in Paris they're yelling outside the Bastille for a change. Just as they've done a hundred times before.

DUKE: If I were king, I'd have put an end to this long ago.

ALBIN: Is the King so gentle and kind?

DUKE: You haven't been presented to his Majesty?

FRANÇOIS: It's the Chevalier's first time in Paris.

DUKE: Yes, you *are* incredibly young, aren't you. How old *are* you?

ALBIN: I only look young. But I'm really seventeen.

DUKE: Seventeen! How much you have to look forward to! I'm twenty-four. And already I regret how much of my youth I've wasted.

FRANÇOIS: (*Laughs.*) Excellent! Excellent! You, my dear Duke, consider every day lost on which you fail to win a woman or kill a man.

DUKE: The trouble is one almost never wins the right woman, and always kills the wrong man. And so, youth is wasted after all. As Rollin says.

FRANÇOIS: What does Rollin say?

DUKE: I was thinking of his new play. At the Comédie. There's a wonderful simile. Do you recall it?

FRANÇOIS: I don't remember verses.

DUKE: Unfortunately I don't either. I remember the sense of the words. He says that — youth that is not enjoyed is like a feathered ball left lying in the sand and never tossed into the air.

ALBIN: (*Precociously.*) Very true!

DUKE: Isn't it? The feathers gradually lose their colors and fall out. The best thing is to toss it into the bush where no one will ever find it.

ALBIN: What do you make of that, Émile?

DUKE: It's more a matter of feeling. If I'd recalled the verses exactly, you'd have less trouble —

ALBIN: You should write verses yourself, Émile.

DUKE: Why do you say that?

ALBIN: The minute you arrived the place burst into flame.

DUKE: Really? Burst into flame?

FRANÇOIS: Sit with us.

> (*Meanwhile two NOBLEMAN enter and sit at a rather distant table. PROSPÈRE seems to be insulting them.*)

DUKE: I can't stay just now. But I'll be back later.

MICHETTE: Stay with me!

FLIPOTTE: Take me with you!

> (*They try to hang onto him.*)

PROSPÈRE: (*Comes toward them.*) Leave him alone! You two won't be in his league for years. He handles only *seasoned* prostitutes.

DUKE: I'll be back. I promise. I wouldn't miss Henri.

FRANÇOIS: Henri was leaving with Léocadie when we arrived.

DUKE: He married her. Did you know?

FRANÇOIS: Really? What will the others say to that?

ALBIN: What others?

FRANÇOIS: Well, she's a very popular girl.

DUKE: And they're leaving Paris together. Or so I hear.

PROSPÈRE: Oh? They told you that? (*Looks at the DUKE.*)

DUKE: (*Looks at PROSPÈRE; then.*) It's ridiculous! Léocadie was created to be one of the world's grand courtesans.

FRANÇOIS: That's no secret.

DUKE: Imagine! Denying such a person her profession! It's monstrous! (*FRANÇOIS laughs.*) I wasn't making a joke. A courtesan is born. The same as a conqueror. Or poet.

FRANÇOIS: You're a royal paradox.

DUKE: I'm sorry for her. And for Henri. He should stay here. Well. Not *here* precisely. But at the Comédie, for example. Although even there they wouldn't understand him. Not as I do. Of course, I could be wrong. But I have feelings where artists are concerned. If I weren't the Duke de Cadignan, I'd be an actor. An actor like —

ALBIN: Alexander the Great.

DUKE: (*Smiling.*) Yes. Like Alexander the Great. (*To FLIPOTTE.*) May I have my sword? (*He replaces the sword in its scabbard; speaking slowly.*) There's no better way to mock the world. A person who can pretend to be anyone he wants, whenever he likes, is luckier than all of us put together. (*ALBIN regards him with surprise.*) Don't let what I say trouble you. It's true only at the moment of utterance. Good-bye.

MICHETTE: Give us a kiss before you go.

FLIPOTTE: Me, too.

(*They hang on him. The DUKE kisses them both and goes out. At the same time the following takes place.*)

ALBIN: What a remarkable man.

FRANÇOIS: True. And the fact that such creatures exist is sufficient reason not to marry.

ALBIN: What sort of women are they?

FRANÇOIS: Actresses. Members of Prospère's troupe. He owns the tavern these days. And yet, they seldom do more than they're doing now.

(*GUILLAUME rushes in breathless. He staggers to the table where the ACTORS are seated, his hand on his heart and breathing painfully.*)

GUILLAUME: I'm safe! I'm safe!

SCAEVOLA: What's all this about? What happened?

ALBIN: What's the matter with that man?

FRANÇOIS: Pay attention. They're acting.

ALBIN: Oh.

(*MICHETTE and FLIPOTTE rush to GUILLAUME.*)

MICHETTE and FLIPOTTE. What? What happened?

SCAEVOLA: Sit here. Have a drink.

GUILLAUME: Wine, Prospère! More wine! God! I ran! My tongue sticking to my mouth! They were right behind me!

JULES: (*Starts.*) We can't be too careful. They're always on our heels.

PROSPÈRE: What happened? (*Aside to the ACTORS.*) Move! Move! Liven it up!

GUILLAUME: Where — where are the women? Ah! (*Throws his arms around FLIPOTTE.*) I needed that! (*To ALBIN, who is seated.*) Damn, boy! I never thought I'd see you alive again! (*As if listening.*) Shh! They're coming! They're coming! (*Running to the door.*) No. No. It's nothing —

ALBIN: Listen! There really is a noise out there. Like hordes of people running past. Is that part of the performance?

SCAEVOLA: (*To JULES.*) He pulls the same trick every time. Stupid.

PROSPÈRE: Why were they chasing you? Tell us.

GUILLAUME: Nothing important. But if they catch me, it's my head. I set fire to a house!

(*During this, several other young NOBLEMEN enter and take their places at the tables.*)

PROSPÈRE: (*Aside.*) Go on! Go on!

GUILLAUME: Go on? What more do you want?

FRANÇOIS: Why did you do it?

GUILLAUME: The President of the Court of Justice lived there. We wanted him to be the first. We'll teach these gentlemen and lords of Paris that it's dangerous to have tenants who can send us poor devils to prison.

GRAIN: That's good! Good!

GUILLAUME: (*Looks at GRAIN in surprise, then continues.*) We'll burn their houses! A few more men like me and there won't be any more judges in Paris!

GRAIN: Death to the judges!

JULES: Yes. But there's one judge we *can't* destroy.

GUILLAUME: I'd like to know who!

JULES: The judge inside *us*.

PROSPÈRE: (*Aside.*) This is insipid. Stop it. Scaevola. Start yelling. It's time.

SCAEVOLA: Wine, Prospère! Let's drink to the death of all the judges in Paris!

(*During these last words, the MARQUIS DE LANSAC, with his wife SÉVERINE, and ROLLIN the poet enter.*)

SCAEVOLA: Death to all those in power! Death!

MARQUIS: You see, Séverine? This is the reception we get.

ROLLIN: I warned you, my dear Marquise.

SÉVERINE: But why should you?

FRANÇOIS: (*Rises.*) What's this? The Marquise? Permit me to kiss your hand. Good evening. How are you, Rollin? You're taking a risk coming here, my dear Marquise.

ROLLIN: But I've heard so much about it. Besides, this appears to be quite a day for adventure. Don't you agree, Rollin?

MARQUIS: Yes. Just imagine, my dear Vicomte. Where do you suppose we've just come from? The Bastille.

FRANÇOIS: Is there still such a noise?

SÉVERINE: It's terrible. It looks as though they're about to swarm the prison.

ROLLIN: (*Declaims.*)

"Just as the flood, which breaks upon the floor
In grim anger that his only child,
The earth, should dare resist —"

SÉVERINE: No, Rollin. We stopped our carriage quite close to them. What a marvelous sight. There's something so magnificent about large crowds.

FRANÇOIS: If only they didn't smell so vile.

MARQUIS: And then my wife insisted that we bring her here.

SÉVERINE: I see nothing so remarkable about this place.

PROSPÈRE: (*To the* MARQUIS.) Ah, so you've come, too, you withered old snake. Did you bring your wife? Afraid to leave her at home? Alone?

MARQUIS: (*With a forced laugh.*) What an original!

PROSPÈRE: See to it nobody runs off with her while she's here. Respectable women would give anything to know what a *real* man is like.

ROLLIN: I simply can't endure this, Séverine!

MARQUIS: I warned you, my dear. But we can leave whenever you like.

SÉVERINE: I don't know what you mean. I think it's charming. Shall we sit?

FRANÇOIS: Marquis, may I introduce the Chevalier de la Tremouille. He's also here for the first time. The Marquis de Lansac. Rollin, our celebrated poet.

ALBIN: Pleased to meet you. (*They all bow and take their places. To FRANÇOIS.*) Is she one of his actresses or — I'm terribly confused.

FRANÇOIS: Don't be stupid. She the real wife of the Marquis. And a woman of great position.

ROLLIN: (*To SÉVERINE.*) Tell me you love me.

SÉVERINE: Yes, of course. But don't ask so often.

MARQUIS: Have we missed any good scenes?

FRANÇOIS: Nothing of importance. That one there is playing an incendiary.

SÉVERINE: Chevalier, are you the cousin of Lydia de la Tremouille, who was married today?

ALBIN: I am, Marquise. That's why I'm in Paris.

SÉVERINE: I recall seeing you in church.

ALBIN: (*Embarrassed.*) I'm flattered, Marquise.

SÉVERINE: (*To ROLLIN.*) Such a nice boy.

ROLLIN: Ah, Séverine! You've never seen a man who hasn't pleased you.

SÉVERINE: Ah, there you're wrong. And I married him on the spot.

ROLLIN: Yet I'm afraid there are frequent times when even he attracts you.

PROSPÈRE: (*Bringing wine.*) Your wine, gentlemen. If only it were poison. But I'm not permitted to sell that to you scum — yet.

FRANÇOIS: The time will come, Prospère.

SÉVERINE: (*To ROLLIN.*) What about those two pretty girls? Why don't they come closer? Now that I'm here at last, I don't want to miss a thing. So far it's all just too proper.

MARQUIS: Patience, Séverine.

SÉVERINE: Undoubtedly the streets are the most amusing place to be these days. You'll never guess what happened to us yesterday as we drove down the Promenade de Longchamps.

MARQUIS: My dear Marquise, I see no reason to —

SÉVERINE: One of the mob jumped onto the step of our carriage and screamed: "Next year *you'll* be in the coachman's seat and *we'll* be in the carriage!"

FRANÇOIS: That's a bit strong.

MARQUIS: The less said about these things the better. Paris is in a fever at the moment. But it will soon pass.

GUILLAUME: (*Suddenly.*) I see flames! Flames! Wherever I look! Tall red flames!

PROSPÈRE: (*Aside to him.*) You're supposed to be a criminal. Not a lunatic.

SÉVERINE: He sees flames?

FRANÇOIS: The best is yet to come, Marquise.

ALBIN: (*To ROLLIN.*) I'm so confused by all this.

MICHETTE: (*Comes over to the MARQUIS.*) I haven't said good evening to you yet, my sweet old little swine.

MARQUIS: (*Embarrassed.*) She *is* joking, my dear Séverine.

SÉVERINE: Are you so certain, my dear? (*To MICHETTE.*) Tell me, my charming girl. How many lovers have you had?

MARQUIS: (*To FRANÇOIS.*) It amazes me how the Marquise adapts herself to any situation.

ROLLIN: Remarkable.

MICHETTE: Do you count yours?

SÉVERINE: When I was your age, my dear — most certainly.

ALBIN: (*To* ROLLIN.) Excuse me, Monsieur Rollin. Is the Marquise acting, or is she really — ? I simply don't know what's happening.

ROLLIN: Reality and acting, my dear Chevalier — can one always detect the difference?

ALBIN: Of course.

ROLLIN: Not I. What makes all this so remarkable is that apparent differences are dissolved into illusion, and illusion into reality. Look at the Marquise over there. Chattering with those creatures as though she were one of them. And yet she's —

ALBIN: Something quite different.

ROLLIN: I thank you, Chevalier.

PROSPÈRE: (*To* GRAIN.) What about your story?

GRAIN: What story?

PROSPÈRE: About your aunt. That put you in prison for two years.

GRAIN: I told you. I strangled her.

FRANÇOIS: Not much of an actor, I'm afraid. Probably a dilettante. I've never seen him here before.

GEORGETTE: (*Enters quickly, dressed like a prostitute of the lowest order.*) Good evening. Has Balthasar come yet?

SCAEVOLA: Georgette. Sit here. Balthasar'll be on time. Don't worry.

GEORGETTE: If he's not here in ten minutes, I'll never see him again.

FRANÇOIS: Pay attention, Marquise. In reality she's the wife of this Balthasar. She plays the role of a prostitute. Balthasar is her bully. In reality, she's the most faithful wife in Paris.

(*BALTHASAR enters.*)

GEORGETTE: Oh, Balthasar! (*Runs to him and throws her arms around him.*) You're here!

BALTHASAR: I settled it myself. (*Everyone is silent.*) It wasn't worth the trouble. I felt sorry for him. When you pick your customers, be more careful, Georgette. I'm tired of killing promising young gentlemen for only a few francs.

FRANÇOIS: Excellent!

ALBIN: What?

FRANÇOIS: He has a remarkable sense of phrase.

(*The POLICE SERGEANT enters in disguise and sits at a table.*)

PROSPÈRE: You've come at just the right moment, Sergeant. He's one of my best actors.

BALTHASAR: I've had enough of this world. I'm no coward. But this is a hell of a way to earn a living.

SCAEVOLA: I believe it.

GEORGETTE: What's wrong with you today?

BALTHASAR: Look, Georgette — you're getting a little too cozy with these young men.

GEORGETTE: Oh! What a child he is. Be reasonable, Balthasar. I *have* to be "cozy" to win their confidence.

ROLLIN: What she says is true.

BALTHASAR: If I ever hear of you having any feeling for these men when they —

GEORGETTE: Listen to him. The stupid ape's dying of jealousy.

BALTHASAR: I heard your sighs today when you were with him. When there was no reason for sighing! None!

GEORGETTE: You expect me to turn it off? Just like *that?*

BALTHASAR: Watch out, Georgette! (*Wildly.*) If you ever deceive me —

GEORGETTE: I wouldn't! I wouldn't!

ALBIN: I don't understand this —

SÉVERINE: There's really no other way to look at it.

ROLLIN: Do you think so?

MARQUIS: (*To SÉVERINE.*) We can leave anytime you like, Séverine.

SÉVERINE: But why? I'm beginning to feel remarkably comfortable here.

BALTHASAR: Oh, Balthasar! I adore you!

(*They embrace.*)

FLIPOTTE: Bravo! Bravo!

BALTHASAR: Who's that idiot?

SERGEANT: I'm afraid this won't —

(*MAURICE and ÉTIENNE enter. They are dressed as young gentlemen, yet it is obvious that their clothes are shabby theatrical costumes.*)

THE ACTORS. Who are they?

SCAEVOLA: Hey! It's Maurice and Étienne!

GEORGETTE: It is! It's them!

BALTHASAR: Georgette!

SÉVERINE: What beautiful young men!

ROLLIN: It's embarrassing, Séverine, to watch how every attractive face excites you.

SÉVERINE: Why else do you think I came?

ROLLIN: At least tell me that you love me.

SÉVERIN: (*With a glance at him.*) You have a very short memory.

ÉTIENNE: Where do you think we've been today?

FRANÇOIS: Listen to this, Marquis. They're a pair of very clever boys.

MAURICE: To a wedding!

ÉTIENNE: You have to dress up for affairs of that sort. Or you'll have the secret police after you.

SCAEVOLA: Make a good haul?

PROSPÈRE: Let's see.

MAURICE: (*Pulling some watches from his jerkin.*) What do I hear? A bid! A bid!

PROSPÈRE: For this one — one louis.

MAURICE: I should hope!

SCAEVOLA: Sure ain't worth no *more!*

MICHETTE: Ooo! Here's a lady's watch! Give it to me, Maurice.

MAURICE: What's your price?

MICHETTE: One look at me? That enough?

FLIPOTTE: No. Give it to *me!* Look at *me!*

MAURICE: Girls, girls! I have that pleasure anytime I want it. And without risking my neck.

MICHETTE: Conceited!

SÉVERINE: I can't believe these actors!

ROLLIN: Of course you can't. There's always a thread of reality that comes through. It's their charm.

SCAEVOLA: Who's wedding was it?

MAURICE: Mlle. de la Tremouille's. She married the Count de Banville.

ALBIN: Did you hear that? They *are* real thieves!

FRANÇOIS: Don't get excited. I know them. I've seen them perform here a dozen times at least. They specialize in playing pickpockets.

(*MAURICE pulls several purses from his jerkin.*)

SCAEVOLA: Ah! So today you can afford to be generous.

ÉTIENNE: It was a very elegant wedding. All the nobility of France was there. And the King even sent a representative.

ALBIN: (*Excited.*) It's true! All of it!

MAURICE: (*Lets the money roll onto the table.*) This, my friends, is for you. To show our loyalty to each other.

FRANÇOIS: Stage props, my dear Albin. (*He rises and takes a few of the coins.*) No reason we shouldn't have some, too.

PROSPÈRE: Of course. Help yourself. It'll be the first honest sou you ever made.

MAURICE: (*Holds up a jeweled garter.*) Who shall I give this to?

(*GEORGETTE, MICHETTE, and FLIPOTTE snatch at it.*)

MAURICE: Patience, my dears! Patience! We must discuss this first. I give it to the one who invents a new way of making love.

SÉVERINE: May I enter the competition?

ROLLIN: You're driving me mad, Séverine!

MARQUIS: Séverine, wouldn't you care to leave? I think —

SÉVERINE: Certainly not. I'm enjoying myself immensely. (*To ROLLIN.*) I'm just getting into the mood.

MICHETTE: How did you get the garter?

MAURICE: There was a real crowd in the church. And, well, when a woman thinks a man is making advances —

(*They all laugh. GRAIN has stolen FRANÇOIS's purse.*)

FRANÇOIS: (*Returning to ALBIN with the money.*) There, you see, nothing but chips. Satisfied?

(*GRAIN tries to steal from the room.*)

PROSPÈRE: (*Going after him; softly.*) Hand over the purse you stole from that gentleman!

GRAIN: I —

PROSPÈRE: *Now!* Or you'll regret it!

GRAIN: You needn't be so rough about it. (*He gives the purse to PROSPÈRE.*)

PROSPÈRE: And don't leave. I don't have time to search you now. And who knows what else you've stolen. Get back to your seat.

FLIPOTTE: I'm going to win the garter.

PROSPÈRE: (*Goes to FRANÇOIS, throws him the purse.*) Here's your purse. It fell from your pocket.

FRANÇOIS: Thank you, Prospère. (*To ALBIN.*) You see? In reality you're sitting with the most honest people in the world.

(*HENRI, who has been present for some time, suddenly rises from his seat at the back.*)

ROLLIN: Henri! It's Henri!

SÉVERINE: Is he the one you're always talking about?

MARQUIS: He's the only reason anyone comes here.

(*HENRI comes forward theatrically. He is silent.*)

THE ACTORS. What's wrong, Henri? What's the matter? What is it?

ROLLIN: Watch the expression on his face. It's a world of passion. True passionate involvement with the criminal he plays.

SÉVERINE: Yes. I like that.

ALBIN: Why isn't he speaking?

ROLLIN: He's in a trance. Watch him now. Watch. He's committed some terrible crime.

FRANÇOIS: He's a bit theatrical this evening. It seems he's preparing for a monologue.

PROSPÈRE: Henri, Henri, where have you been?

HENRI: I just killed a man —

ROLLIN: What did I tell you!

SCAEVOLA: Who?

HENRI: My wife's lover — (*PROSPÈRE looks at him momentarily with the sense that it might be true. HENRI looks up.*) Yes. I did it. Why are you staring at me? That's how it happened. Is it so strange? You all know what my wife is. It was bound to end like this.

PROSPERE: And she — where is she? Where is she?

FRANÇOIS: There. You see? Now Prospère acts as though he believes it. That's why it seems so real.

(*Noise outside, though not too loud.*)

JULES: What's that noise out there?

MARQUIS: Do you hear it, Séverine?

ROLLIN: Sounds like troops passing by.

FRANÇOIS: No, no. Those are our beloved citizens of Paris. Listen to them shout! (*There is an uneasiness among those present. The noise outside dies away.*) Continue, Henri! Continue!

PROSPÈRE: Yes, Henri. Tell us. Where is your wife? Where did you leave her?

HENRI: I'm not worried about her. It won't kill her. One man or another.

What does a woman like her care. There are thousands of other handsome men in Paris. Who cares which one it is!

BALTHASAR: Kill them all! Kill all those who steal our wives!

SCAEVOLA: Kill all those who steal what's ours!

SERGEANT: (*To PROSPÈRE.*) These are revolutionary speeches!

ALBIN: This is frightening. They mean what they're saying!

SCAEVOLA: Down with the usurers of France! The bastard he found with his wife steals the bread from our mouths!

ALBIN: Can we leave?

SÉVERINE: Henri! Henri!

MARQUIS: Séverine!

SÉVERINE: Please, my dear, would you ask him how he discovered his wife's infidelity? Or shall I ask him myself?

MARQUIS: (*Hesitantly.*) If you please, Henri. How did you happen to — apprehend the two together?

HENRI: (*Who has long been sunk in thought.*) Do you know my wife? She's the most beautiful and the most depraved creature alive. And I love her. We've known each other for seven years. But only yesterday she became my wife. In these seven years there wasn't a single day, not one, that she didn't lie to me. Everything about her lies. Her eyes. Her lips. Her kisses. Her smiles.

FRANÇOIS: He's a bit declamatory this evening.

HENRI: She was had by every old man and every young man. By anyone who attracted her. By anyone who paid for her. And I knew it.

SÉVERINE: Not every man can make that claim.

HENRI: And yet she loved me, my friends. Can you understand that? Any of you? She would come back to me. Time after time. From wherever she was. From whoever she was with. From the handsome. From the ugly. The clever. The stupid. From the tramp and the gentleman. Came back to me. Always.

SÉVERINE: (*To ROLLIN.*) If only you could understand what her coming back to him meant. It's what love is all about —

HENRI: Oh, I suffered. I was tortured. Tortured.

ROLLIN: This is quite strong.

HENRI: And yesterday I married her. We had a dream. No. *I* had a dream. I wanted to take her away from here. Into solitude. Into the country with its peace and silence. We wanted to live our lives like other happy couples. We even dreamed of having a child.

ROLLIN: (*Softly.*) Séverine!

SÉVERINE: All right, all right —

ALBIN: François, this man is telling the truth!

FRANÇOIS: Yes, yes. The love story is true. Only the murder is fiction.

HENRI: I was late one day. There was one man she had forgotten. Otherwise — I think — there wasn't a single one of them missing. I caught them together. And now he's dead.

THE ACTORS: Who? Who? How did it happen? Where is he? Are they after you? How did it happen? Where is she?

HENRI: (*Growing more and more agitated.*) I walked her to the theater. Tonight was to be the last time. I kissed her. At the door. She went up to her dressing room. And I took off like a man who hadn't a trouble in the world. But after I'd walked only a hundred yards, it began. Inside me. Do you understand? A terrible restlessness. Something forcing me to turn back. I turned and went back. But I felt ashamed. I walked away again. But after another hundred yards I again felt gripped. And I went back. Her scene was over by now. She has little to do. Stand on stage half-naked for a while and she's done. I stood in front of her dressing room door. I heard whispering. I couldn't make it out. Then it stopped. I pushed open the door. (*He screams like a wild animal.*) It was the Duke de Cadignan! I killed him!

PROSPÈRE: (*Who finally believes it to be the truth.*) You're mad!

(*HENRI looks up, staring at PROSPÈRE.*)

SÉVERINE: Bravo! Bravo!

ROLLIN: Séverine! What are you doing?! The moment you applaud you drag all this down to the level of ordinary theater! The delightful shuddering sensation is lost!

MARQUIS: I didn't find your "shuddering sensation" particularly delightful! I suggest we applaud and remove ourselves from this — spell!

PROSPÈRE: (*To HENRI, during the noise.*) Henri. Save yourself. Leave here at once.

HENRI: What — ! What — !

PROSPÈRE: That's enough now. Hurry. Get away.

FRANÇOIS: Quiet! Let's hear what Prospère is saying!

PROSPÈRE: (*After a moment's thought.*) I told him to escape before the guard at the city gate is notified. The handsome Duke was a favorite of the King. They'll stretch you on the rack, Henri! Why didn't you kill that bitch of a wife of yours instead?

FRANÇOIS: The ensemble work is magnificent! Magnificent!

HENRI: Which of us is mad, Prospère? You or me?

(*The noise outside has grown increasingly louder. PEOPLE enter; yells and shouts are heard. At their head is GRASSET, followed by LEBRÊT. They surge down the stairs. Shouts of "Liberty!" "Liberty!" are heard.*)

GRASSET: Here we are, my friends! In here!

ALBIN: What is this? Is this part of the show?

FRANÇOIS: No —

MARQUIS: What is the meaning of this?

SÉVERINE: Who are these people?

GRASSET: In here! My friend Prospère always has an extra barrel of wine! (*Noise from the streets.*) And we've earned it! Friends! Brothers! We've taken it! We've taken it!

CRIES FROM OUTSIDE. Liberty! Liberty!

SÉVERINE: What's happened!

MARQUIS: Let's go! Let's leave here at once! The mob's crowding in!

ROLLIN: How do you suggest we get out?

GRASSET: It's fallen! The Bastille has fallen!

PROSPÈRE: What's that? Is it true?

GRASSET: Are you deaf?

(*ALBIN puts his hand to his sword.*)

FRANÇOIS: No! You mustn't! Or we're lost!

GRASSET: (*Staggers down the steps.*) If you hurry you can see a merry sight out there! The head of our beloved Delaunay stuck on the top of a pole!

MARQUIS: Is the man crazy?

SHOUTS. Liberty! Liberty!

GRASSET: We've lopped off a dozen heads! The Bastille's ours! Paris belongs to the people!

PROSPÈRE: Listen to him! Listen to him! Paris is ours!

GRASSET: Your sudden courage is astonishing, Prospère. Shout all you like. Your skin's safe now.

PROSPÈRE: (*To the noblemen.*) What do you say to this, you swine! The performance is over!

ALBIN: What did I tell you!

PROSPÈRE: The people of Paris have conquered!
(*They laugh.*)

SERGEANT: Silence! I order this performance to cease immediately!

GRASSET: Who is that idiot?

SERGEANT: Prospère, I hold you responsible for these revolutionary speeches!

GRASSET: Is he insane?

PROSPÈRE: The performance is over! Don't you understand? Tell me, Henri! You can tell them now! We'll protect you! Paris will protect you! (*HENRI stands there dazedly.*) Henri really *has* murdered the Duke de Cadignan!

ALBIN, FRANÇOIS, MARQUIS: What's that? What is he talking about?

ALBIN and OTHERS: What's the meaning of this, Henri!

FRANÇOIS: Henri! Say something!

PROSPÈRE: He found the Duke with his wife! And he killed him!

HENRI: It's not true!

PROSPÈRE: There's nothing to be afraid of now! You can shout it to the world! I could have told you an hour ago that the Duke was your wife's lover! My God! I was just about to tell you! Bellowing Brimstone knew! We knew! Didn't we!

HENRI: Who saw them? Where were they seen?

PROSPÈRE: What difference does it make now? I think he's gone mad! You've killed him! What more could you do?

GEORGETTE: Damn, is it true or not?

PROSPÈRE: Yes, it's true!

GRASSET: Henri! We're friends from this moment on! Long live Liberty! Long live Liberty!

FRANÇOIS: Say something, Henri!

HENRI: She was his mistress? The Duke de Cadignan's mistress? I didn't know. He's alive.
(*All are greatly moved.*)

SÉVERINE (*To the others.*) Where is your truth now?

ALBIN: My God!

(*The DUKE DE CADIGNAN pushes his way through the crowd on the stairs.*)

SÉVERINE: (*Seeing him first.*) The Duke!

SEVERAL OTHERS: The Duke!

DUKE: Why, yes. What is it?

PROSPÈRE: Are you a ghost?

DUKE: Not to my knowledge. Let me through.

ROLLIN: I'll wager this is all part of the performance. Even the mob is part of Prospère's troupe. Bravo, Prospère! It was sensational!

DUKE: What are you all doing in here? While you're playacting in here, out there — ! Don't you know what's happening? They just carried Delaunay's head past on a pole! Why are you looking at me like that? (*He descends the stairs.*) Henri —

FRANÇOIS: Watch out for Henri!

(*HENRI hurls himself at the DUKE like a madman and stabs him in the throat.*)

SERGEANT: (*Rising.*) This is going too far!

ALBIN: He's bleeding!

ROLLIN: This is murder!

SÉVERINE: The Duke is dying!

MARQUIS: Dear Séverine, I can't believe I brought you here! Today of all days!

SÉVERINE: But why? (*With difficulty.*) It was a rare opportunity! One doesn't see a real duke murdered every day!

ROLLIN: I still don't understand —

SERGEANT: Silence! No one will leave this room!

GRASSET: What does he want!

SERGEANT: I arrest this man in the name of the law!

GRASSET: Idiot! *We're* the law now! Get this rabble out of here! A man who murders a duke is a friend of the people! Long live Liberty!

ALBIN: (*Draws his sword.*) Make room there! My friends! Follow me!

(*LÉOCADIE rushes in and down the stairs.*)

VOICES: Léocadie!

OTHER VOICES: His wife!

LÉOCADIE: Let me through. I want my husband. (*She comes forward, sees what has happened, and screams.*) Who did that? Henri! (*HENRI looks at her.*) Why did you do it?

HENRI: Why — ?

LÉOCADIE: Yes. I know. For my sake. Oh, don't say it. No. I'm not worth it. I'm not worth it.

GRASSET: (*Beginning his speech.*) Citizens of Paris! Let us celebrate our victory! Chance has led us through the streets of Paris to this amiable resort! We couldn't have found a better place! Our cries of "Long live Liberty!" could nowhere have sounded more beautiful than over the dead body of a duke!

SHOUTING VOICES: Long live Liberty! Long live Liberty!

FRANÇOIS: We'd better go. The crowd's gone mad. Come on.

ALBIN: Do we leave the body here?

SÉVERINE: Long live Liberty! Long live Liberty!

MARQUIS: Have you gone mad?

CITIZENS and ACTORS: Long live Liberty! Long live Liberty!

SÉVERINE: (*At the head of the noblemen as they make their way toward the exit.*) Rollin — wait outside my window tonight. I'll throw down the key as before. We can enjoy each other for an hour or so. I feel so deliciously excited!

SHOUTING ACTORS: Long live Liberty! Long live Liberty!

LEBRÊT: Look at the bastards! They're running away!

GRASSET: Only for tonight. Let them go. They won't escape.

END OF PLAY

FLIRTATION

A Play in Three Acts

Cast of Characters

Hans Weiring *a violinist at the Josefstadt Theater*
Christine *his daughter*
Mitzi Schlager *a milliner*
Kattrin Binder *wife of a stocking-weaver*
Lina *her nine-year-old daughter*
Fritz Lobheimer *a young gentleman*
Theodore Kaiser *a young gentleman*
A Gentleman

Time and Place

Vienna in the 1890s

Flirtation

ACT ONE

Fritz's apartment. An elegant and comfortably furnished room. FRITZ and THEODORE enter, FRITZ in the lead, his overcoat tossed across his arm. He removes his hat upon entering, his walking stick still in hand.

FRITZ: (*From off.*) You're sure no one called?

SERVANT: (*From off.*) No one, sir.

FRITZ: (*Entering.*) Shall I have him dismiss the carriage?

THEODORE: Yes. I thought you had.

FRITZ: (*In the doorway.*) You can send off the carriage. And you might as well leave, too. I won't be needing you anymore today. (*To* THEODORE.) Take off your things.

THEODORE: (*At the writing-table.*) Some letters for you. (*He tosses his overcoat and hat onto an easychair, while still keeping hold of his walking stick.*)

FRITZ: (*Going to the table.*) Ah!

THEODORE: You're a past master at hiding your emotions.

FRITZ: From Papa! (*Breaks the seal on the other letter.*) From Lensky.

THEODORE: Don't tell me. (*FRITZ rushes through the letter.*) News from your father?

FRITZ: No. They want me to spend Pentecost with them on the estate.

THEODORE: You're a fool not to. You're due for a rest. (*FRITZ turns toward him from the writing-table.*) I'd suggest six months. Horseback riding, fresh air. Not to mention a dally or two with the milkmaids.

FRITZ: There's not a cow within miles.

THEODORE: You know what I —

FRITZ: Come *with* me!

THEODORE: Can't.

FRITZ: Why?

THEODORE: Doctor's orals. And if I did, it'd be only to keep you there. I know you, Fritz.

FRITZ: Stop!

THEODORE: You need fresh air. Country air made you into an actual human being today.

FRITZ: Thanks a lot.

THEODORE: But you're already coming apart. Have we re-entered the "danger zone"? (*FRITZ gestures angrily.*) And what about the time we had with those two girls recently? You were a real charmer. But back to the old rut, as they say. All you think about is *that woman.*

FRITZ: Where do you get your energy!

THEODORE: Did I say to forget her? No! Just think "trouble!" The whole affair gives me the shakes. Stop putting her on a pedestal. She might turn out to be a winner. She's not a demon. She's a charmer. She's a woman. And she's there to have fun with. Like all women who are young and lovely and temperamental.

FRITZ: What do you mean, it gives you the shakes?

THEODORE: Any day I expect you to run off with her.

FRITZ: Be serious.

THEODORE: (*After a short pause.*) And *that* barely scratches the surface.

FRITZ: You're right. There are dangers.

THEODORE: Caution's the word.

FRITZ: (*To himself.*) Dangers —

THEODORE: Like?

FRITZ: (*With a glance toward the window.*) She was mistaken once already.

THEODORE: Explain.

FRITZ: It doesn't —

THEODORE: Make some sense, Fritz.

FRITZ: She has anxiety attacks.

THEODORE: Due to?

FRITZ: Nerves. (*Ironically.*) Guilty conscience? I don't know.

THEODORE: What was she mistaken about?

FRITZ: Like earlier today.

THEODORE: Well, what?

FRITZ: (*After a short pause.*) She thinks we're being watched.

THEODORE: Ah!

FRITZ: (*Going to the window.*) She imagines seeing someone on the corner. Could you recognize anyone from here?

THEODORE: I doubt it.

FRITZ: She has fits. Cries. Wants nothing to do with me. And then she wants us to die together.

THEODORE: Yes! Well!

FRITZ: (*After a short pause.*) Today I had to go down for a look. Not a soul. (*THEODORE is silent.*) At least it's something. People don't just disappear. Say something!

THEODORE: Like what? No. People don't just disappear. But they *do* hide in doorways.

FRITZ: I looked.

THEODORE: That must have been a sight!

FRITZ: No one! She hallucinates!

THEODORE: Just be more careful.

FRITZ: Her husband suspects nothing. I'd have noticed. I dined with them last night after the theater. Very pleasant. Ridiculous!

THEODORE: Fritz. Just drop it. The whole can of worms. For *my* sake. It makes me nervous. I know. It's not easy. But I've done all I can to help you find something else to —

FRITZ: What are you — ?

THEODORE: That girlfriend of Mitzi's? The one you dated a few weeks ago? You really seemed to like her.

FRITZ: She was lovely. It's what I need to get over this. Tenderness. Sweetness. Silence —

THEODORE: Right. It's why women exist. "Interesting" women give me a pain. They're meant to be pleasant. Not "interesting"! I know what happiness is. It's freedom from emotional scenes. From danger. From tragic relationships. It's an affair that begins at the drop of a hat and ends as simply as a summer day.

FRITZ: You're right.

THEODORE: Women are simple. They're honest. They're healthy. But we turn them into demons. Or angels.

FRITZ: She's precious. She's faithful. And just too good for me.

THEODORE: You never learn! If you don't stop this —

FRITZ: I will! You're right! I need to recover.

THEODORE: I'll just wash my hands of it! Your tragic affairs bore me. As does your conscience! Take my advice. Live by the maxim that says: I come first, you come second. Because if not, you might as well cut your throat.

(*A bell rings.*)

FRITZ: What — ?

THEODORE: The bell. Go see. You're white as a ghost! Fritz! It's Mitzi and Christine.

FRITZ: (*Pleasantly surprised.*) What — ?

THEODORE: I invited them.

FRITZ: (*Going out.*) You could have told me. I just sent off the servant.

THEODORE: Pity!

FRITZ: (*From off.*) Mitzi! How are you! (*FRITZ enters with MITZI in the lead, a package in her arms.*) Where's Christine?

MITZI: She'll be along. Evening, Theo! (*THEODORE kisses her hand.*) Theodore invited us. I hope you don't —

FRITZ: Marvelous! But Theodore overlooked one small item.

THEODORE: Theodore overlooks nothing. (*He takes the package from MITZI.*) Did you bring it all?

MITZI: What else! (*To FRITZ.*) May I?

FRITZ: I'll put it on the buffet.

MITZI: I brought a treat! Something Theo *didn't* put on the list.

THEODORE: (*Suspiciously.*) Oh?

MITZI: A chocolate-creme torte!

THEODORE: Nibble-nibble-nibble!

FRITZ: Where's Christine?

MITZI: Walking her father to the theater. She'll take a streetcar from there.

THEODORE: Such a loving daughter!

MITZI: Especially lately. Since the funeral.

THEODORE: Who died?

MITZI: Her father's old sister.

THEODORE: Her aunt, then.

MITZI: Not exactly. An old maiden lady who lived with them. Her father's very lonely now.

THEODORE: He's rather small, isn't he? With short gray hair?

MITZI: (*Shaking her head.*) Wrong again. His hair is *long*.

FRITZ: Do you know him?

THEODORE: I went with Lensky to the Josefstadt the other day. I happened to notice the men playing the bass viols.

MITZI: He plays the violin.

THEODORE: (*To MITZI who is laughing.*) What's so funny? How should *I* know? Silly!

MITZI: I like your apartment, Mr. Fritz. Beautiful. Is there a view?

FRITZ: You see into Strohgasse from here. But in the next room —

THEODORE: Loosen up. Call him Fritz.

MITZI: We'll drink a loving cup at supper.

THEODORE: Great! I can't wait! How's your mother?

MITZI: (*Suddenly turning toward him with a troubled expression.*) Oh, goodness! She had another —

THEODORE: Don't tell me! A toothache! She's a martyr! What about seeing a dentist?

MITZI: Doctor says it's rheumatism.

THEODORE: (*Laughing.*) Oh, well! Rheumatism!

MITZI: (*Holding an album.*) What lovely things! (*Turning the pages.*) Who's this? Why, it's you, Mr. Fritz! In a uniform! Are you in the army?

FRITZ: Yes.

MITZI: A dragoon! Black or yellow regiment?

FRITZ: (*Smiling.*) Yellow.

MITZI: (*As if in a dream.*) Yellow!

THEODORE: She's slipping away, Fritz. Mitzi! Wake up!

MITZI: And a lieutenant!

FRITZ: Nothing less.

MITZI: How handsome you must be in your furs!

THEODORE: Your knowledge is staggering. I say, Mitzi! I'm in the reserves, too.

MITZI: The dragoons?

THEODORE: Yes.

MITZI: You didn't tell me!

THEODORE: I prefer being loved for myself.

MITZI: Oh, Theo! Next time wear your uniform!

THEODORE: Maneuvers are in August.

MITZI: I'd die before then!

THEODORE: Love is fleeting!

MITZI: But August! It's only May! Tell him, Mr. Fritz! (*To FRITZ.*) Why did you run out on us yesterday?

FRITZ: I don't —

MITZI: After the theater.

FRITZ: Didn't Theodore excuse me?

THEODORE: Of course Theodore excused you.

MITZI: Excuses, excuses! Poor Christine! Promises should be kept!

FRITZ: I'd rather have been with you and —

MITZI: Mean that?

FRITZ: But I couldn't. I was with friends and — and couldn't break away. But you saw —

MITZI: We saw the beautiful woman you couldn't break away from. From the gallery. You were in a loge.

FRITZ: I saw you, too.

MITZI: You sat as far back as you —

FRITZ: Not all the time.

MITZI: But most of the time. Behind a woman in black velvet. You were always (*Mimicking.*) peeking out.

FRITZ: Were you spying on me?

MITZI: Oh, it means nothing to *me!* But if I were Christine — Theodore had time for us afterwards. (*To THEODORE.*) Didn't *you* have friends to go to supper with?

THEODORE: (*Proudly.*) Didn't *I* have friends to go to supper with?
(*A bell rings.*)

MITZI: There's Christine!
(*FRITZ hurries out.*)

THEODORE: Mitzi. Spare us your reminiscences of the military.

MITZI: What?

THEODORE: You didn't learn all you know from books, my dear.
(*FRITZ enters with CHRISTINE, who carries some flowers. She greets them with mild embarrassment.*)

CHRISTINE: Good evening. (*To FRITZ.*) Are you glad we came? You're not angry?

FRITZ: Don't be silly. At times Theodore's head is on straighter than mine.

THEODORE: Is your father playing yet?

CHRISTINE: Yes. I walked him to the theater.

FRITZ: Mitzi told us.

CHRISTINE: (*To MITZI.*) And Kattrin delayed me, too.

MITZI: That awful woman!

CHRISTINE: She's all right. She's kind.

MITZI: You trust everybody.

CHRISTINE: I have no reason not to trust her.

FRITZ: Who's — ?

MITZI: A stocking-weaver's wife. Jealous of anyone younger than her.

CHRISTINE: She's still young.

FRITZ: Let's forget Kattrin. What's that you've got?

CHRISTINE: Flowers.

FRITZ: (*Takes them from her and kisses her hand.*) Angel! Let's find a vase.

THEODORE: Goodness, Fritz! They're to be scattered across the tablecloth. After it's been set, of course. Actually they should fall from the ceiling. But that might be a problem. (*FRITZ laughs.*) So the vase it is! (*Hands CHRISTINE the vase.*)

MITZI: Oh! It's getting dark!

(*FRITZ has helped CHRISTINE remove her jacket and places it, along with her hat, which she has also removed, on a chair in the background.*)

FRITZ: We'll light the lamps in a second.

THEODORE: Lamps? Candles, Fritz! Candles! Good Lord! Come along, Mitzi, you can help.

(*THEODORE and MITZI light the candles; those in the branched candelabrum on the trumeau, one on the writing-table, and then two on the sideboard. During this FRITZ and CHRISTINE converse.*)

FRITZ: How have you been?

CHRISTINE: Fine. Now.

FRITZ: Now?

CHRISTINE: I missed you.

FRITZ: But I saw you yesterday.

CHRISTINE: Saw, yes, far off. (*Shyly.*) That wasn't nice of you, Fritz.

FRITZ: Mitzi mentioned it. You're such a child, Christine. I couldn't get away. You can understand that.

CHRISTINE: But who were those people? In the loge?

FRITZ: Friends. Who they were has nothing to do with it.

CHRISTINE: And the lady in the black velvet dress?

FRITZ: Christine, I don't remember how people dress.

CHRISTINE: (*Coaxingly.*) Oh!

FRITZ: Well, maybe in special cases. Like the dark gray blouse you wore. The day we met. And the black and white blouse you had on last night.

CHRISTINE: This one?

FRITZ: Well. It looks different from a distance. And this locket.

CHRISTINE: (*Smiling.*) When did I wear it?

FRITZ: In the garden? By the tracks? When we watched the children playing?

CHRISTINE: Yes. You do think of me sometimes.

FRITZ: More than you know.

CHRISTINE: Not more than I do about you. All day long. But I'm only happy when I'm with you.

FRITZ: Don't we see each other enough?

CHRISTINE: Enough!

FRITZ: In summer we might see less of each other. I might travel for a few weeks.

CHRISTINE: (*Frightened.*) You're going away?

FRITZ: I don't know. I might want to be alone. For a week or two.

CHRISTINE: Why?

FRITZ: I only said it was *possible!* I get into moods! You might not want to see me for a few days as well. I'd understand.

CHRISTINE: No, Fritz, never.

FRITZ: You can't be sure.

CHRISTINE: I can. I love you.

FRITZ: I love you, too. Very much.

CHRISTINE: You're everything to me, Fritz. I — I can't imagine not seeing you. I —

FRITZ: (*Interrupting.*) Don't, Christine.

CHRISTINE: (*Smiling sadly.*) Fritz, I know it's not forever.

FRITZ: Don't misunderstand. One day maybe we'll be — (*Laughs.*) inseparable. But — but we don't know. We're only human.

THEODORE: (*Indicating the candles.*) Better than some old gas lamp staring us in the face.

FRITZ: Theo's a born party man!

THEODORE: Then suppose we think about supper!

MITZI: (*Excited.*) Oh! Come on, Christine!

FRITZ: Let me show you where things are.

MITZI: First we need a tablecloth.

THEODORE: (*In a British accent.*) "A tablecloth!"

FRITZ: What?

THEODORE: The clowns at the Orpheum. "This is a tablecloth." "This is a tin plate." "This is a piccolo."

MITZI: When'll you take *me* to the Orpheum, Theo? You promised. And Christine and Mr. Fritz can come, too. (*She takes the tablecloth from FRITZ, which he has removed from the cupboard.*) Then *we'll* be the friends in the loge!

FRITZ: Yes, yes.

MITZI: And the woman in the black velvet can go home alone.

FRITZ: This fuss about the woman in black is silly.

MITZI: Nothing against her. There. And the silverware?

(*THEODORE meanwhile has reclined on the divan. He speaks as FRITZ approaches him from the front.*)

THEODORE: You'll excuse me —

(*MITZI and CHRISTINE set the table.*)

MITZI: Have you seen the photograph of Fritz? In his uniform?

CHRISTINE: No.

MITZI: So smart!

THEODORE: (*From the divan.*) I love evenings like this.

FRITZ: Don't blame you.

THEODORE: I'm utterly comfortable. You?

FRITZ: Pity it has to end.

MITZI: Is there a coffee-maker, Mr. Fritz?

FRITZ: Yes. Light it now. It takes an hour.

THEODORE: (*To FRITZ.*) A girl like this is worth ten of those female demons of yours.

FRITZ: There's no comparison.

THEODORE: You know something? We actually hate the women we love and love the ones we couldn't care less about.

(*FRITZ laughs.*)

MITZI: You're laughing! Let *us* in on the joke!

THEODORE: Not for the ears of babes. We're being profound. (*To FRITZ.*) If we never saw them again — would we be less happy?

FRITZ: Never again? Parting is painful no matter *how* you've looked forward to it.

CHRISTINE: Fritz, where are the knives and forks?

FRITZ: (*Goes toward the back, to the sideboard.*) Here, my dear. (*MITZI has gone to THEODORE on the divan and runs her fingers through his hair.*)

THEODORE: Little kitten!

FRITZ: (*Opening the packages brought by MITZI.*) Magnificent!

CHRISTINE: (*To FRITZ.*) Everything here is so neat.

FRITZ: I suppose. (*He arranges the food: cans of sardines, cold cuts, butter, cheese.*)

CHRISTINE: Fritz? Is there something you want to tell me?

FRITZ: Tell you?

CHRISTINE: (*Very shyly.*) Who the lady was?

FRITZ: No! And don't make me angry! (*More gently.*) Look. We agreed. No questions. It makes our relationship so beautiful. When we're together the world disappears. So, no more of that. And I promise, too. No questions.

CHRISTINE: You can ask me anything.

FRITZ: But I don't. I don't *want* to know anything.

MITZI: (*Returning to them.*) Lord, what a mess you've made! (*She takes the food and places it on the table.*) There!

THEODORE: What's there to drink, Fritz?

FRITZ: Oh, I think I'll find something! (*Goes into the anteroom.*)

THEODORE: (*Rises from the divan and goes to inspect the table.*) Good!

MITZI: There now. I don't think we've forgotten anything.

FRITZ: (*Returning with some bottles.*) Here we are! This should do it.

THEODORE: And the roses? They're supposed to fall from the ceiling.

MITZI: Oh, God! The roses! (*She takes the roses from the vase, stands on a chair and lets them fall onto the table.*) There!

CHRISTINE: She's lost her mind!

THEODORE: Mitzi! Not *on* the plates!

FRITZ: Where would you like to sit, Christine?

THEODORE: Do you have a corkscrew?

FRITZ: (*Taking one from the sideboard.*) Here. (*MITZI attempts to open one of the bottles.*) Here, give that to me.

THEODORE: Let me do that. (*He takes the bottle from FRITZ along with the corkscrew.*) In the meantime you might — (*Goes through the motions of playing the piano.*)

MITZI: Oh, Fritz! That would be lovely! (*She goes to the piano and opens it, after removing the articles to a chair.*)

FRITZ: (*To CHRISTINE.*) Shall I?

CHRISTINE: Please. I've wanted to hear you for so long.

FRITZ: (*At the piano.*) Do you play?

CHRISTINE: (*Turning away.*) Oh, God!

MITZI: Christine plays beautifully. Sings, too.

FRITZ: You never told me.

CHRISTINE: You never asked.

FRITZ: Who taught you to sing?

CHRISTINE: No one. Well, my father for a while. But I'm not very good. And since auntie died — she lived with us — the house has been very quiet.

FRITZ: What do you do all day?

CHRISTINE: Oh, I keep busy.

FRITZ: At home?

CHRISTINE: Yes. And I copy manuscripts.

FRITZ: Music manuscripts?

CHRISTINE: Yes.

FRITZ: You must make a fortune! (*The others laugh.*) Well, *I'd* pay a fortune for it! It can't be easy.

MITZI: She's crazy! All that trouble! (*To CHRISTINE.*) If I sang like you, I'd be on the stage today.

THEODORE: Talent is no requirement, my dear! And you are delightfully idle all day, eh, Mitzi?

MITZI: Believe me! With two little brothers to dress every morning! And help with their lessons every evening!

THEODORE: I don't believe a word of it.

MITZI: Then don't! And till last fall I worked from eight in the morning till eight at night!

THEODORE: (*Gently teasing her.*) And where would *that* have been, I wonder?

MITZI: *That* would have been in a milliner's shop. My mother wants me to go back.

THEODORE: (*As before.*) Why'd you leave in the first place?

FRITZ: (*To CHRISTINE.*) You'll have to sing for us.

THEODORE: Supper first. Then you can play.

FRITZL: (*Rising; to CHRISTINE.*) Come, my dear. (*He leads her to the table.*)

MITZI: The coffee! It's boiling over! And we haven't even eaten!

THEODORE: It's no tragedy.

MITZI: But it's boiling! (*Blows out the flame.*)
  (*They all sit at the table.*)

THEODORE: What's your wish, Mitzi? But one thing's for sure. The chocolate-creme torte comes last. First there are all kinds of pickled things. (*FRITZ pours the wine.*) Fritz! For God's sake! We do it differently these days! (*He rises and affects a solemn grandness, bottle in hand. To CHRISTINE.*) *Vöslauer Auslese,* eighteen hundred and — (*Mumbles the rest of the date; then serves MITZI.*) *Vöslauer Auslese,* eighteen hundred and — (*As above; then serves FRITZ.*) *Vöslauer Auslese,* eighteen hundred and — (*As above; then serves himself.*) *Vöslauer Auslese,* eighteen hundred and — (*As above; then he sits down.*)

MITZI: (*Laughing.*) He's always so crazy!

FRITZ: (*Lifting his glass; they all touch glasses.*) Prosit!

MITZI: Long life, Theodore!

THEODORE: (*Rising.*) Ladies and gentlemen!

FRITZ: Not yet!

THEODORE: (*Sits down.*) I can wait.
  (*They eat.*)

MITZI: I always like a speech. I have a cousin who does it in rhyme.

THEODORE: What regiment's *he* in?

MITZI: Oh, stop it now! He delivers his speeches by heart. And in rhyme. And it's absolutely wonderful, Christine! He's an elderly gentleman by now.

THEODORE: Elderly gentlemen frequently speak in rhymed verse.

FRITZ: You're not drinking. Christine! (*He touches glasses with her.*)

THEODORE: (*Toasts MITZI.*) To old gentlemen who speak in rhymed verses!

MITZI: (*Happily.*) To young gentlemen! Even when they have nothing to say! Mr. Fritz, for example. How about the loving cup now, Mr. Fritz? And Christine has to drink it with Theodore.

THEODORE: Not with *this* wine! Here's the one for the occasion! (*He rises, takes another bottle, and performs the same ceremony as before.*) Xeres de la Frontera, mille huit cent cinquante — Xeres de la Frontera — Xeres de la Frontera — Xeres de la Frontera.

MITZI: (*Sips the wine.*) Ah!

THEODORE: You could have waited, Mitzi! Well now, before we pledge ourselves to brotherhood, let us drink to the good fortune which — well, and so forth.

MITZI: That's enough of that!

(*They all drink. FRITZ takes MITZI's arm, and THEODORE takes CHRISTINE's, and glasses in hand they perform the ceremony of the pledge. FRITZ kisses MITZI and THEODORE tries to kiss CHRISTINE.*)

CHRISTINE: (*Smiling.*) Do I have to?

THEODORE: Of course. Otherwise what's the sense in it? (*He kisses her.*) There! And now to our places, *s'il vous plaît!*

MITZI: This room is like an oven!

FRITZ: Yes. The candles Theodore lighted.

MITZI: And the wine. (*She leans back in the fauteuil.*)

THEODORE: Oh, all right, Mitzi! You can start with the best after all! (*He cuts a piece of the torte and pops it into her mouth.*) There, you little kitten! How's that?

MITZI: Mmmmm!

THEODORE: (*Giving her another piece.*) I think the time's come! Fritz! Play something!

FRITZ: Christine?

CHRISTINE: Please.

MITZI: Something smart! (*THEODORE fills the glasses.*) Oh, I couldn't drink another drop! Really! (*She drinks it down.*)

CHRISTINE: (*Sipping.*) Such a heavy wine —

THEODORE: (*Indicating the wine.*) Fritz?

(*FRITZ empties his glass and makes his way to the piano. CHRISTINE sits down beside him.*)

MITZI: Play "The Double Eagle March."

FRITZ: "The Double Eagle March." How does it go?

MITZI: Theo? Can you play "The Double Eagle March."

THEODORE: I can't even play the piano!

FRITZ: I *know* it. I just can't —

MITZI: Let's see. La, la, lalalala, la —

FRITZ: I remember now. (*He plays it, but not quite correctly.*)

MITZI: (*Going to the piano.*) No, like this. (*Picks out the melody with one finger.*)

FRITZ: Yes, yes. (*Plays as MITZI sings along.*)

THEODORE: More recollections of the military, Mitzi?

FRITZ: (*Again plays it incorrectly, and stops.*) I can't play it. I can't remember. (*He improvises on the piano.*)

MITZI: (*After the first measure or so.*) What's that supposed to be?

FRITZ: (*Laughs.*) What do you mean? I wrote it!

MITZI: Well! It's not for dancing!

FRITZ: Try it and see.

THEODORE: (*To MITZI.*) Shall we, Mitzi? (*He takes MITZI by the waist and they dance.*)
> (*CHRISTINE stands at the piano and looks down at the keys. A bell rings offstage. FRITZ suddenly stops playing while THEODORE and MITZI continue dancing.*)

THEODORE and MITZI: What was that? Well!

FRITZ: The bell! (*To THEODORE.*) Someone else you've invited?

THEODORE: Not me. Just don't answer.

CHRISTINE: (*To FRITZ.*) What is it?

FRITZ: Nothing. (*The bell rings again.* FRITZ *rises without moving from the piano.*) You can hear the piano clear into the hallway. And see the lights from the street.

THEODORE: Don't be silly. You're not at home.

FRITZ: But it makes me nervous.

THEODORE: Well, what could it be? A letter? A telegram? You can't be having a caller at (*Looks at his watch.*) nine in the —
> (*The bell rings again.*)

FRITZ: I have to answer. (*Goes out.*)

MITZI: That's not very nice of him. (*She strikes a few keys on the piano.*)

THEODORE: That's enough of that. (*To CHRISTINE.*) What is it? Has the bell upset you, too?
> (*FRITZ returns, his composure somewhat unsettled.*)

THEODORE and CHRISTINE: (*Together.*) Well, who was it? — Who was it?

FRITZ: (*With a forced laugh.*) Excuse me for a moment. Please. Make yourselves comfortable in there.

THEODORE: What's wrong?

CHRISTINE: Who is it?

FRITZ: Nothing. Just a few words. To the gentleman outside.

(*FRITZ has opened the door to the adjoining room and leads CHRISTINE and MITZI inside; THEODORE is the last to enter and turns to look questioningly at FRITZ.*)

FRITZ: (*Quietly, with a frightened expression.*) It's him!

THEODORE: Oh!

FRITZ: Go on in! Go!

THEODORE: Don't do anything stupid. It could be a trap.

FRITZ: Go on! Go!

(*THEODORE goes in. FRITZ hurries through the room and goes into the hallway, leaving the stage empty for some moments. Then he returns with an elegantly dressed GENTLEMAN of about thirty-five, who enters the room first. The GENTLEMAN is dressed in a yellow overcoat, wears gloves, and holds his hat in his hands.*)

FRITZ: (*Entering.*) Excuse me! I kept you waiting. I regret —

GENTLEMAN: (*In an easy voice.*) That's quite all right. I regret having disturbed you.

FRITZ: Not at all. Would you care to — ? (*Indicates a chair.*)

GENTLEMAN: Yes, I see I *have* disturbed you. A small party?

FRITZ: A few friends.

GENTLEMAN: (*Sits down; in a friendly manner.*) A masquerade, no doubt.

FRITZ: (*Embarrassed.*) Sorry?

GENTLEMAN: Your "friends" appear to have come in women's hats and coats.

FRITZ: Yes, well. (*Smiling.*) Friends might also include women.

GENTLEMAN: (*After a silence.*) Life can be rather amusing at times. Yes.

(*He stares at FRITZ who bears up under his glance for a while, then looks away.*)

FRITZ: To what do I owe the honor?

GENTLEMAN: Of course. (*Quietly.*) It seems my wife left her veil here.

FRITZ: Your wife? Here? Your — (*Smiling.*) You can't be serious.

(*The GENTLEMAN rises suddenly, very stern, almost furious, while he props himself with his hands on the back of the chair.*)

GENTLEMAN: I said she left her veil! (*FRITZ also rises and the two men stand opposite one another. The GENTLEMAN raises his fist as if to bring it down on FRITZ in a rage of loathing.*) Oh! (*FRITZ wards off the blow and takes a step backward. The GENTLEMAN speaks after a long pause.*) Here are your letters. (*He tosses the packet of letters which he has removed from his overcoat pocket onto the writing-table.*) I suggest you return her letters to *you*. (*FRITZ motions for him to keep away. The GENTLEMAN points his words sternly.*) I wouldn't want anyone to find them. Afterward.

FRITZ: (*Strongly.*) They won't be found. (*The GENTLEMAN looks at him. Pause.*) Is there anything else?

GENTLEMAN: (*With scorn.*) Anything else!

FRITZ: I'm at your disposal.

GENTLEMAN: (*Bowing coolly.*) Good. (*He looks about the room; upon seeing the table laid out, and the women's hats and coats again, an expression of near rage crosses his face.*)

FRITZ: (*Noticing the GENTLEMAN's perusal of the room.*) I am completely at your disposal. I'll be at home tomorrow. Till twelve.

(*The GENTLEMAN bows and turns to leave. FRITZ accompanies him to the door, which the GENTLEMAN gently refuses. When he is gone, FRITZ goes to the writing-table and stands there for a moment. Then he hurries to the window, looks through a slit in the blinds, and we are aware of him following the GENTLEMAN along the sidewalk with his eyes. He turns from the window and stands looking at the floor; then he goes to the door of the adjoining room and opens it half-way.*)

FRITZ: (*Calling into the room.*) Theodore? May I see you for a moment?

(*THEODORE enters. The scene moves at a swift pace.*)

THEODORE: (*Excitedly.*) Well?

FRITZ: He knows!

THEODORE: He knows *nothing!* I warned you to be careful! You probably admitted it! You're a fool, Fritz! An absolute fool!

FRITZ: (*Pointing at the packet of letters.*) He returned my letters.

THEODORE: (*Struck.*) Oh! (*After a pause.*) That should teach you to write letters!

FRITZ: It was he she saw today. On the corner. This afternoon.

THEODORE: What happened? Say something!

FRITZ: Theodore? Do me a favor?

THEODORE: I'll straighten it out. Don't worry.

FRITZ: It's too late for that.

THEODORE: I see —

FRITZ: In any case, I wish you'd — my God! We can't keep the girls in there forever!

THEODORE: They can wait! What?

FRITZ: Contact Lensky. Tonight.

THEODORE: Of course. At once.

FRITZ: You won't find him now. But he'll be at the café. Between eleven and twelve. Bring him here.

THEODORE: Don't look like that! These things turn out.

FRITZ: Not this time.

THEODORE: Last year? Remember? Billinger and Herz? The same thing.

FRITZ: Stop it! He should have shot me! On the spot! At least it would have been over!

THEODORE: Hm —

FRITZ: It's useless! Why go through it!

THEODORE: Don't be a child! It's luck! You could just as easily —

FRITZ: (*Not listening to him.*) She suspected. We both suspected. We both knew.

THEODORE: Oh, Fritz!

FRITZ: (*Goes to the writing-table and locks the letters in the drawer.*) She must be in hell! Do you think he — ? Theodore! Tomorrow! Find out what happened!

THEODORE: I'll try.

FRITZ: And I want no delays.

THEODORE: Probably the day after tomorrow.

FRITZ: (*Afraid.*) Theodore!

THEODORE: Fritz! Cheer up! Believe in yourself! It'll turn out. Don't worry. (*Talking himself into a happy mood.*) I don't know *why*. But it *will*.

FRITZ: (*Smiles.*) You're a real friend, Theodore! What do we tell the girls?

THEODORE: I don't care. Send them home.

FRITZ: No. Look happy. Christine mustn't suspect. I'll be at the piano. You call them in. (*THEODORE turns with dissatisfaction at having to go.*) What'll you tell them?

THEODORE: That it's none of their business.

FRITZ: (*Has seated himself at the piano; turns to THEODORE.*) No, no.

THEODORE: Something to do with a friend. What can they say? (*FRITZ plays a few notes.*) Ladies, if you please! (*He opens the door and MITZI and CHRISTINE enter.*)

MITZI: About time! Is he gone?

CHRISTINE: (*Rushing to FRITZ.*) Fritz? Who was it?

FRITZ: (*Continues playing.*) Questions, questions!

CHRISTINE: Fritz! Please! Tell me!

FRITZ: Nothing to say. You don't know them.

CHRISTINE: (*Coaxing.*) Fritz? The truth?

THEODORE: Persistent, isn't she! Not a word. You promised.

MITZI: Christine! Don't be silly! The boys have a *secret!* Let them be important, if they want!

THEODORE: Let's see now. I was waltzing with Mitzi — (*Like a British clown.*) Maestro, if you please!

(*FRITZ plays as THEODORE and MITZI dance.*)

MITZI: (*After a few moments.*) Oh! I can't! No more!

(*MITZI sinks into a fauteuil. THEODORE kisses her and sits beside her on the arm of the chair. FRITZ remains at the piano; then takes CHRISTINE by both hands and looks at her.*)

CHRISTINE: (*As though waking.*) Why did you stop?

FRITZ: (*Smiling.*) Enough for today.

CHRISTINE: I wish *I* played like you.

FRITZ: You play a lot?

CHRISTINE: No time. Always something. Around the house. Besides, it's a terrible piano.

FRITZ: Could I play it sometime? And see your room?

CHRISTINE: (*Smiling.*) It's not like yours.

FRITZ: And — you'll tell me about yourself. Everything. I know nothing.

CHRISTINE: There's not much. But I don't have secrets. Like some.

FRITZ: Have you been in love?

(*CHRISTINE merely looks at him. FRITZ kisses her hands.*)

CHRISTINE: Only you. No one else. Ever.

FRITZ: (*With an almost painful expression.*) No! Don't! You don't know a thing about it! Your father. Does *he* love you, Christine?

CHRISTINE: Oh, God! I used to tell him everything!

FRITZ: Don't be ashamed. We all have secrets. That's life.

CHRISTINE: I wish I knew you loved me. At least —

FRITZ: Don't you?

CHRISTINE: If you always talked like —

FRITZ: You're not comfortable there.

CHRISTINE: I'm fine. (*She leans her head against the piano. FRITZ rises and strokes her hair.*) I like that.

(*The room is silent.*)

THEODORE: Fritz? Cigars?

(*FRITZ goes to the sideboard where THEODORE has already looked. MITZI has by now fallen asleep. FRITZ hands THEODORE a box of cigars.*)

FRITZ: Black coffee? (*He pours two cups.*)

THEODORE: Ladies? Black coffee?

FRITZ: Mitzi?

THEODORE: Let her sleep. And don't *you* drink any. Get to bed. Soon. Get a good rest. (*FRITZ looks at him and laughs bitterly.*) Nothing to be done, old chum. Just don't make it worse. Be reasonable.

FRITZ: Lensky? You'll bring him? Tonight?

THEODORE: Don't be stupid. Tomorrow.

FRITZ: Please.

THEODORE: Yes. All right.

FRITZ: Now! Mitzi! Wake up!

MITZI: Coffee! You're drinking without us! I want some!

THEODORE: Here you are.

FRITZ: (*Going to CHRISTINE.*) Tired?

CHRISTINE: (*Smiling.*) The wine. A little headache.

FRITZ: The night air will see to that.

CHRISTINE: Are we leaving? You're coming, aren't you?

FRITZ: No. There are things I —

CHRISTINE: Now? But it's late!

FRITZ: (*Almost sternly.*) Christine! Stop that! (*Gently.*) I'm exhausted. We were in the country all day. Theodore and I. Walked for hours.

THEODORE: And a great time was had by all! We'll all go together next time.

MITZI: That'll be smart! In your uniform! Both of you!

THEODORE: You have a real feeling for nature, Mitzi!

CHRISTINE: When will I — ?

FRITZ: (*Rather on edge.*) I'll write.

CHRISTINE: Good-bye. (*She turns to go.*)

FRITZ: (*Noting her sadness.*) Christine. Tomorrow.

CHRISTINE: (*Happily.*) Really?

FRITZ: The garden. By the tracks. Like the other day. Six? All right? Happy? (*CHRISTINE nods.*)

MITZI: (*To FRITZ.*) Coming with us, Fritzie?

THEODORE: What a remarkable knack for informality!

FRITZ: No. I'm staying.

MITZI: Lucky you! All that way ahead of us! Ugh!

FRITZ: Mitzi! You hardly touched the torte! Here. Let me pack it for you.

MITZI: Is it proper?
    (*FRITZ packs the torte.*)

CHRISTINE: She's like a child.

MITZI: (*To FRITZ.*) Just for that I'll help you put out the candles. (*She extinguishes one candle after another, except for the one on the writing-table.*)

CHRISTINE: The window. Shall I open it? It's so close. (*She opens the window and stands looking out at the house across the street.*)

FRITZ: There you are! (*He hands MITZI the package.*) Now for some light. The stairs are dark.

MITZI: Are they out?

THEODORE: It's late.

CHRISTINE: (*At the window.*) The air's so cool.

MITZI: A lovely May night! (*She is at the door. FRITZ holds a candle.*) Well! Thank you! It was a wonderful time!

THEODORE: (*Urges her on.*) Go, go, go!

MITZI: Oh, pooh!

THEODORE: Watch out for the steps!

MITZI: Thanks for the torte!

THEODORE: Shh! You'll wake the whole neighborhood!

CHRISTINE: Good night!

THEODORE: Good night!

(*The sound of FRITZ closing and locking the door is heard. As he enters the room and places the candle on the writing-table, the main door of the apartment building is heard opening and closing. FRITZ goes to the window and waves to them below.*)

CHRISTINE'S VOICE: (*From the street.*) Good night!

MITZI'S VOICE: (*In high spirits.*) Good night, little sweetheart!

THEODORE'S VOICE: (*Scolding.*) Mitzi!

(*THEODORE's words, their laughter, and the footsteps fade away. THEODORE whistles the melody of "The Double Eagle March," which is the last sound we hear. FRITZ looks out for a few seconds longer, then sinks into the fauteuil beside the window.*)

ACT TWO

Christine's room. Unassuming and neat. CHRISTINE is dressing to go out. KATTRIN enters after having knocked.

KATTRIN: Good evening, Miss Christine!

CHRISTINE: (*At the mirror; turns.*) Good evening!

KATTRIN: Going out?

CHRISTINE: No rush.

KATTRIN: My husband was wondering. Will you eat with us this evening? At the Lehngarten. There'll be music.

CHRISTINE: Thanks, Mrs. Binder. Not this evening. Some other time? You're not angry with me?

KATTRIN: Heavens! It's just us! You'll have a better time, I'm sure. (*CHRISTINE looks at her.*) Your papa's at the theater?

CHRISTINE: Not yet. He'll be home first. Curtain's at seven-thirty now.

KATTRIN: I always forget. I'll wait for him here. Is that all right? It's the passes for the new play. I thought maybe he could get some. Do you think?

CHRISTINE: I'm sure. No one goes in weather like this. Such beautiful evenings!

KATTRIN: We never get to the theater, our kind. Except we have a connection. Well, you know. Don't let me keep you, Miss Christine. I know you have to go. He'll be disappointed. My husband. And someone else, too, of course.

CHRISTINE: Someone else?

KATTRIN: My husband's cousin. Franz. He's coming, too. My husband's cousin Franz is very well set up, you know.

CHRISTINE: (*Indifferently.*) Oh?

KATTRIN: Makes a good salary. Nice young man. So honest. He respects you, you know.

CHRISTINE: Well. Good-bye, Mrs. Binder.

KATTRIN: A person could say almost anything they want about you. Would he believe it? Never. (*CHRISTINE looks at her.*) There *are* such men.

CHRISTINE: Good-bye, Mrs. Binder.

KATTRIN: Bye! (*Not too maliciously.*) You wouldn't want to be late for your rendezvous, Miss Christine.

CHRISTINE: What do you want from me?

KATTRIN: Want? Nothing! And you're right. A person is only young once.

CHRISTINE: Good-bye.

KATTRIN: But if I could give you a little advice, dear? Be more careful.

CHRISTINE: I don't — ?

KATTRIN: Well. Vienna's a big city. Why meet him a few steps from your own home?

CHRISTINE: That's *my* business, Mrs. Binder!

KATTRIN: I didn't believe it when my husband told me. But he *did see* you. Go on, I said to him. Not Miss Christine! She doesn't take walks in the evening. Not with fashionable young gentlemen. At least she's smarter than to be caught. And in her own neighborhood, too! Well then, he says to me, ask her yourself. But it didn't surprise him, you know. I mean, you never visit anymore. I mean, you'd rather run around with that Mitzi Schlager person. What kind of company's that, he said, for a respectable young lady! Men are common creatures, Miss Christine! Of course he told Franz right off. And you should've seen him! Franz, I mean. My husband's cousin? Oh, he was mad! He'd go through fire for you, he said. And anyone says anything against you has got him to reckon with! He talked about how handy you are around the house. And always so kind to your old aunt. Rest her soul! And how modest. And you're alone most of the time. And so on. (*Pause.*) How about some music? You want to come?

CHRISTINE: No.

HANS WEIRING: (*Her father, enters carrying a twig from a lilac bush.*) Good evening, my dear! Oh, Mrs. Binder! How are you?

KATTRIN: Very well.

WEIRING: And your daughter Linny?

KATTRIN: Fine, Lord be praised!

WEIRING: Wonderful. (*To CHRISTINE.*) Why aren't you out, Christine? In weather like this!

CHRISTINE: I was just going.

WEIRING: Good. The air's like perfume. Don't you think, Mrs. Binder? Wonderful weather. I just came through the garden. By the tracks? Lilacs! Glorious sight! And I think I committed a crime! (*He hands the sprig of lilac to CHRISTINE.*)

CHRISTINE: Father! Thank you!

KATTRIN: Be glad the guard didn't catch you!

WEIRING: Go sometime, Mrs. Binder. The garden smells the same as before I picked it.

KATTRIN: But if we *all* did that — ?

WEIRING: Then we'd have to see to it, wouldn't we?

CHRISTINE: Good-bye, Father!

WEIRING: If you wait, you can walk me to the theater.

CHRISTINE: I — I promised Mitzi I'd come by for her.

WEIRING: Good. Young people belong together. See you later.

CHRISTINE: (*Kisses him; then.*) Good-bye, Mrs. Binder. (*CHRISTINE goes off as WEIRING looks lovingly after her.*)

KATTRIN: They're very close, those two girls.

WEIRING: Yes. She needs someone. No good sitting at home all day. And alone, too. She has little enough out of life.

KATTRIN: Yes, well —

WEIRING: I come home after rehearsal and there she is, sewing. And the minute we finish eating she's at her music manuscripts.

KATTRIN: Well, when you're not rich, you're not rich! Doesn't she sing?

WEIRING: For her old father. But it's no living for her.

KATTRIN: What a shame.

WEIRING: She knows that. And I'm glad. At least she won't be disappointed. Oh, I could get her into the chorus at the theater —

KATTRIN: Yes! And with *her figure!*

WEIRING: But she'd never have a career.

KATTRIN: Girls are such a trouble to raise. Five, six years, my little Linny will be a big girl! Oh!

WEIRING: Sit down?

KATTRIN: Thank you. I expect my husband. Any time now. I came to invite Christine —

WEIRING: Oh?

KATTRIN: There's music. At the Lehngarten tonight. She needs cheering up.

WEIRING: No harm in that. And after her sadness this winter. She's not going?

KATTRIN: Maybe because my husband's cousin is coming, too. Franz?

WEIRING: Could be. Doesn't like him. She told me.

KATTRIN: But he's so proper! Franz! And well set up! Any girl'd be interested who isn't —

WEIRING: Too well set up herself — ?

KATTRIN: *Any* girl'd be interested!

WEIRING: Mrs. Binder. For a girl like Christine there are other things than to belong to a man who just happens to be well set up.

KATTRIN: More's the pity. Not many princes today anymore. And if so, they wouldn't be around long. And as for marriage — ? Ha! (*WEIRING is at the window. Pause.*) Can't be too careful with girls. Especially who she goes around with.

WEIRING: Youth can't be wasted. What use is patience and virtue when all you end up with is a stocking-weaver.

KATTRIN: My husband is a stocking-weaver, but he's a good and honest man! I have no complaints!

WEIRING: (*Trying to appease her.*) But I didn't mean *you*, Mrs. Binder! I mean — did *you* waste *your* youth?

KATTRIN: I don't remember it.

WEIRING: Don't talk silly. Those memories are the best part of your life.

KATTRIN: I don't have any memories.

WEIRING: Now, now.

KATTRIN: And if I *did*, what would be left but regret!

WEIRING: Regret is better than *nothing*. Better than life that slips away without happiness or love.

KATTRIN: But that old woman! Your sister! I know. It still hurts to talk about it.

WEIRING: Yes.

KATTRIN: You were so close. It's not easy to find a brother like you. That's what I always said. (*WEIRING turns from her.*) You were still so young and you were father and mother to her. It must be a comfort to know you protected such a poor creature.

WEIRING: I thought so, too, once. When she was still young. I thought I was being so sensible. So noble. But then the gray hair came. And the wrinkles. And her youth was gone. And that young girl — so slowly you hardly noticed it — was suddenly an old woman. That's when I realized what I'd done.

KATTRIN: But, Mr. Weiring — !

WEIRING: I still see her. Sitting across from me. In the evening. Quiet. Resigned. Smiling. Still wanting to thank me for something. But I want to throw myself at her feet. Ask forgiveness for protecting her so well from danger. And from happiness.

(*Pause.*)

KATTRIN: Such a brother is a blessing. Nothing to regret.

MITZI: (*Enters.*) Good evening! Goodness, it's so dark in here! I can hardly see. Oh! Mrs. Binder! Your husband's waiting downstairs. Is Christine home?

WEIRING: No. She left. About fifteen minutes ago.

KATTRIN: Didn't you run into her? She was coming by for you.

MITZI: No. We must have missed each other. Your husband says you're going to hear music tonight.

KATTRIN: Yes. He's all excited. What a charming hat, Miss Mitzi. Is it new?

MITZI: Heavens, no. Last year's done over.

KATTRIN: You did it all yourself?

MITZI: Of course.

WEIRING: How talented.

KATTRIN: Yes. You worked in a milliner's shop for a year.

MITZI: I might be again soon. My mother, you know. Well, what can I do!

WEIRING: It's time I —

KATTRIN: And I'll go down with you.

MITZI: Me, too. Don't forget your topcoat. It gets nippy later on.

WEIRING: Really?

KATTRIN: Oh, yes! You shouldn't be so careless.

(*CHRISTINE enters.*)

MITZI: She's back!

KATTRIN: Goodness! Such a short walk!

CHRISTINE: Yes. Hello, Mitzi. I have a headache. (*She sits.*)

WEIRING: Are you all right?

KATTRIN: Probably the air.

WEIRING: What is it, dear? Please, Mitzi. Light the lamp.

(*MITZI prepares to leave.*)

CHRISTINE: I can do that.

WEIRING: I want to see your face.

CHRISTINE: Father, it's nothing. Really. The evening air.

WEIRING: (*To MITZI.*) Please. Will you stay?

MITZI: Of course.

CHRISTINE: But, Father. It's nothing.

MITZI: My mother should make such a fuss over me when I have a headache!

WEIRING: (*To CHRISTINE, who is still seated.*) You look tired.

CHRISTINE: (*Rising from the easychair.*) No. I can even stand. (*Smiles.*)

WEIRING: There. Doesn't she look better? (*To KATTRIN.*) Amazing what a smile can do. Well, good-bye, Christine. (*Kisses her.*) That'll drive your headache off.

KATTRIN: (*Softly to CHRISTINE.*) Have a little tiff?

(*CHRISTINE is indignant.*)

WEIRING: (*At the door.*) Mrs. Binder!

MITZI: Good-bye.

(*WEIRING and KATTRIN go off.*)

MITZI: It's that sweet wine last night that gave you the headache. I should have had one, too. But it was nice at Fritz's. Don't you think?

CHRISTINE: Mitzi! He didn't come!

MITZI: Stood you up? It serves you right!

CHRISTINE: What did I do?

MITZI: You spoil him. You're too good for him. It makes men arrogant.

CHRISTINE: Oh, don't be silly!

MITZI: Believe me. I get so mad when I think about it. Doesn't meet you when he says he will, doesn't walk you home, goes to the theater with strange women, stands you up whenever he takes a notion. And you? Not a word. You sit there mooning over him with your lovesick eyes.

CHRISTINE: Stop it! It's not like you! Are you fond of Theo?

MITZI: "Fond?" Yes, I'm "fond" of him. But no man, not even Theo, can make me sick over him. They're not worth it.

CHRISTINE: I've never seen you like this.

MITZI: Yes, I know. I never dared. I liked you too much. I knew falling in love would be a blow to you. Especially the first time. But we're friends. I'll help you.

CHRISTINE: Mitzi!

MITZI: There, there. Men aren't worth a hill of beans. And where would you be without me. Hm? Never believe a word a man says.

CHRISTINE: *Men!* What do I care about *men!* All I want is *him!*

MITZI: Christine? Has he — ? I should have known. You should have handled this differently.

CHRISTINE: Stop!

MITZI: There's nothing I can do, Christine. You should have known. You can't go around trusting just *anyone.*

CHRISTINE: I don't want to listen! I don't!

MITZI: (*Placatingly.*) There, there.

CHRISTINE: Please go. Don't be angry. I just want to be alone.

MITZI: Angry! Why should I be angry? Yes, I'll go. I'm sorry I upset you. Really. (*As she turns to go to the door.*) Christine! It's Fritz!

FRITZ: (*Enters.*) Good evening.

CHRISTINE: (*Jubilant.*) Fritz! Oh, Fritz! (*She rushes to him and throws her arms around him.*)

(*MITZI slips out knowing she is unneeded.*)

FRITZ: (*Freeing himself.*) But —

CHRISTINE: She said you'd left me! Say you haven't! Not yet!

FRITZ: Who said such a thing? What is it? (*Caressing her.*) Dear Christine. I knew I'd frighten you by coming.

CHRISTINE: But you're here —

FRITZ: There. Calm down. Did you wait for me?

CHRISTINE: Where were you?

FRITZ: I couldn't help it. I had things to tend to. I went to the gardens. I didn't find you. I was about to go home — but I wanted so much to see you!

CHRISTINE: (*Happily.*) Did you!

FRITZ: To see where you live. Just once. So I came. I hope you don't mind.

CHRISTINE: No.

FRITZ: No one saw me. I knew your father was at the theater.

CHRISTINE: They can think what they like!

FRITZ: (*Looking around.*) So this is your room. Lovely.

CHRISTINE: No, it's not bright enough. (*She begins to remove the shade from the lamp.*)

FRITZ: No, that would be too bright. It's better this way. And here's the famous window you talk about. You work here. Lovely view. (*Smiles.*) All those roof tops to look out over. What's that over there?

CHRISTINE: It's the Kahlenberg.

FRITZ: I should have known — it's so much nicer than my place.

CHRISTINE: Oh!

FRITZ: It must be nice living so high up. To see out over all those roof tops. Lovely. And the streets must be very quiet.

CHRISTINE: It's noisy in the daytime.

FRITZ: Carts driving by?

CHRISTINE: Not often. There's a locksmith's shop across the street.

FRITZ: What a nuisance. (*He has sat down.*)

CHRISTINE: You get used to it. I don't hear it anymore.

FRITZ: (*Rises again quickly.*) I feel like I've been here before. It's so familiar. I knew it would be like this. (*He goes through the motions of looking more closely around the room.*)

CHRISTINE: Oh! Please! Don't look at anything!

FRITZ: What are these pictures?

CHRISTINE: No!

FRITZ: But I want to see them. (*He takes the lamp to light them.*)

CHRISTINE: "Departure" and "Homecoming"!

FRITZ: "Departure" and "Homecoming"!

CHRISTINE: They're not very good. But father has a better one in his room.

FRITZ: And this?

CHRISTINE: A girl looking out of a window. It's winter outside. It's called "Forsaken."

FRITZ: I see — (*He sets down the lamp.*) And this is your library. (*He sits beside the small bookshelf.*)

CHRISTINE: I wish you wouldn't —

FRITZ: Why? Ah! Schiller. Hauff. The Encyclopedia. Oh, damn!

CHRISTINE: It only goes up to *G*.

FRITZ: (*Smiling.*) I noticed. *The Book of General Knowledge.* Do you look at the pictures?

CHRISTINE: Of course.

FRITZ: (*Still seated.*) And who's the gentleman on the stove?

CHRISTINE: (*Didactically.*) That's Schubert.

FRITZ: (*Rising.*) Of course.

CHRISTINE: Father likes him very much. Father composed songs, too. Beautiful ones.

FRITZ: And now?

CHRISTINE: Not now.

(*Pause.*)

FRITZ: (*Sits again.*) It's very pleasant here.

CHRISTINE: You really think so?

FRITZ: Oh, yes. What's this! (*He picks up a vase of paper flowers from the table.*)

CHRISTINE: Oh, God, he found something else!

FRITZ: What are these doing here! They even look dusty!

CHRISTINE: They can't be.

FRITZ: Artificial flowers always look dusty! You should have only *real* flowers. From now on I'll — (*He breaks off and turns to hide his emotion.*)

CHRISTINE: You'll what? What were you — ?

FRITZ: Nothing. Nothing.

CHRISTINE: (*Rises; tenderly.*) Please tell me.

FRITZ: I was going to say that tomorrow I'll send you real flowers. (*FRITZ turns from her.*)

CHRISTINE: And you already regret it? Yes. Because tomorrow I'll be a thing of the past. (*FRITZ turns from her.*) I know. I can feel it.

FRITZ: Don't!

CHRISTINE: But it's *your* fault! All the secrets! Telling me *nothing* about yourself! I don't even know what you do all day!

FRITZ: That's hardly a mystery. I hear a lecture. I visit a coffeehouse. Read a bit. Play the piano. Make a few social calls. And it's all terribly unimportant. Too tedious to talk about. I really have to go now.

CHRISTINE: But you just arrived.

FRITZ: Your father will be back soon.

CHRISTINE: Not for hours. Fritz. Please stay. Just for a moment. Please.

FRITZ: And then I — well. Theodore's waiting for me. We have some matters to discuss.

CHRISTINE: Today?

FRITZ: It can't wait.

CHRISTINE: But you'll see him tomorrow.

FRITZ: I might not be in Vienna tomorrow.

CHRISTINE: Not in — ?

FRITZ: (*Noting her anxiety; calmly, gaily.*) Is that so strange? I'll be gone for a day or two.

CHRISTINE: Where?

FRITZ: Where?! Somewhere or other! God! Don't look at me like that! To the estate. To see my parents. Is that so — ?

CHRISTINE: You haven't told them about me, have you.

FRITZ: You're such a child. When we're together, we don't need anyone else. You should know that.

CHRISTINE: But I don't. And you shouldn't hide from me. I know *nothing* about you and I want to know *everything*. We're together for an hour in the evening, and that's all. And then you're gone, and still I know *nothing*. I want to cry sometimes!

FRITZ: I don't understand.

CHRISTINE: I want to see you, but it's like you're not in the same world — like you've disappeared — swallowed up —

FRITZ: (*Rather impatient.*) Christine —

CHRISTINE: It's true — it's true!

FRITZ: Come here. (*CHRISTINE goes to his side.*) We both know one thing.

That you love me. (*As she starts to speak.*) No, I don't want to hear it. Not about eternity. Not about forever. All we have is *right now*. It's all we can understand. The only thing that's really ours. (*He kisses her. Pause. Then he rises.*) I like your room. (*At the window.*) So remote. All these roof tops to look out over. Quiet. Here with you. (*Softly.*) So safe.

CHRISTINE: Why can't you always be like this? I could almost believe —

FRITZ: What?

CHRISTINE: That you love me as much as I thought. That day you kissed me for the first time.

FRITZ: (*Passionately.*) I *do* love you! (*Embraces her, then pulls himself away.*) No. Please. I have to leave.

CHRISTINE: Are you sorry you said it? Fritz. You're free. You can stand me up anytime you like. You haven't promised *me* anything, and I haven't asked *you* for anything. I don't care what happens to me. But I want you to know. You're the only man I ever loved, or ever will love. When you're tired of me —

FRITZ: (*More to himself.*) Don't — (*A knock is heard at the door. Alarmed.*) That's Theodore!

CHRISTINE: (*Concerned.*) He knows you're here?

THEODORE: (*Enters.*) Good evening. I'm sorry, I —

CHRISTINE: Is it so important? Couldn't you wait!

THEODORE: No. I looked all over for him.

FRITZ: (*Softly.*) You could have waited downstairs!

CHRISTINE: What are you whispering?

THEODORE: (*Deliberately loud.*) Wait downstairs? I didn't know if you were here. I couldn't take the risk.

FRITZ: (*As if answering himself.*) So — you'll be going with me tomorrow.

THEODORE: (*Understanding.*) Yes.

FRITZ: Good.

THEODORE: (*Sitting down.*) Excuse me. I rushed all the way.

CHRISTINE: Please. (*Busies herself at the window.*)

FRITZ: (*Softly.*) Any news? What have you found out about her?

THEODORE: (*Quietly to FRITZ.*) No. I came because I know how careless you are. Why are you doing this! You should be sleeping. You need rest. (*CHRISTINE approaches them.*)

FRITZ: The room's lovely.

THEODORE: Charming. (*To CHRISTINE.*) Are you home all day? It's very livable. A bit above my taste.

FRITZ: That's what I like about it.

THEODORE: Fritz has to go now. We'll be starting out early tomorrow.

CHRISTINE: Then you're going away?

THEODORE: He'll be back.

CHRISTINE: Will you write?

THEODORE: He'll be back tomorrow.

CHRISTINE: No. He won't.

(*FRITZ suddenly shudders.*)

THEODORE: (*Noting FRITZ's reaction.*) You've very sentimental, Miss — Christine, I should say. Well. Kiss each other and don't mind me.

(*FRITZ and CHRISTINE kiss. THEODORE takes out a cigarette case, puts a cigarette in his mouth and searches for a match in his overcoat pocket. When he fails to find one, he addresses CHRISTINE.*)

THEODORE: Excuse me, Christine. Do you have a match?

CHRISTINE: Over there. (*She points toward the bureau.*)

THEODORE: Empty.

CHRISTINE: I'll bring you some. (*She hurries into the next room.*)

FRITZ: (*Looking after her; to THEODORE.*) God, I could almost believe it myself!

THEODORE: Believe what?

FRITZ: That she was meant for me. That I could be happy. But it's a pack of lies.

THEODORE: Don't be stupid. You'll have a good laugh out of it someday.

FRITZ: Not much time for that.

CHRISTINE: (*Returns with some matches.*) Here.

THEODORE: Thanks. Well. Good-bye. (*To FRITZ.*) What more do you want!

FRITZ: (*Looks once more around the room as if trying to encompass it all.*) It's hard to leave.

CHRISTINE: That's right. Make fun of me.

THEODORE: Come on. Good-bye, Christine.

CHRISTINE: See you soon. (*THEODORE and FRITZ go out. CHRISTINE stands there anxiously, then goes to the door which has been left ajar. Softly.*) Fritz.

FRITZ: (*Returns and takes her in his arms.*) Good-bye.

ACT THREE

Christine's room. The same as in the previous act. CHRISTINE is alone and seated at the window, sewing. She puts down her work. LINA, Kattrin's nine-year-old daughter, enters.

LINA: Hello, Miss Christine!

CHRISTINE: (*Very absentmindedly.*) Hello, Lina. What do you want?

LINA: Mother sent me for the tickets. For the theater.

CHRISTINE: Father's not home yet. Do you want to wait?

LINA: No. I'll come back. After we've eaten.

CHRISTINE: That'll be fine.

LINA: (*Turns on her way out.*) Mother says hello and do you still have a headache?

CHRISTINE: Not anymore.

LINA: Good-bye, Miss Christine. (*As LINA turns to go, she meets MITZI in the doorway.*) Hello, Miss Mitzi!

MITZI: Hello, little silly!

(*LINA goes off. CHRISTINE rises as MITZI approaches her.*)

CHRISTINE: Are they back?

MITZI: How should I know?

CHRISTINE: No letter? Nothing?

MITZI: No.

CHRISTINE: Not you either?

MITZI: What would Theodore and I write about?

CHRISTINE: Two whole days!

MITZI: It's not forever. Why think the worst? I don't understand you. And you look terrible. Your eyes are red. You've been crying. Your father's sure to know if he comes home and sees you like this.

CHRISTINE: (*Simply.*) I told him.

MITZI: (*Almost frightened.*) You what?!

CHRISTINE: I told him everything.

MITZI: That was bright! But you never were good at hiding things. Does he know who?

CHRISTINE: Yes.

MITZI: Was he angry? (*CHRISTINE shakes her head.*) Well? What did he say?

CHRISTINE: Nothing. He went off quietly. Like always.

MITZI: It was silly of you! Do you know why he didn't say anything? He thinks Fritz will marry you.

CHRISTINE: Do you have to talk about it!

MITZI: Know what I think?

CHRISTINE: What?

MITZI: They probably never left town.

CHRISTINE: They *did!* I *know* they did! I went past his house yesterday. The blinds were down. There was no one there.

MITZI: Oh, I believe that! No question they're gone. They just won't be back. At least as far as *we're* concerned.

CHRISTINE: (*Frightened.*) Mitzi!

MITZI: It won't be the first time.

CHRISTINE: How can you be so calm!

MITZI: If not today, then tomorrow. Or six months from now or — it all boils down to the same thing.

CHRISTINE: You're wrong! You don't *know* Fritz! He's not that way! I *know!* He was in this room! Recently! He just pretends he's indifferent sometimes. But he loves me. (*As if guessing MITZI's reply.*) Oh, I know! It's not forever! But it won't just end all at once!

MITZI: You're right. I *don't* know him that well.

CHRISTINE: He'll come back. Theodore, too. I *know* he will. (*MITZI gestures as if to say: It's all the same to me.*) Mitzi? Do me a favor?

MITZI: If you'll calm down, yes. What?

CHRISTINE: Go to Theodore's apartment. It's not far. Just for a look. Ask if he's back. If he's not, maybe someone will know when.

MITZI: Me? Chase after a man? Not a chance.

CHRISTINE: He'll never know. You might meet him on the way. It's almost one. He usually goes to lunch.

MITZI: Go yourself.

CHRISTINE: I wouldn't dare. He can't stand that. Besides, I know he's not there. But Theodore could be home. And he'd know where Fritz is. Please, Mitzi!

MITZI: You can be so childish.

CHRISTINE: Do it for *me!* Go and see. There's nothing to it.

MITZI: If it means that much. All right. But it won't do much good. They *couldn't* be back yet.

CHRISTINE: Thank you, Mitzi. You're so good.

MITZI: I know. I know. Just don't do anything foolish. All right? I'll be back.

CHRISTINE: Thank you!

(*MITZI goes off. CHRISTINE is alone. She straightens the room, assembles her sewing, and so on, then goes to the window and looks out. After a moment or so WEIRING appears in the doorway, afraid to enter any farther. He is deeply agitated and watches CHRISTINE at the window with some apprehension. CHRISTINE then turns, sees him, and is startled. WEIRING attempts a smile. He moves farther into the room.*)

WEIRING: Well, Christine — (*He speaks as though calling her to him. CHRISTINE crosses to him wanting to go down on her knees. He resists her kneeling.*) Christine. I — I think — we should forget this — this whole affair. (*CHRISTINE lifts her face to him.*) Both of us.

CHRISTINE: Didn't you hear what I told you this morning?

WEIRING: Yes, Christine. But I haven't told you what *I* think.

CHRISTINE: Father, I don't understand.

WEIRING: Come here. Calm down now. Listen to me. Like *I* listened this morning. I think we must —

CHRISTINE: Don't. If you can't forgive me, I'll get out. Just don't —

WEIRING: You're still so young. Didn't you ever think this might be a mistake?

CHRISTINE: I know what I've done. If it's a mistake then I can take care of myself.

WEIRING: Why go on like this? So it was a mistake. We'll have a wonderful life together. There are so many wonderful things. Why throw it all away because you have to give up your first — or what you thought was your first happiness?

CHRISTINE: (*Anxious.*) Why — should I have to give it up?

WEIRING: You know you weren't happy. I've known for a long time. You wouldn't look like this if you'd loved someone worthy of you.

CHRISTINE: What do you know — ? What have you heard — ?

WEIRING: Nothing. But you told me yourself what he is. What can a young man like that know? How could he possibly appreciate you? And as for your love for him —

CHRISTINE: (*Her fears growing.*) Did you go to see him?

WEIRING: He's away. On a trip. Forget him, my dear. One day you'll find someone who's worthy of you.

(*CHRISTINE has hurried to the bureau to get her hat. The following six speeches go very rapidly.*)

WEIRING: What are you doing?

CHRISTINE: I'm going.

WEIRING: Where?

CHRISTINE: To him —

WEIRING: You can't.

CHRISTINE: You're hiding something from me! Let me go!

WEIRING: (*Holding her back.*) Be reasonable! He may have gone on a long trip. There's nothing for you there. I'll go with you tomorrow morning. Or this evening.

CHRISTINE: You'll go with me?

WEIRING: Promise. Stay. People would laugh if they saw you.

CHRISTINE: What do you *know?*

WEIRING: I know that I love you. That you should stay with me —

(*CHRISTINE pulls away from him and opens the door as MITZI appears.*)

MITZI: (*Cries out softly as CHRISTINE rushes to her.*) Don't frighten me like that!

(*CHRISTINE retreats into the room at the sight of THEODORE who stands in the doorway. He is dressed in black.*)

CHRISTINE: What — ? (*When she receives no reply, she looks directly at THEODORE who tries to avoid her gaze.*) Where is he? (*Frightened when she receives no reply, she looks at their embarrassed and saddened faces. To THEODORE.*) Answer me! (*THEODORE tries to speak. CHRISTINE looks at him, then looks around her and begins to interpret their expressions. She utters a fearful cry when suddenly she comprehends the situation.*) He's dead?

WEIRING: My dear —

THEODORE: You know all there is.

CHRISTINE: I *don't* know. I don't know *anything*. How did it happen? Father. Theodore. (*To MITZI.*) Even *you* know how it happened!

THEODORE: It was an unfortunate —

CHRISTINE: How?

THEODORE: He was killed.

CHRISTINE: I don't —

THEODORE: In a duel.

(*CHRISTINE screams and WEIRING supports her, giving THEODORE a sign that he should leave. Noticing this, CHRISTINE grabs hold of THEODORE.*)

CHRISTINE: Don't go. Tell me. I want to know!

THEODORE: What more do you — ?

CHRISTINE: Why there was a duel —

THEODORE: I don't know.

CHRISTINE: Who was it — who killed him? Tell me!

THEODORE: No one — that you'd know —

CHRISTINE: Who?

MITZI: Christine!

CHRISTINE: (*To MITZI.*) Tell me! Father? (*There is no reply. She turns to leave.* WEIRING *restrains her.*) Then I'll find out for myself!

THEODORE: It was senseless.

CHRISTINE: You're lying to me!

THEODORE: Christine —

CHRISTINE: (*After a silence.*) Because of a woman?

THEODORE: No —

CHRISTINE: Yes. Because of a woman. (*Turning to MITZI.*) For *that* woman. For that woman he *loved!* And *I?* What am *I?* What did *I* mean to him? Theodore. Didn't he *tell* you anything for me? Didn't you *find* anything? A letter? A note? (*THEODORE shakes his head.*) And that evening — when he was here — when you came for him. He knew that he might never — and he left here. To be killed. For someone else. No. No. Didn't he know what he meant to me?

THEODORE: He knew. On that last morning when we rode out. He even spoke of you.

CHRISTINE: He *even* spoke of me? *Even?* And what else? Of how many others? Of how many other things that meant as much to him as *I* did? Of his father? His mother? His friends? His room? The springtime? The city? Everything? Everything else that was a part of his life? And that he had to leave just the same as he had to leave me? And he spoke to you of everything. And *even* of me!

THEODORE: (*Moved.*) He loved you very much.

CHRISTINE: Fritz? I was a pastime for him. But I worshipped him. He should have known. I gave him everything I had. I would have died for him. He was my God. He was my happiness. And he left here. Smiling. To be killed for another woman.

WEIRING: Christine —

THEODORE: (*To MITZI.*) You could have spared me this! (*MITZI looks angrily at him.*) I've had enough to deal with these last few days!

CHRISTINE: (*With sudden decision.*) Theodore. Take me there. I want to see him. Once more.

THEODORE: (*Looks away; hesitantly.*) No —

CHRISTINE: You can't keep me from seeing him!

THEODORE: It's too late.

CHRISTINE: To see his body? I —

THEODORE: He was buried this morning.

CHRISTINE: And I didn't know. Dead for two days? And you didn't tell me? Damn you! Damn you, all of you! Damn you!

THEODORE: (*Deeply moved.*) I had so much to think about. I had to tell his parents, and I — Only his closest friends and relatives were —

CHRISTINE: But not me —

MITZI: They would have asked who you were —

CHRISTINE: Then I'm less important than they were? Than his relatives? Less than — than *she?*

WEIRING: (*To THEODORE.*) Please go.

THEODORE: I'm terribly — I had no idea —

CHRISTINE: Of what? That I loved him? — Take me to his grave.

WEIRING: No.

MITZI: Don't, Christine.

THEODORE: Later. Tomorrow. After you're calm.

CHRISTINE: And in a month I'll have consoled myself. Hm? And in *six* months? I'll be able to laugh again? — And when will the *next* lover come along?

WEIRING: Christine —

CHRISTINE: I can find my own way.

WEIRING: Don't go.

MITZI: Don't go.

CHRISTINE: I'd be better off — Leave me alone.

WEIRING: *She* might be there. Praying.

CHRISTINE: I'm not going there to pray. (*She rushes out.*)

  (*Silence.*)

WEIRING: Go after her. Please.

  (*THEODORE and MITZI follow her. WEIRING moves tiredly from the door to the window and looks out.*)

END OF PLAY

THE TRANSLATOR

Carl R. Mueller has since 1967 been professor of theater at UCLA where he has taught theater history, criticism, dramatic literature and playwriting in the Theater Department of the School of Theater, Film, and Television. He has won many awards, including the Samuel Goldwyn Award for Dramatic Writing, and in 1960–61 was a Fulbright Scholar in Berlin. A translator for almost forty years, he has translated and published works by Büchner, Brecht, Wedekind, Hauptmann, von Horváth, Hofmannsthal, Hebbel, and Stringberg, among others. Most recently he is the co-translator of the complete plays of Sophocles, which are soon to be published. His translations have been staged in every part of the English-speaking world.